SPECIAL DISTRICT GOVERNMENTS
in the United States

SPECIAL DISTRICT GOVERNMENTS
in the United States

BY JOHN C. BOLLENS

Foreword by John M. Gaus

GREENWOOD PRESS, PUBLISHERS
WESTPORT, CONNECTICUT

85105

Library of Congress Cataloging in Publication Data

Bollens, John Constantinus, 1920-
    Special district governments in the United States.

    Reprint of the ed. published by University of
California Press, Berkeley.
    Bibliography: p.
    Includes index.
    1. Special districts--United States. I. Title.
[JS425.B6 1978]   352'.0073'0973   77-26250
ISBN 0-313-20065-3

Reprinted with the permission of The University of
California Press

Reprinted in 1978 by Greenwood Press, Inc.
51 Riverside Avenue, Westport, CT 06880

Printed in the United States of America

Foreword

LIGHT FROM A DARK CONTINENT

Forty years ago Mr. H. S. Gilbertson wrote of American county government that it was "the Dark Continent of American Politics." Early in the first chapter of this book Mr. Bollens states that the term could now better be applied to the special districts which are his subject. I claim at once the privilege of an old friend to qualify his remark. Few people have thought of special districts as a substantial branch of our system of government at all, certainly not sufficiently to regard them as a unity, a continent, a "maine," as John Donne might say. The author has created as well as discovered this new continent. And through his assault upon the darkness that envelops it, he brings light upon the world of government of which it is a part. The book shares this quality with other studies of area and function made in recent years—I think of those by Anderson, Bosworth, Fesler, McKinley, Parks, Ostrom, and Weidner, for example—in which the specific and particular theme is treated in such a way as to illumine the general questions of the changing relations of population, environment, and government.

I suggest that Mr. Bollens has both discovered and created a continent because he brings some order and common significance out of the bewildering variety of the many particular institutions and practices which he describes. There have been excellent studies of particular districts or types of districts. But I learn from Mr. Bollens' labors to put rural soil conservation districts, "rurban" fringe water and fire protection districts, and urban housing districts within a common perspective and to search for likenesses that give new insights into government generally. I learn from him of the far greater substantive and quantitative importance of this group of governments in comparison with the various classes of general governments (national, state, local) that I had known. And I have learned from him also that in some respects the special districts reveal better than other units of government the service role of government, government as public housekeeping supplementing and supporting private housekeeping. Special districts are a sort of cutting edge in the evolution of functions. They are the constant and ubiquitous evidence of that creeping socialism which is the product of galloping consumption and birth rates and population densities and new techniques of transportation. I would prefer to have social change come by creeping rather than with the tempo of catastrophic explosion, and so I am glad to learn more about these districts.

They illustrate well, I find from Mr. Bollens, the intractable nature of political boundaries, which resisted even a British Boundaries Commission undertaking a study in what I had thought was the favoring atmosphere of the catastrophe of war and blitzkrieg. (The commission was dissolved.) They reflect clearly the role of professional-functional influence operating through several levels of government, sometimes in alliance with citizen interest groups, as against the claims of the total balanced need of any one level or unit. And they cause one to search for a more humane political theory evolved from observing how people really act in contrast to speculation as to how they ought to act when they participate in government.

One might dismiss special districts as unimportant (until a special tax or assessment bill is delivered). One might overlook them as surface features of the landscape. The geological metaphor perhaps warrants enlarging, since so many of them have to do with soil and water. The geologist dare not dismiss a kame or esker, or faint indications of a fault line as unimportant. He has to spend long hours in the field, and in many fields, and hunt for clues that seem to go underground from one exciting spot to somewhere else as yet unknown; and then ponder his notes and graphs and drawings to see what generalization will fit. Mr. Bollens has been out in the field with his geological-political hammer, talking with par-

vii   FOREWORD

ticipants in district activities, poring over documents and statistics, and trying to make the superficial, that is the surface landscape features, tell what lies below. I gather that they tell us, through him, that there are some underlying fault lines where the pressure of needs in certain areas has led to the fracturing of the old strata, or levels, of government. Or maybe some volcanic energies, deep below, have here and there forced new structures up. And all of these changes lie concealed in part by the glacial till and debris from more spectacular and more recent movements. For one with Mr. Bollens' industry and patience and objectivity, there is so much to learn from the superficial about what lies below it.

And so he comes to us here with his field notes, comparisons, questionings, tentative hints of explanation, and hypotheses of the direction of stresses and fault lines, suggestions to others who are exploring or who may be induced to explore these surface features for what may lie below. From such efforts a science is cumulated, as the wise Charles Van Hise preached and practiced in his own geological studies and proposals for public policy. Mr. Bollens' career has been in places and institutions which have been contributory to the qualities he has himself brought to his task. His earlier years and formal education leading to the doctorate in political science were spent in the Middle West, where he was first challenged by these problems of government. He has subsequently served on the staffs of the Municipal League of Seattle and King County, the Bureau of Public Administration of the University of California at Berkeley, and the Department of Political Science of the University of California at Los Angeles, where the Bureau of Governmental Research of the University and the Haynes Foundation, also located in Los Angeles, have enlarged his opportunities for research in the field in which he was already making contributions. The Puget Sound, San Francisco Bay, and Los Angeles regions, with their rapid growth and numerous governmental units, offer many examples relevant to the theme of this book. Populations drawn widely from every part of the United States and starting a new life have apparently been more ready to adjust older forms of government, and to invent new ones appropriate to the unprecedented conditions they faced.

Mr. Bollens has drawn upon the resources of both the governmental research institutions and the universities. He has moved out from the particular and local experience with special districts, a rich one in the West, to whatever experience elsewhere in the nation might seem to offer relevant comparison and throw light on the institution generally. As he thought about the resultant data in his notebooks and documents, the outlines of a branch or class of government, to be put alongside municipal or county or state government for purposes of study and understanding, seemed to have appeared. It is to me significant that other scholars of and from the Pacific Northwest and Los Angeles have similarly accepted the challenge of their regions to produce studies of regional problems present throughout the United States, which also give us new insight into government generally—for example, Charles McKinley's *Uncle Sam in the Pacific Northwest* and Vincent Ostrom's *Water and Politics.*

All writers on questions of local and state government face the insoluble problem of treating comparatively variations of a particular practice or institution among forty-eight states or among thousands of local governments, while at the same time indicating that in any one state or local government the practice or institution must be examined as part of a particular local setting, with its own peculiar governmental, social, physical, cultural, and historic characteristics. Too much emphasis on the first, and you are accused of counting sewer covers and lampposts. Too much on the second, and meaningful generalization is strangled by the local variables.

Mr. Bollens has given considerable detail, but it is detail essential to our understanding; he has recognized that the particular device must be interpreted as part of the entire unit, and has presented samples in his case studies; and he has dared to generalize, always tentatively and with modesty. If the reader is at first overwhelmed by the particulars, whether of device or locality, let him note and ponder the deductions and speculations. Since special districts are a reflection of social change, appropriately Mr. Bollens' concluding suggestions will be affected by time. But to study and appraise a political institution as he has done is to fulfill both a civic obligation and the duty of scholarship.

JOHN M. GAUS

Harvard University
Cambridge, Massachusetts

Preface

Special districts have been too long neglected in the study of government in the United States. This book is an attempt to rectify this situation and fill many of the voids of information and interpretation in a basic phase of American government. The work has been arduous and time-consuming because many fragments of knowledge, some difficult to locate, have had to be pieced together. The project has spanned several years. This written record is the result of analyzing and blending data gathered from several sources: many laws and court decisions, widely scattered and frequently elusive written materials in a broad range of subjects, field interviews with public officials and private citizens, and field observations of district organizations and operations from coast to coast.

The endeavor has been richly rewarding since special districts are constantly fascinating, often mysterious, and increasingly important. If it is possible to view one's own thinking somewhat objectively, this last statement does not merely indicate that the author has become enamored of a subject that has been close at hand for some time. Special districts are particularly fascinating because some of their characteristics are very much out of the usual governmental pattern and because they seemingly offer clues and insights into a better understanding of other parts of our governmental system. They are mysterious and phantom-like because many of them have been in the realm of the unknown. One need not write a mystery novel to deal with the mysterious. Locating special districts in a geographical sense and subsequently acquiring information about them are no simple tasks. Their importance is evident in many ways—number, types, geographical extent, areas, functions, personnel, finance, and other characteristics treated in general and in particular in the pages that follow.

A few words should be said about the terms that are used in this study. Special districts (sometimes known legally by other names, as noted in the first chapter) constitute a specific class of separate governmental units which possess substantial fiscal and administrative independence and are not merely parts of other governments. Organizations that are adjuncts to governmental units are identified as dependent districts or authorities. A few authorities are actually special district governments, but when they are discussed an effort has been made to show that they fall within the category of special districts. When school districts are treated separately from other special districts, the two groupings are identified as school and nonschool districts. Thus the term "special district" or "district" means that school and nonschool districts are being considered together. Furthermore, although school districts constitute more than four-fifths of the total of all special districts, they are only one of five major groups of such governments. Therefore this study attempts to provide a reasonable balance in the discussion of the various groupings of districts, and at the same time to give sufficient, but not overextended, consideration to school districts. Dependent entities which are not separate governments and which legally have the word "district" in their titles are designated as "dependent" when necessary for clarity. Dependent districts are discussed separately in chapter 7.

The nomenclature of several kinds of nondistrict governments also requires explanation. To avoid confusion, municipal corporations known variously as cities, villages, towns, and boroughs are all generally identified as cities or municipalities. The word "town," when used in this study, therefore refers to a different and separate class of governmental units found exclusively in New England, unless it is used specifically with another geographical designation, such as New York State. In addition, the appellation "county" includes parishes in Louisiana, for the parish in that state corresponds to the county in other states.

Since beginning this study, I have been much gratified to note the increased desire for more knowledge about special districts, expressed by scholars and operating officials in periodicals and at conferences. Another pleasing parallel development is the more comprehensive collection of data about districts by the Governments Division of the United States Bureau of the Census. This latter undertaking has been useful as well, for throughout this study, for purposes of uniformity and comparability, I have utilized the Census Bureau's determinations as to which special districts are independent governments. To suggest minor modifications, it seems to me, would have been unduly petty, and would have diverted this research project from its main purposes.

One never travels the long road of research entirely alone, although stretches of it sometimes induce loneliness and introspection. My appreciation is extended to numerous public officials, academic people, full-time researchers, civic leaders, and lay citizens who discussed various phases of the subject during my transcontinental field work. They were most hospitable and, although frequently humble about their specialized knowledge, much more helpful than they realized. My thanks also go to librarians, scholars, and practitioners who suggested certain materials in specialized fields and sources generally familiar only to individuals working closely with specific governmental operations in a single state. Allen D. Manvel and Robert F. Drury of the Governments Division of the United States Bureau of the Census kindly furnished desk space and access to data during a number of extremely humid days in Washington. Barbara J. Hudson and her able staff at the Bureau of Public Administration Library on the Berkeley campus of the University of California have been most coöperative and helpful, just as they were in many of my previous research efforts. My use of many materials in this library again convinced me of the excellence of its collection. It is a lasting memorial to the late Samuel C. May who was the bureau director for many years. Dorothy V. Wells, librarian of the Bureau of Governmental Research, University of California, Los Angeles, has also supplied numerous valuable items.

I am additionally grateful to William N. Cassella, Jr., Howard A. Dawson, Roy E. Huffman, Victor Jones, W. Robert Parks, and Coleman Woodbury who read and commented on portions of the manuscript before its publication. Acknowledgment is further gladly given to William Anderson for his stimulating insights growing in part out of his pioneer work, originally published in 1934, on determining and enumerating all governmental units in the United States. My thanks also go to Stanley Scott with whom I have had worthwhile discussions and who has been interested in the subject since its inception. Jean Eberhart has competently shouldered most of the secretarial work and Virgene R. Bollens has been a fine source of help and encouragement.

This study was supported by a grant from the John Randolph Haynes and Dora Haynes Foundation of Los Angeles, a charitable and educational trust organized "for the purpose of promoting the well-being of mankind." As in all projects financially aided by the Foundation, the author has had complete freedom of investigation and expression. The presentation, conclusions, and recommendations are solely those of the author. I wish to express my appreciation to the Foundation for the grant which greatly facilitated the progress and completion of the project.

Finally, my gratitude is expressed to two individuals. John M. Gaus, whom I knew initially as a fine teacher and friend and subsequently as a continuing friend and counsel, read the manuscript and graciously consented to write the foreword. More than any other person he has helped to shape the course of my research activities during the last decade. The late Edwin A. Cottrell, formerly of Stanford University and at the time of his death a consultant and trustee of the Haynes Foundation, was deeply interested in the subject and did much to encourage the development of the research effort. He has been in my thoughts often as the study has proceeded.

JOHN C. BOLLENS

University of California
Los Angeles, California

Contents

CHAPTER ONE

General Characteristics

Special districts, a varied class of governmental units, have without much notice and concern become a significant part of the governmental pattern of the United States. They are furthermore becoming increasingly important despite a widespread lack of general understanding and knowledge about them. Only one kind of special districts, the school district, is reasonably well known, although subject to frequent misconceptions, and many nonschool districts are erroneously regarded as parts of other governments. Special districts, particularly those in the nonschool categories, constitute the "new dark continent of American politics," a phrase applied earlier in the century to counties.[1]

What are special districts? Much of the analysis that follows seeks to answer this question fully, but a general statement is appropriate here. In common with all other kinds of governmental units, special districts have certain essential characteristics. They are organized entities, possessing a structural form, an official name, perpetual succession, and the rights to sue and be sued, to make contracts, and to obtain and dispose of property. They have officers who are popularly elected or are chosen by other public officials. They have a high degree of public accountability. Moreover, they have considerable fiscal and administrative independence from other governments. The financial and administrative criteria distinguish special districts and other governments from all dependent or subordinate districts and from most authorities which, lacking one or both of these standards, are not governmental units. However, some entities legally identified as authori-

[1] H. S. Gilbertson, *The County: The "Dark Continent" of American Politics* (New York: National Short Ballot Organization, 1917).

1

ties, especially those in public housing, meet the requirements and are considered as special district governments. Special districts are also to be distinguished from the field offices or districts of national and state governments.[2] Unlike most other governments, individual special districts usually provide only one or a few functions. In this respect they most closely resemble the townships in a number of Midwestern states, but it is not difficult to differentiate them. Townships are largely limited to one geographical region, commonly include a rectangular area of 36 square miles, constitute a territorial subdivision of the county, and are overwhelmingly rural units of government. Special districts have none of these general features. Furthermore, although individually performing fewer functions than many townships, collectively they undertake a much broader range of services than townships in general. Special districts are therefore a clearly distinguishable class of local governmental units.

GENERAL EVIDENCE OF SIGNIFICANCE

Numbers and Geographical Extensiveness

One test of the significance of special districts is their number in relation to the over-all total for all governmental units. There are more than 79,000 of them, constituting about two-thirds of the approximately 116,000 governmental units in the United States.[3] This means that about thirteen of every twenty governments are special districts—eleven in the school category and two in the nonschool category. In addition, they are not only very numerous but also geographically widespread. These two characteristics are both evident in the fact that in thirty-five states special districts are more numerous than any other class of government.[4] Even the school

---

[2] For a consideration of the elements required of all governments, and their enumeration by classes, see *Governments in the United States in 1952*, U.S. Bureau of the Census, Governments Division (Washington: 1953), pp. 1–7.

[3] The report by the Census Bureau that school districts decreased by 7,715 in the two years after its count of governments in 1952, which was used to derive these figures, seemingly does not significantly alter the comparisons made here. Apparently gains in nonschool districts partially offset the school district loss. However, comparable data on very recent numerical changes in nonschool districts and other governments are not available.

[4] The exceptions are Alabama, Florida, Georgia, Louisiana, Maine, Massachusetts, North Carolina, South Carolina, Tennessee, Utah, Vermont, Virginia, and West Virginia.

and nonschool categories separately often outrank numerically each of the other governmental classes. School districts alone in twenty-nine states, and nonschool districts alone in fourteen states, are more numerous than any one class of other governments. Tens to thousands of special districts exist in every one of the states, and at least one such district is found in a large majority of the 3,049 counties in the country.

The large number, relative proportion, and geographical dispersion of special districts are not the only criteria for demonstrating their significance. Numerically they have been very much in flux, most noticeably since 1942. Unlike other governments in the United States which, with the minor exception of townships, remained virtually unchanged in total number, special districts declined by almost one-third in the period from 1942 to 1952. A closer look at this development indicates that it actually consists of two countertrends, each of consequence in itself. While one group of special districts, the school district, was decreasing by almost two-fifths (38.0 per cent), nonschool districts were increasing by almost one-half (48.4 per cent). The number of school districts has been decreasing faster and the number of nonschool districts has been growing faster than any other class of governmental units. Then, too, the number of kinds of nonschool districts has substantially increased since the early 1940's. The highly significant changes in numbers and types of governments in the United States have been occurring in the special district category. Rapid growth in particular is evidence of increasing significance. In this instance, rapid decrease has been important, too, for it generally involves territorial enlargement of the remaining districts and further strengthening and reinforcement of the district concept in the field of public education.

Finances and Personnel

Special districts are also consequential because of the extensiveness of their collective activity. In the fiscal year ending in 1955, school and nonschool districts spent $8.2 billion and $1.6 billion, respectively. This combined total of approximately $9.8 billion easily outranked the collective expenses of counties, townships, and towns, and stood close to the $10.5 billion figure for cities. At

TABLE 1

FINANCES AND PERSONNEL OF GOVERNMENTS IN THE UNITED STATES

Governmental class	Annual expenditures (fiscal year 1955)	Debt (end of fiscal year 1955)	Monthly payroll (October, 1955)	Number of employees (October, 1955)
National government	$72,409,000,000	$274,374,000,000	$845,700,000	2,378,000
States	20,357,000,000	11,198,000,000	340,400,000	1,250,000
Cities	10,541,000,000	15,973,000,000	413,800,000	1,436,000
Counties	5,130,000,000	3,140,000,000	147,800,000	597,000
Townships and towns	1,130,000,000	860,000,000	30,800,000	199,000
School districts	8,192,000,000	7,259,000,000	452,800,000	1,455,000
Nonschool districts	1,605,000,000	5,837,000,000	33,200,000	116,000

SOURCE: *Summary of Governmental Finances in 1955*, U.S. Bureau of the Census, Governments Division (Washington: 1956), pp. 24, 32; *State Distribution of Public Employment in 1955*, U.S. Bureau of the Census, Governments Division (Washington: 1956), pp. 8, 10. The figures for expenditures and debt have been rounded to the nearest million, those for monthly payroll to the nearest hundred thousand, and those for number of employees to the nearest thousand.

the same time the outstanding debt of all special districts was more than $13 billion, more than two-fifths of which was owed by non-school districts. The indebtedness of the school and nonschool groups of special districts each exceeded that of counties, townships, and towns combined, and the total district debt was more than that of all state governments together. Payrolls further illustrate the large amount of activity. The monthly payrolls for October, 1955, totaled $486 million for all special districts, more than nine-tenths of which went to school districts. The total for all district payrolls was thus larger than that for any other class of state and local governments. In the same month special districts also stood first among state and local governments in the number of persons employed. Slightly more than 1,570,000 people were professionally engaged in district activities. To state it in another way, about two of every five employees working for a local government were paid by some type of special district. More than nine-tenths of the district figure related to school districts.

A Possible Symptom

It is therefore evident that special districts are important in many aspects, including number, geographical extensiveness, finances, and personnel. Not so readily apparent but also of great possible significance is that the current number, the total operational extent, and particularly the sustained recent growth of various kinds of special districts may be symptomatic of weaknesses in other governments. The analysis of specific features of special districts, including their diversity, flexibility, and complexity, may furnish keys to a better comprehension and subsequent improvement of the governmental system of the United States.

CAUSES

Since special districts are expanding in over-all importance, the reasons prompting their establishment as part of the United States pattern of government are of growing consequence. As is true of many governmental institutions, there is no single all-inclusive cause. Instead, a series of factors is usually behind the formation of a particular district. Furthermore, the reasons are sometimes intertwined and interdependent, making it difficult to determine which is the controlling one and to separate it entirely from the others. The problem is further complicated by another difficulty. Because special districts have been so widely accepted in a relatively short period of time, or because it has been so quickly forgotten that they are separate governmental units, reports and individuals concerned with them do not usually analyze the causes bringing them into existence. Despite these difficulties, a number of reasons for the creation and continuance of most special districts can be identified.

Unsuitability of Other Local Units: Area

High-ranking among the reasons for special districts is the unsuitability of existing general local governments in terms of their area, financing, functions, or administration, or of the attitudes of those controlling them. There may be legal or operating inadequacies, or unwillingness by a government to perform a certain function. In many instances no general local government is permitted, equipped, or willing to undertake the service desired. Consideration of the inappropriateness of existing governments in these various respects will explain the establishment of numerous special districts.

Frequently the area appropriate to a particular function wanted by residents or property owners does not coincide with that of any existing general local government. The territory of the general unit may be smaller or larger. Thus the area of service need does not correspond to the boundaries of a local government presently in operation. Despite the post–World War II upsurge in annexation by cities, the limits of most governments are rigidly or relatively inflexible. Such inflexibility is a crucial problem when the area of the general unit is smaller than the territory needing the service. In other circumstances, the functional need can encompass part or all of several existing units and cross over numerous boundaries, sometimes interstate or even international. Furthermore, long-term contracts between general governments to handle a functional need in an area larger than a single unit, although increasing in number, are not in general use. Therefore, when existing governments are smaller territorially than the area having a specific need, the district device is frequently utilized as a substitute for land absorption, consolidation of general units, or contractual agreements.

A comparable type of unsuitableness similarly develops when an operating government is larger territorially than the area wanting a service. Under these conditions area rigidity normally intervenes, because the general government performs functions and finances them with substantial uniformity throughout its entire territory. Here the factors of area and financing inadaptability are intermeshed, since many general governments are not permitted to make additional charges in one section in exchange for performing an extra service. Furthermore, the area unsuitability of general governments is frequently the outgrowth of such ecological factors as population shifts, technological changes, especially in transportation, and new knowledge and methods concerned with soil and water.

Unsuitability of Other Local Units: Finances and Functions

Legal and operating limitations on financing the services of existing units are another heavy contributor to the formation of special districts. The legal obstacles usually take the form of state constitutional and legislative restrictions on the tax and debt limits of general governments. When these maximums are reached, no methods of performing added or more intensified functions are available unless the restrictions are liberalized or eliminated. Despite the unrealistic nature of many of them in relation to financial needs of general units, their modification is frequently difficult to accomplish. Consequently, a general government attaining its tax or debt limit is prevented from expanding functionally. However, residents of exactly or approximately the same area are not often legally prevented from organizing a special district possessing the power to levy taxes or to incur debt, or both. Thus, special districts are sometimes created as a direct means of circumventing financial restrictions placed on general governments. This has happened in such widely separated geographical locations as urban sections of Illinois and rural lands in the Columbia River Valley of the Pacific Northwest, and in the development of housing authorities which are special district governments. Moreover, creating a new special district is at times easier than winning popular approval for a tax increase by a general government for the performance of the same function.

The district device is also utilized to pool the financial resources of an area that includes at least several governments which feel that their individual financing ability is inadequate to undertake a function. In addition to wanting a new governmental unit made responsible for financing the service, existing general units in these circumstances often favor the establishment of a district for another reason. They regard such an arrangement as having greater permanency or consistency of performance than an intergovernmental contract under which the function would be jointly handled by all general governments or undertaken by one of them on behalf of the others.

The financial unsuitability of a general government such as the county works in two additional ways to foster special districts. One, mentioned previously, is that often this unit cannot legally set up a taxing or assessment area in a part of its territory in order to finance additional service. The second is that, since financial costs must be spread uniformly throughout its area, other general governments within its borders, usually cities, oppose its assumption of a function that they are already performing for their residents. Arguing that their residents would be paying twice for the same service, they advocate the establishment of a special district made up of the territory of the county but excluding them. This is the reason for the creation of most of the county library districts in Missouri.

The range of functions that can legally be performed by a general government does not always include a service that is desired by some people. This lack of functional authorization in existing units stimulates the creation of special districts. Numerous general governments show little disposition to seek additional functions but are at the same time reluctant to relinquish authority. Counties and townships in Illinois, for example, though not aggressively trying to increase their functional authorization, vigorously oppose suggestions and efforts to take away functions previously granted them. State legislatures often oppose attempts to make a function requested by one general unit available to all general units of the same type. New functions have been conferred upon general governments in a number of states, but the requests have frequently far outdistanced the legal permission. Then, too, there has been little or no service expansion by such general units as counties and townships in many states, either because of the lack of legal permission or because of the negative attitude of the general government itself even when the additional service is legally permissible.

Unsuitability of Other Local Units: Administration and Attitude

The status of the administrative structure and processes and the quality of the operational performance of an established general unit contribute to the formation of special districts. Some general governments, lacking modern administrative organization or procedures, or both, have not sufficiently matured to handle properly particular functions that are wanted. Administratively they are simply not capable of assuming new responsibilities. Sometimes the low caliber of present operations has decisive effect. There may be evidence or charges of inefficiency, mismanagement, or unsavory political behavior. Professionalized performance of public work may be absent or irregular. Unsatisfactory administrative structure or performance in an existing unit therefore works in two directions to encourage the growth of special districts. First, a function that could legally be handled by an existing general unit is entrusted instead to a special district. Second, a function already being performed by a general unit is transferred to a special district.

The attitude of a general government is sometimes the predominant factor accounting for the creation of special districts. A general government may have or could develop suitable area, financing, functions, and administrative organization and methods for a specific activity, and the interested people may want the general government to perform the service. Nevertheless, the general government's reaction, as reflected by its governing body members, is often negative. This attitude takes several forms. The general government may refuse to perform a function which is already legally authorized or which would be granted upon request to the legislature. It may be extremely slow and reluctant to assume a new activity. It may exercise the function but at a level below that desired by certain people. It may seek to stop rendering a present service.

These various degrees of antagonism, resistance, unresponsiveness, and abdication by a general unit are most often countered by the establishment of special districts. Frequently the governing body of a general government does not want to exercise more functions, or to exercise its existing functions more intensively. Many times a general government is glad to have another government supply the service. Sometimes, when intergovernmental rivalry is strong, it even advocates the establishment of a new unit to undertake the assignment. Some general governments are anxious to increase their functional span and expand their operations, but many of them are not so inclined. Established ways of performing functions and familiarity with particular services are contributors to this attitude. Also, the elective status of governing body members and the desire of many of them to keep the tax rate low, in part at least as an aid to reëlection, should not be overlooked as powerful influences in shaping a negative response. Then, too, such an attitude can more firmly entrench the legal inadequacy of certain aspects of the general government, such as financing and administrative arrangements. A government not wanting a function will hardly facilitate its acquisition or performance by changing in other ways.

The Desire for Independence

The desire for independence is a further reason for the creation of special districts. People and groups possessing a major interest in one function frequently resist having that function allocated to an established general government or even to another special district. The desire to have an activity performed apart from any existing government sometimes grows out of an unfounded allegation or a well-based conviction regarding the condition of the particular government. At other times it is rooted in great concern for a single function. Under any of these circumstances the advocacy of separate status is generally expressed in terms of keeping (or taking) the function "out of politics," which may simply mean protecting the function from the highly partisan approach and unprofessional administration of an existing unit. Administrative personnel desiring increased job protection are sometimes in the forefront in presenting this argument. The phrase "out of politics," however, has other connotations, which are less often openly expressed and represent the feelings of many lay and professional functional specialists. It may mean keeping or placing a certain group in control of the function instead of transferring it to another organization where the influence of this group may be substantially lessened. It may mean that individuals and groups with a special interest feel that they have a better chance of obtaining public funds for a specific function if that function is separated from competing demands within a general government. It may mean that there is expectation of greater zeal and fervor for an activity when it is independent. In practice, these meanings are all included within the term of keeping or taking the function "out of politics."

The desire for independence is also advanced in support of a government that is small either in operations or in area, and often in both. In various localities throughout the United States there are strong feelings in favor of simple localism as well as of governmental separatism. The attitude is commonly expressed as "grass-roots" government. Therefore, instead of making an existing government more complex through functional enlargement, a new more simplified unit is created. This action is often related to a primary interest in one function, but it is also an outcropping of the belief that government can be better observed and controlled if it is kept small. In this line of reasoning large numbers of governments are regarded as preferable to huge operations by fewer governments. The desire for independence, in any one of its various expressions, may be a forceful factor stimulating the use of special districts even when established general units do not have or can overcome legal inadequacies.

Advocacy by Existing Governments

Existing governmental units at all levels sometimes advocate the creation of special districts. Rivalry between local governments may have this result. For example, a local government may not have legal authorization to provide a specific service which is desired. Instead of suggesting that the interested people seek to

become part of a local government of another class and thus obtain the function, it recommends the establishment of a special
district. A government follows this course when it is unwilling to
see a neighboring government strengthened. Sometimes a district
results as a compromise when two different local governments
both want to perform the function. Another circumstance, mentioned earlier in connection with financial unsuitability of existing
general units, occasionally develops when one local government
is located within the territory of another and is subject to financial
charges made by the latter for services rendered. Already performing the desired function, the first government advocates the
creation of a special district that does not include its territory.
Finally, when various local units have a common functional problem but refuse to merge territorially or to effect an intergovernmental contract, a special district is often strongly advocated and,
as the need becomes more urgent, ultimately utilized.

The influence of the state and national governments on the
establishment of special districts is exerted differently. One of the
most important means is through the impact of professional functional specialists. Their primary objective is the enhancement of
a single public activity and their promotional work may be undertaken with little consideration of its effect on existing governments.
They look upon the special district as a convenient method of
overcoming the functional deficiency, for their basic concern is
the accomplishment of the job by government, regardless of the
government involved. Even though not directly urging the cir-
cumvention of existing units, they frequently point out the difficulty of using them and suggest the special district as an alternative
that will be immediately useful. Recommendations favoring special
districts may be incorporated in officially published reports but
appear more often in memoranda to regional offices and in com-
munications sent to individuals in specific communities.[5] The rep-
utation of persons who are specialists in a governmental function
but not necessarily specialists in governmental structure and procedure is frequently impressive in decisions about satisfying service needs.

---

[5] An example of special district advocacy in a study sponsored by the national
government is *A Water Policy for the American People*, U.S. President's Water
Resources Commission (Washington: 1950), I, 184.

Financial aid by state and national governments for certain functions also influences the development of special districts. Programs are sponsored by these levels of government to remove or lessen a functional shortcoming. Again, performance of the service is emphasized without much regard for its best location governmentally. In turn, at times in response to the availability of aid from other governments, the financial inability of general government units accelerates the creation of special districts under existing laws and the passage of legislation authorizing new types of districts. The legislature or people of a state could, however, make the existing general units adequate to accept responsibility for such programs. Instead, new districts are often legally authorized. Soil conservation districts and housing authorities (districts) in many states are the product of specific policies of the national government since the 1930's. Furthermore, encouragement of the establishment of special districts by other governments extends even further than financial assistance. National and state administrators sometimes draw up model provisions for consideration by state legislators in enacting district enabling laws. Adoption of many of the suggested provisions may be a condition of receiving money grants from the government that initially presented the recommendations.

Expediency and Area Condition

Expediency is important among the reasons for the creation of special districts. Setting up such a district is an easy method of responding to a need, and can often be done quickly on the basis of existing enabling laws. People want immediate relief to satisfy a need that seems particularly compelling at the time. With some frequency, then, the motivation for utilizing special district governments is nothing more than the urgency of a service deficiency and the need for a quick answer. Although the possibility of using a general government, sometimes only after its reorganization, is not deliberately bypassed, neither is it consciously investigated. When general governments are considered as an alternative, expediency may still enter into the situation. Reluctance to wait until a long-range, possibly better solution can materialize influences the decision that supplementing existing governments is much easier than reorganizing or supplanting them. Additions to the governmental scene are usually accomplished with much greater facility than revisions or substitutions. Furthermore, additions are more likely to be supported by the governments that would otherwise be affected by reorganization.

The actual functional needs and the limited financial resources of an area are two of the underlying causes of some special districts, even when the area desires to utilize general governments. An area that is not substantially developed may really need only a few services. Yet it may be impossible to obtain limited functions from a general government. Thus, the reluctance or legal inability of a general unit to provide substantially different quantities of service prompts people who desire only limited functions to turn to special districts. Even when the legal means exist, a general government may refuse limited service because of the difficulty of determining an equitable charge for one or several of the many functions it performs. Then, too, an area may not contain financial resources sufficient to support a general array of functions. Despite a fairly extensive range of needs, a general government may not want the responsibility for providing services in an area that may become a heavy financial liability. Again, the answer is a special district, which can operate at a low financial level as well as on a restricted functional basis.

Unadorned Self-Interest

Many of the reasons for the establishment of special districts contain various shadings of self-interest on the part of groups and individuals. Some actions in favor of special districts, however, are so baldly based on complete selfishness that they warrant brief separate consideration. One illustration relates to the actions of private concerns anxious to sell equipment and supplies. Judging that their business opportunities will be enhanced, they sometimes provide the principal stimulus for the establishment of special districts. The organization of supporting "citizen groups," the payment of election fees, and the circulation of district formation petitions and nominating papers of sympathetic governing body candidates are all techniques that have been employed by businesses acting wholly in their own self-interest. The result in one instance was the creation of a sanitary district which laid sewer pipes far in excess of the needs of both the present and the foreseeable future population. Another example of self-interest is the desire of local residents to realize a return on tax money collected in their area. This self-centered attitude explains the establishment of a number of road districts in Missouri. Another far from altruistic reason for creating road districts is that they provide employment opportunities, in construction and maintenance, for governing body members and their relatives and friends.

CREATION

The creation of special districts is usually based on state enabling legislation that can be utilized anywhere in the state. Occasionally, however, a state legislature will pass a special act for the formation of a certain district in a certain locality. Sometimes, as in Rhode Island fire districts, the special act is passed after local approval is gained. Less often the legal basis of creation is a state constitutional section or amendment, an interstate compact, or an international agreement, but in most of these situations, too, action by the state legislature is part of the process. Local charters, common in many cities and some counties, are virtually unknown in special districts.

The state legislature therefore occupies the key initiating position in the establishment of practically all special districts. It generally authorizes their formation by enacting the procedure for bringing them into legal existence. Furthermore, in these enabling laws, the state legislature decides upon the major governmental characteristics of the districts, such as area, function, organization, and financial authority. It may require the area of the district to include or exclude certain other governments, although frequently no area stipulations are mentioned. It permits the performance of a specific function or functions. It authorizes financing, which may or may not include taxation, bond issuance, and service charges. It establishes the number of governing body members, the method of selecting them, and the length of their terms of office. The state legislature is thus the usual source of rules for the creation and operation of special districts, and has, moreover, the freedom to change the conditions of their continuance; it may even abolish them by rescinding the supporting laws. Most types of special districts are not protected from legislative action by state constitutional provisions or local charters, a fact that could be of major importance in a comprehensive reform movement.

An Abundance of Laws

There are many hundreds of general state laws that permit the formation of special districts, and new laws are added frequently. In addition, numerous acts relate to a particular phase of district operations and have reached such proportions, especially in the school district field, as to require compilation in lengthy codes. Basically there are many district enabling laws because there are so many needs to be met, and because each type of district usually performs only one or several functions. But the number of enabling laws far outdistances the number of district functions. This is because highly comparable but somewhat different acts are sometimes passed to authorize the establishment of districts to perform the same function or functions as a type previously authorized.

The events leading to district formation frequently occur in this sequence. Many district formation laws, although general in application, originate through sponsorship by a few individuals or a group in a single area seeking a governmental solution to a local problem. The proposal is introduced and passed in the legislature, often without opposition because the matter is judged to be one of local concern. Other areas may subsequently decide to use the provisions of the enabling law. Sometimes, however, after the law has been enacted, a group with a similar problem elsewhere in the state objects to certain features of the legislation. It may then seek to amend the law, but will probably encounter opposition from persons who have formed districts under the law and who want no changes. Or, the dissatisfied group may immediately seek a new law relating to the same function or functions but differing in some respects. Numerous legislators have concluded that it is easier, and more satisfactory to all interested parties, to pass a new district enabling law than to amend an old one. This practice, utilized much more extensively in connection with special districts than with any other class of governments, results in a number of functionally similar districts operating under different enabling laws, some of which show evidence of poor draftsmanship. It also increases the amount of district legislation and adds to the widespread confusion about special districts. The abundance of district formation acts also demonstrates the ease with which a matter of local option can pass the state legislature.

Legislative authorization for a proposed district can at times be obtained much more readily than public approval in the area. Consequently, some district formation laws have never been used. Others are no longer in use, either because their original legal unworkability was never rectified or because all districts organized under their provisions are currently inactive. Yet both categories remain legally in existence because there is no impetus for their repeal. In all likelihood there are more unused and no longer used enabling laws for special districts than for any other class of governmental units. These unrepealed acts serve as a warning about the unrealism of studying district formation laws alone and emphasize the necessity for ascertaining which laws are in operation in order to obtain an accurate picture of special districts in action.

Formation and Dissolution Diversity

The profusion of district enabling laws causes a great diversity of formation procedures. Petitioning is the most common first step in creating a special district. Only occasionally is a resolution by one or more of the governing bodies of governments in the proposed district territory substituted for the petition. Voting registration and property ownership are the two most widespread requirements for signing petitions, and both are extensively utilized. They appear predominately as separate rather than combined requirements. Some states, such as Illinois, make more frequent use of the voting qualifications. Others, like Missouri, largely stipulate property ownership, whereas Nebraska, for example, calls for about equal use of both bases. Occasionally petition signers must be both property owners and residents, or they may merely be residents without necessarily being registered voters or property owners.

The percentage or absolute number of required signatures varies widely with the different petitioning bases. As few as twenty electors or 3 per cent, or as many as 5,000 voters or a majority may be required. Among property owners from as few as one to as many as two-thirds of the total, or hundreds of individual owners possessing property valued at not less than $1,000 to $2,000, may be the stipulation. There is usually little uniformity of requirements within the same state. In general, however, the number or percentage of voters tends to be substantially less than one-half of the total, whereas the number of property owners or the percentage of property owners or of land owned tends to be more than one-half. Many districts functioning in agricultural or rural areas, such as drainage, irrigation, and soil conservation districts, use property ownership as the basis for petitioning. The signatures, whether of registered voters or property owners, may usually be obtained anywhere within the territory of the proposed district. Under a few laws they must be acquired proportionately from persons residing or owning property in specific portions, such as cities and unincorporated territory, of the proposed district area. The petition customarily describes the boundaries and sometimes the tax levies and bond issues required for district activation.

In addition to two major qualifications for petition signers, there are two principal classes of officials to whom most of the completed petitions are transmitted. They are the governing body of the county in which the district is to be located, and the presiding judge or the entire membership of an intermediate level of the courts whose jurisdiction embraces the contemplated boundaries of the district. A petition proposing an intercounty district is frequently sent to the governing body of the largest county or of the county in which the largest part of the district will be situated. A similar procedure is often followed when the court receives the petition and operates solely within one county. Less often the petition receiver is the governing body of a city, a county government board or official, or a state government board, committee, department, or official. For example, at the state level, typical examples are the state engineer, the irrigation board, the board of health, the state soil conservation committee or board, and the department of roads and irrigation.

There is considerable variance in the responsibilities of those receiving the petition. Many of the receivers are limited to determining the sufficiency and correctness of the petition, giving adequate publicity to these facts, and calling an election if one is required. Others can change proposed boundaries, usually by reducing them after public hearings. Still others can stop the formation attempt by deciding that the district is not necessary. This infrequent right is seldom used, however.

As there are two major qualifications for petition signing and two main groups for receiving petitions, there are also two widely practiced methods of completing the formation attempt. One is by election decision of the voters who in some instances must be property owners in the proposed district. The other is through exclusive legal action, often an order, by an agency or official of another government, generally the one that initially received the petition. A frequent combination of steps involving the first method consists of petition by less than a majority of voters or property owners, or by owners of less than a majority of the land, followed by a local election. Overwhelmingly, the election requirement is a simple majority of the votes cast. Far less often the stipulation involves separate majorities in the different sections or governmental areas within the district or, very rarely, a two-thirds or three-fourths majority. In rather unusual situations an individual possesses more than one vote on the basis of one vote for each designated amount of land owned. Occasionally the total balloting must equal a certain percentage of the vote cast in the area at the last general election, a requirement that is difficult to meet when the preceding election included national or state-wide offices.

The second method—exclusive legal action by another government—is the predominant or the only practice in some states and in some types of special districts, such as housing authorities. A common combination is petition by a majority of the property owners or by the owners of a majority of the land, followed by a nonelection decision. Under some groupings of petition and nonelection requirements, districts that are not supported, or are at times openly opposed, by a majority of the people within the affected territory can be brought into existence. Furthermore, when a small number or proportion of signatures is required on the petition and the petition receiver makes the sole legal judgment on activation of the district, it is sometimes possible to bring a substantial amount of land into the district, especially for purposes of taxation, whose owners may have definite justification for staying out.

Many districts have a dissolution procedure that exactly duplicates the formation process. A district may automatically cease to exist when its area is brought within the territorial limits of a city. This is by no means a universal practice, however, for in numerous circumstances a district must have a city within its boundaries in order to be created. Occasionally a highly unusual dissolution procedure is in effect. Noxious weed eradication districts in Nebraska, for example, have a twenty-five-year time limit which becomes operative unless abolition action is completed sooner. Automatic dissolution after a defined period is unknown in other classes of governments in the United States. Dissolving a district can be legally more difficult than creating it. Many districts established by the legal action of another government must be dissolved by election. Moreover, some of them require an extraordinary vote for dissolution as compared to a majority vote for formation. Two examples are irrigation and library districts in California, which can be established through majority consent but which need a two-thirds vote to be abolished.

In numerous situations it is currently a legal impossibility to abolish certain types of districts, simply because no procedure for eliminating them has ever been enacted. As an illustration, there is no abolition process for many kinds of districts in Illinois, including fire protection, sanitary, hospital, tuberculosis sanitarium, street lighting, and water. Many districts become inactive without formally dissolving under an authorized procedure or seeking to obtain such a procedure when it does not exist. Numerous school districts as well as a number of other governmental units, such as cities, have become inoperative. This practice can lead to confusion and to mistaken impressions by the casual observer. The governmental landscape is cluttered with many ghosts.

FUNCTIONS AND TITLES

Although most special districts individually provide only one or a few functions, they collectively supply an extremely broad range of activities, some of which are not usually undertaken by government. In some states they perform in total more services than some of the classes of general governments, such as counties and townships in certain states, and a number of less populous cities and New England towns. Most special districts, however, separately furnish only one function or a narrowly limited number of services and are therefore unique among the principal classes of governments in the United States.[6] In this respect they are most strikingly different from the national government, but are also very unlike states, counties, cities, and many New England towns. Even townships, which have been declining in functional importance, possess more functions than many types of special districts. Most districts provide one or two services, and those supplying more are exceptions to the usual pattern.

Eleven Categories

The functions performed by special districts are so numerous that they do not easily lend themselves to classification, but a helpful grouping into eleven categories is possible. They are health and sanitation; protection to persons and property; road transportation facilities and aids; nonroad transportation facilities and aids; utilities; housing; natural resource and agricultural assistance; education; parks and recreation; cemeteries; and miscellaneous. The following enumeration of functions under each category is substantially all-inclusive and was formulated only after detailed analysis of the district powers in use under the laws of each state. The practice of considering district powers actually in operation, employed throughout this study, provides a realistic approach because numerous district laws are no longer in use or have never been utilized, and far from all districts perform the full extent of the authority granted them.

---

[6] Even this basic differentiation is lessening to some extent. In recent years, for example, California, Colorado, and Michigan legislatures have passed acts permitting the establishment of districts possessing a wide range of functions.

In the health and sanitation category, special districts provide sewage, garbage, and refuse disposal; drainage; general and special hospitals; water pollution control; mosquito abatement; pest extermination; food inspection; and various other sanitary and health measures and activities. In the protective field they supply policing and fire fighting and prevention.

Districts that furnish transportation facilities construct and maintain streets, pleasure drives, highways, sidewalks, bridges, tunnels, and terminals. They provide street and highway lighting as well as parking facilities. They plant and care for roadside trees. They own and operate mass transit facilities, including those in such densely populated places as the Boston and Chicago areas. In the nonroad transportation field, special districts build, manage, and control airports, harbors and ports, and their facilities. They operate airplanes and boats, regulate navigation, and supply watercourse improvements.

In the utilities category special districts supply water, lighting, power, telephone, heat, ice, and fuel. In the housing category they build and operate low-rent public housing projects, clear slum areas, and engage in urban redevelopment. There are many districts that provide natural resource and agricultural assistance. Some of them are concerned with the use or control of water and engage in irrigation, flood control, water conservation, reclamation, drainage, diking, and levee construction. Others revitalize and preserve the quality of the soil, eradicate debilitating weeds, eliminate predatory animals, undertake forestation, abate pests, and build fences and gates to protect agricultural holdings.

In education, special districts provide instruction and other educational services, and range from kindergarten to the collegiate level. In addition, they build and operate libraries. In the parks and recreation category, special districts acquire and manage both city and regional parks as well as playgrounds and other recreational facilities, prevent beach erosion, and erect community centers. The function of acquiring and administering cemeteries stands as a separate division of district activities because it is not readily classifiable elsewhere and represents a substantial numerical total. The remaining functions of special districts are classified as miscellaneous because of their great diversity. Among other matters, special districts construct and direct veterans' memorial buildings, provide planning and zoning, license vehicles and businesses, and acquire and maintain marketing facilities.

Some of the various functions of special districts are performed by only a few districts, and others are performed by thousands. Especially prevalent are the districts that undertake education, drainage, soil conservation, irrigation and water conservation, housing, street and highway construction and maintenance, fire protection, and urban water supply. Most districts engage in service rather than regulatory activities, many of them of an income-producing nature. When a district possesses more than one function, the functions are very often complementary and closely related, such as fire protection and water or water and sewage disposal. Special districts obviously have a tremendous impact upon many people in numerous localities, and some of them individually have an effect of considerable magnitude.

Helpful and Confusing Titles

Unlike other governments, a special district very often has the function it performs as part of its official title or designation. The national government of the United States, the state government of New Hampshire, Republic County (Kansas), West Bloomfield Township (Michigan), and the City of Magnolia (Arkansas) are all official designations of units in other classes of governments, but none contains a functional word in its title. The official names of most special districts offer a strong contrast. Frequently the name of the geographic location or region covered by the district is adopted as part, and often the first portion, of the official appellation. Thus, in Florida, there are such representative examples as the Indian River Mosquito Control District, the West Coast Inland Navigation District, the Maryland Manor Special Sanitary District, and the South Interbay Special Light District. Similarly, special districts active in Missouri include the Cape Special Road District, the Little River Drainage District, the Eminence Fire Protection District, and the Jackson County Library District. Many thousands of school districts follow a similar practice of being legally known by a name in which the geographical location precedes the term "school district" or a more restricted term relating to a specific level of education, such as elementary school, high school, or junior college. The official names of some districts contain a number, such as the East Jefferson Waterworks District Number One of Jefferson Parish (County), Louisiana, and the Sixth Taxing District of Norwalk, Connecticut. This form of designation may well serve its purpose of identification but is utterly devoid of the romantic quality inherent in the names of many other governmental entities.

The function appearing as part of the official name of a district does not always accurately indicate the range of the district's activities. Instead, it sometimes reveals merely one activity in which the district may legally be involved but which it may not actually be exercising. Furthermore, the functional designation in the title is at times overgeneralized and therefore not very meaningful. Thus, protection districts in California could be thought of as performing any one of a number of protective functions, whereas they actually safeguard against overflow water.

Generally the insertion of a too limited or too nebulous functional word into the formal designation of a special district causes much less confusion than another difficulty involving titles. The word "district" is usually part of the official appellation, but not always. Some special district governments are legally known as authorities, although it should be stressed that not all authorities are special districts. In addition, other words such as board, commission, association, and area are employed in place of district. Again, terms that are more generally employed in other types of governments are sometimes used by districts; examples are village in Maryland, community in Oregon, and precinct in New Hampshire. Usually terms such as these have been used in some states to designate some kinds of districts, while at the same time the word "district" has been applied to other kinds.

Among governments, special districts are not alone in having bewildering titles, for municipal corporations in some states furnish numerous examples, but in a smaller range. This, however, does not lessen the difficulty of recognizing a special district when it exists under an ambiguous name. Even the term "special district" is not always entirely satisfactory, for an important minority of such districts have more than one purpose rather than a single one. There is, however, no movement toward adoption of a different word. Some special districts, therefore, are special mainly in the sense that they are not yet regarded as traditional units of government.

AREAS

Compared with other governments, special districts often have highly unusual area characteristics.[7] A major differentiation is one of location rather than of territorial size. Special districts can nearly always occupy any part of the area of all other kinds of special districts; only occasionally are they specifically excluded from doing so. Furthermore, the area of a special district can in many instances cover a segment of or all the territory of other governments that are not special districts. Territorially, therefore, most kinds of special districts do not have to be mutually exclusive of one another or of other governments. The result is that many types of special districts pile upon one another and other governments in the same area.

In contrast, no city may be situated on any portion of the territory of another city. Counties are also territorially exclusive of one another, as are townships, towns, states, and nations. A general government of one class, however, does sometimes overlap at least one of another class. Counties overlie the boundaries of cities in most states and of townships in states that have township organization. Some townships also contain cities within their borders. Nevertheless, the more general area flexibility of special districts in relation to other types of districts and other classes of governments largely accounts for the overlapping of governments in the United States.

Mandatory Inclusion and Exclusion

In addition to the optional right of most districts to overlie the area of other governmental units, the frequent initial requirement that another government must be part of the district territory also

---

[7] A basic indication of the uniqueness is that in the judgment of the Census Bureau a few special districts do not even have area since they are associated with an undefined rather than an explicitly defined territory. *Local Government Structure in the United States*, U.S. Bureau of the Census, Governments Division (Washington: 1954), p. 3. Notable examples are several districts that provide bridge facilities. This condition is completely unknown to other classes of governmental units in the United States.

contributes to overlapping. At least one city must be included within the boundaries of numerous kinds of districts. Most often only one city is required, but the mandatory inclusion of two or more cities is not unknown. Even though the district and the city are sometimes coterminous (which adds to the confusion), they are separate and independent governments. In a similar but less frequent pattern an entire county must be included within the district borders, and often the district and the county occupy exactly the same total area. Furthermore, several types of districts must have all or parts of two and sometimes more counties within their area, which means that they not only occupy at least part of the area of other governments but also cross over their boundaries. Infrequently a district is required by its enabling law to have another district within its boundaries. As mentioned previously, the existence of one district in the territory of other districts is not unusual.

The most common legal restriction on the area of districts is that certain ones can be organized only in unincorporated territory. In a practical sense this requirement excludes cities from the district territory. Although appearing with only moderate frequency, such formal exclusion does reduce governmental overlapping to some extent; it is, however, inapplicable to other districts, counties, and, in states where they are functioning, townships. As an illustration, a district that may not have a city within its borders may still cross over county, district, and township lines. It may even be interstate or international under appropriate written agreements. Another restriction, used even less often, stipulates that the territory of a district must be entirely within one county.

Considerable Freedom

The areal flexibility of many districts is rooted in the wide territorial discretion assured to them by state laws. Much state legislation places no restrictions upon area, or simply requires that the territory of the district, wherever located, be compact and contiguous. Such legal provisions furnish many districts broader area possibilities than counties, cities, and townships have. In order to facilitate the performance of the district operation, far more districts are composed of contiguous territory than is legally required.

However, a number of districts consist of noncontiguous territory—that is, part of the district area is separated from the remainder by land that is not included within the district. Some drainage and irrigation districts in several states are examples. Another prominent illustration is the Golden Gate Bridge and Highway District whose famous bridge spans San Francisco Bay from San Francisco to the north and whose area includes one city-county, four entire counties, and part of another county. The northernmost county, however, is separated from the remainder of the district by a county that is not part of the district.

Another noteworthy area feature of special districts is the freedom of most of them from the three standards of minimum assessed valuation, territorial size, and population. The absence of a population requirement puts special districts in direct contrast with cities in many states. Very few districts are legally required to have a particular minimum assessed valuation within their borders, or to contain a certain number of acres or square miles. When a minimum area requirement exists, it sometimes relates to a large-scale district undertaking and calls for a substantial amount of land to be included. As illustrations, reclamation districts in the state of Washington must contain not less than 1 million acres and Nebraska rural fire protection districts must have at least 36 square miles. Both of these minima greatly exceed the actual size of many other local governments in the United States.

Effect of Other Governments

A few kinds of districts must possess a specific minimal number of inhabitants. This usually occurs when a city or sometimes a county, possessing not less than a stated number of inhabitants, must be included within the proposed district. At times, when a district must contain at least two cities, they must have a minimum aggregate population. Such districts therefore cannot have less than the population of the city (or cities) or the county that is to be within their territorial limits. Only rarely is an exact district population minimum directly stipulated, irrespective of the presence or absence of other governments within the district.

Several kinds of districts are limited to a maximum area. Some of these restrictions are determined by the area of a government functioning within the borders of the district. The boundaries of some districts required to have a city within their territory may extend only a specified number of miles beyond the limits of the city. Housing authorities in North Carolina, for example, may not extend more than 10 miles beyond the corporate limits of the city that must be part of the district. The area of the city itself and the nature of its borders therefore directly affect the total territory that can be brought within the district. Other districts have their territorial size conditioned by the population size of the cities they adjoin. The territorial extent of a suburban improvement district in Arkansas adjacent to a city of 5,000 can be only one-fifth as large as the maximum permitted to the same type of district bordering a city of 50,000. In addition, there are further area gradations for districts adjoining cities of two intermediate population groups.

Potentialities and Handicaps

This consideration of various aspects of the area of special districts illustrates that one of their outstanding characteristics is area flexibility. Many of them are legally empowered to contain a large amount of territory without regard to the boundaries of other governments that cover all or part of the same land. Quite often they cross city, township, town, and county lines (as well as other district boundaries), and include both urban and rural land. Such authorization furnishes them great latitude in both location and territorial extent. Fifteen special districts include area within more than one state as the result of the adoption of interstate compacts. A few function under international agreements and are international in that the facility they operate, such as a bridge, has its terminal points in two different countries.

Despite their area potentialities, many special districts are actually small in comparison with cities. Some encompass only a fraction of a square mile. But others, often including some of the same types utilized in small areas (such as water districts), embrace the major portion of a state. In some states, usually in rural sections, one special district possesses the smallest area and another the largest of all governments functioning below the state level. An occasional district is territorially larger than some of the smaller states in other parts of the Union. Although many districts have small areas, collectively they include most of the territory of the United States, and in some sections of the country they themselves constitute two or more layers of government. Both school and soil conservation districts include a very large portion of the United States. Below the state level, the county is the only governmental unit that rivals the total amount of territory within special districts. Cities, towns, and townships contain far less of the total land of the nation.

Many types of special districts have additional area flexibility through legal authorization to annex territory not originally part of the district. The existing boundaries of other governments are usually no obstacle in such annexation actions. At times the enlargement procedure is quite easy. Frequently annexation can be initiated within either the district or the territory under consideration, and a combined, over-all vote of both areas or a nonvoter action, such as a court order, decides the issue. Sometimes a very small percentage or number of individuals can start the proceedings.

Ease of annexing is not universal, however. A number of districts are legally unable to change their boundaries through annexation once they have been established. In some states no kind of district is able to annex, and in others there are many that cannot do so. There is some indication that occasionally this was a legislative oversight rather than a purposeful omission.

The annexation process utilized by many districts is confining. Often the people in the area to be absorbed have the exclusive right to initiate the action. In addition, the landowners and not the voters in the area under consideration must frequently sign the petition. The difficulty may be increased when the landowners do not have equality in signing the petition but instead are weighted according to the amount of land owned. Under some laws signatures must be obtained from those owning more than one-half of the value of the land. Thus a small minority of landowners or even one person may control the outcome of an annexation attempt. At times a large percentage or a large number of signatures must be obtained, with the result that the required number of signers may exceed the number of individuals already in the district. Still another hurdle arises from the voting requirement that separate popular approval in each area, or at least in the area to be annexed, must be forthcoming. The requirement of an extraordinarily large majority may be another barrier. The prevalence of such restrictive features means that many districts, when being established, have considerable area latitude but subsequently are severely confined. This reduces the ability of districts to encompass the entire natural areas of functional demand as such areas enlarge. It also accounts, in part, for the proliferation of special districts.

One final characteristic should be noted because of its distinguishing nature and importance. The general lack of information and knowledge about the location and limits of special districts after their establishment makes even their approximate boundaries largely unknown. Such a deficiency, fostered by the numerousness and the pyramiding of districts, prevails among many district residents and among practically all outside persons, a number of whom may indirectly be very much affected by district activities. Incoming residents usually know in advance, or soon learn about, the other governmental areas within which they are locating, such as a state, county, township, or city. But many of them do not discover their special district areas until the tax and service bills arrive. Even this kind of revelation is not always forthcoming, for such charges sometimes appear in the consolidated bill of another government which is serving as the collection agency for the district. Many individuals think that one of the other governments to which they are contributing financially is furnishing a service that is actually being supplied by a special district.

In this sense many special districts are phantom governments. People who receive services from them often do not know that they exist or exactly where they function. Although most districts have definite areas and boundaries which limit their jurisdiction, there is seldom visible evidence of these facts. Districts often create a crazy-quilt pattern of governmental areas and boundaries with only very slight public knowledge that they do so. Their phantom-like quality does not diminish their collective and sometimes individual importance. It merely increases the difficulty of comprehending a class of governments which is of rising significance.

GOVERNING BODIES

The most noticeable feature of the governing bodies of special districts is the division between direct election and appointment in the selection of their members. The members are elected in the majority of districts, but the margin of difference over appointment is not overwhelming. Some types of district governing bodies, in school districts, for example, are predominantly elected throughout various sections of the nation. Others, such as those in housing authorities, are always appointed. Some districts, such as soil conservation districts, usually have both appointive and elective governing personnel. The diversity is also evident in comparisons between states. Appointment of the members of the district governing bodies is the dominant requirement in some states, such as Alabama and Mississippi. Other states, including Arizona and Oregon, largely stipulate election, and still others, such as Utah, make fairly equal use of the two methods. Sometimes no uniform process of selection is provided in special acts relating to the creation of even the same functional type of district in the same state. Water districts and sewer districts in Maine are illustrative.

Whether elected or appointed, governing bodies have numerous characteristics in common. The official title of the members is usually director, commissioner, or trustee, with supervisor and board member appearing less frequently. Occasionally the collective designation is citizen committee or prudential committee. Total membership is almost always an odd number, usually three to five, though it may range from eleven to as many as thirty-six. Infrequently a single person governs the district. Many district governing bodies are therefore smaller than those of most other governments and, although some are unwieldy in size, none approaches the total membership of the governing bodies of certain counties. A few districts have an even number of board members, which at times results in deadlocked votes.

The terms of office generally range from two to six years but three- and four-year terms are most prevalent. Governing body members, however, sometimes hold office for five or six years, and occasionally for only one year; a frequent combination involves three members serving for three years. There is much less uniformity in the length of the term when there are five members. Occasionally members who are appointed serve indefinitely at the pleasure of the appointing authority. Staggered or overlapping terms are frequent for both elective and appointive offices. Election methods are few in number and well known in many other governments; election is either at large or on a district basis, but the former is the more general practice. Conversely, appointment procedures are much more diversified and are frequently complex.

Appointment Methods

Most often a single group or individual from another government acts as the appointing authority. Many times the authority that receives the formation petition and creates the district also chooses the governing body. The most frequent selecting agent is the governing body of the county in which the district is situated. Another customary appointing authority is a court or the presiding judge of a court, usually at an intermediate level of the state judicial system within whose jurisdiction the district lies. Appearing less often in the role of appointer is the governing body of a city, the mayor of a city, or the governor of a state. The governor usually appoints when the district covers a large area and handles a function, such as port or airport, which may be judged to have state-wide effect. The governing bodies of a few types of districts are chosen at the state level by an administrative official, an administrative agency, a committee, or the legislature. Generally, when the legislature does the appointing, it accepts the recommendation of the legislative delegation from the area involved.

At times a joint appointing responsibility, either dual or triple, of different units, levels, or branches of government adds to the variety and complexity of selecting the members of district governing boards. Selection decisions by the governing body or chief executive of at least two governments at the local level may be required. The various combinations are two or more cities, one or more cities and counties, a town and a village, or any of these units plus special districts. Each government may appoint a specified number separately, or may agree jointly upon selections for the entire membership. Action by different levels of government may be necessary. Separate appointments by the governor, the county governing body, and the city governing body constitute one system currently in operation. Another consists of independent appointment action by the county governing body and the governor. Occasionally one unit of government recommends, another has the right to approve or disapprove, and other nominations must be submitted in the event of disapproval. The five commissioners of the Albany Port District in New York are appointed by the governor; four are nominated by the mayor of Albany and one by the mayor of Rensselaer. Three of the trustees of the Metropolitan St. Louis Sewer District are chosen by the mayor of St. Louis with the approval of a majority of the judges in the circuit court in the city. The other three are appointed by the county supervisor (executive) of St. Louis County, similarly with majority consent by the circuit court in the county.

Different branches of government and sometimes different levels of government are jointly concerned in the selection of the governing members of some districts. Under the most complex method, individual appointments to the board are made by the judges of two different levels of courts, the county governing body, and the mayor of the largest city within the district. The procedure may be interstate or even international, with selection by the governors of two states or by the governor of one state and the appropriate authority of another country. Occasionally most of the members of a district governing body, appointed in various ways, choose others to serve with them. Under some of these procedures there is serious doubt as to the degree of effective control that people residing within the district and influenced by its operations can exercise over the governing body.

The appointed board membership of some special districts includes at least one person serving by reason of his official position with another government, often a government that is within the territory of the district. In California, for example, when a county sewerage and water district contains incorporated area the presiding officer of each city within the district is an ex officio member of its governing body. It is unusual to have a special district governing body consist entirely of ex officio members, and in such instances most of them do not hold office with the same government. One of the few examples of this type of district is the consolidated health district in New York, whose members are the mayor of the city, supervisor of the town, and village mayor or president of the village board of trustees of the participating governments. All of them are officeholders in other governments, but no two come from the same governmental unit. In general, ex officio members do not receive additional compensation for their increased assignments in various districts.

Many officials of other governments who are on district governing boards are not ex officio members. Instead, they serve because the governing body of a government within the district has the right to appoint a representative to the board and decides to select him from its own membership. This is a discretionary right to choose either a private individual or a public official. Although service by officials of other governments on district governing bodies, whether ex officio or not, may facilitate intergovernmental coöperation, it may also unduly divert these individuals from the main task for which they were initially elected or appointed.

The governing bodies of some special districts are selected partly by election and partly by appointment. The most prominent example of this hybrid arrangement is found in soil conservation districts in many states. The usual pattern is a board of five members, two appointed by a state soil conservation committee and three elected by the local district voters. It is also possible for the membership of housing authorities in certain Massachusetts localities to be a mixture of elected and appointed members. Four are elected at the town meeting and the fifth is appointed by a state housing board.

How can these many types of special districts, governed wholly or partly by appointed board members, still be independent units of government? It is because, like special districts with elected governing boards, they conduct their fiscal and administrative activities without substantial review or modification by other governments, including those appointing board members. Within the framework of state legislative and constitutional limits on their finances and any general state supervision of governments, they determine their own budgets and financing programs and carry out policy and administrative decisions which they have formulated. Appointed board members are not legally subject to important control by the appointing authority. Most members are selected for definite terms and cannot be removed by the appointing agent except upon substantiation of serious charges. This tenure right also strengthens their autonomy. In actual practice appointees have wide freedom during their period of service.

But what about district governing bodies with ex officio members? Such a district is an independent unit of government when the ex officio representatives from one other government do not constitute a majority. If a district is governed directly by the governing body of another unit, such as a county or a city, it is not an independent government but a dependent district or adjunct of another government. There are many dependent districts but they are not special districts in the sense of being separate governmental units.[8]

The key test of a special district as a separate unit of government is not whether its governing body is appointed or elected or even ex officio. Some districts have elected governing bodies which are under close administrative and fiscal surveillance by another government; they are therefore dependent districts. The basic determinant is whether the district possesses substantial freedom from other governments in its fiscal and administrative operations.

Numerous Influences

The selection method and the number of members on the governing board sometimes depend upon the size of the district or the number of governmental units within the district territory which are participating members. The state legislation does not always provide for the selection method and a fixed number of members. Sometimes decisions about appointment or election of the governing body and the number of members are made by the district voters at the election to create the district or by the circulators of petitions to form the district. Election of members has usually been favored. Determination of the appointing authority depends at times on whether the district is in one or more counties. Under one method, the county governing board chooses the governing body when the district includes only unincorporated territory within one county, and the governor selects the members when the area is

---

[8] Dependent districts are considered separately in chap. 7.

intercounty. Other times the number of governments within the district determines both the appointing authority and the number on the board. One variation of this procedure is to have the mayor appoint a council-determined number when the area of the district is entirely within one city, and to have the mayor of each city choose one member when the district includes more than one city.

Sometimes the appointing authority is determined by the location of the major portion of the district. Thus appointments are made by the presiding judge of the court in the county containing the largest part of the district area. Sometimes the size of the district fixes the number on the board and the areas from which they are elected. In North Dakota, for example, irrigation districts of less than 10,000 acres have three directors elected at large, but those of more than 10,000 acres have three to seven governing board members elected by districts. In some situations the governing body is composed of representatives selected by governments within the district territory, such as cities, counties, and special districts. These districts frequently are of the same functional type as the one on which they have representation, but cover a smaller area. In such arrangements, each of the governments usually has an equal number of members on the governing body regardless of population. Occasionally, however, representation of the participating governments is founded partly upon assessed valuation, most commonly when the district is empowered to levy taxes. Such flexibility in the methods of selection can raise obstacles to the smooth functioning of district governments, either because the governing board is so large as to be unwieldy, or because it consists of an even number of members.

Eligibility, Salary, and Service

The most usual eligibility requirements for governing body membership are residence, voting registration, and property ownership in the territory of the district. Sometimes it is necessary to have all three, but ordinarily one or two are sufficient. Only occasionally is there a more specialized requirement, such as in California memorial districts where the governing body members must be veterans. In practice, however, the members of many special districts are drawn heavily from occupations on which district activities have a direct bearing. Water and port districts are two frequent cases in point.

Compensation is generally nominal or nonexistent. This is true of large as well as of small operations, as indicated by the highly important Port of New York Authority and the Hartford County (Connecticut) Metropolitan District, whose boards receive no salary. Frequently a small sum is paid for each regular meeting attended. Only a few governing body members receive as much as $1,000 a year. In scattered instances members receive relatively high pay for their services. For example, the directors of the Chicago Transit Authority are each paid an annual salary of $15,000, and the chairman's salary is even higher. A very large number of district board members serve more than a single term of one to six years, for many of them are reappointed or reëlected. Frequently their tenure is terminated only because of their own desires, poor health, or death. Many who are elected run for reëlection without opposition.

A widespread practice has developed among board members who obtain office on an elective basis. A member who has decided not to seek reëlection resigns before the election so that his successor, often selected by the remainder of the board membership, can run as the incumbent. This seems to dissuade some individuals who might otherwise become candidates. The technique is not completely unknown to other governments, but is more common among special districts. Sometimes, however, the decision by a governing board member not to seek reëlection has created a situation where there are more offices to be filled by election than people formally seeking them. In some district elections not a single name appears on the official ballot. Under such circumstances a limited number of write-in votes, often cast for a reluctant or perhaps unknowing person, is sufficient. This sequence of events is highly extraordinary in elections held by other governmental units.

In some states elected district members serve longer average periods than appointed members. This is because the individual or a majority of the group initially making the appointment may meet strong and successful opposition at the polls before the time of reappointment, while at the same time elected board members have few, if any, opposing candidates. In numerous districts at least one member has been serving continuously for a decade or a quarter of a century. Some have been on the governing body almost all of their adult life.

The chairman or president of the district governing body is seldom directly elected or appointed to the position. When this is the procedure, however, he sometimes serves a shorter term than his associates on the board. Much more commonly, the presiding officer is elected or appointed as a regular member and is elevated to the chairmanship or presidency by vote of the board membership. Although frequently the presiding term is one year, or lasts until the board composition changes through subsequent elections or appointments, continuance in the position over an extended period is not unusual.

Board Activities and Administration

There is considerable variation in the amount and nature of the work performed by district governing bodies. Most of them convene once or twice a month, a small number meet every week, and a few hold annual meetings. Many handle directly all policy considerations and most of the administrative details, especially in the smaller districts. Some boards confine themselves to setting broad policies, generally overseeing administration, and assigning administrative activities to district administrators and employees. Some provide little policy initiation or administrative guidance. Most district governing boards have complete freedom in shaping the administrative organization because state laws are generally silent on the matter. This power is often unused because of the limited amount or volunteer nature of the activity undertaken by many districts.

More than one-third of the nonschool special districts have no paid employees, a condition that is most apparent in fire protection and soil conservation districts. The average number of employees of all nonschool special districts is slightly more than nine. About 5 per cent of such districts have more than twenty-five employees, and only 1 per cent employ at least 100 individuals. Twelve districts employ more than 1,000 persons each, and of these the Chicago Transit Authority stands first with approximately 17,000.[9] On the other hand, the employment level of school districts is much higher. Employing more than nine-tenths of the total district personnel, they average about twenty-three paid persons, more than four-fifths of whom are full-time. Most special districts have an administrative organization, although at times it is skeletal.

District officials and employees are almost always appointed directly by the governing body members or with their ultimate approval. Usually the board creates an administrative organization centering on an individual who handles details arising between board meetings, or who coördinates or manages administrative operations. This person is called the manager, executive secretary, executive director, engineer, clerk, or superintendent. The last title is the prevalent one in school districts. In some medium-sized and large special districts the governing body does not organize the administration around a single person. Instead, it employs coequal managers of business and technical affairs and has each report to the board. Other employees include technical, professional, clerical, and laboring personnel. In the larger district establishments there is often an elaborate administrative structure, with numerous departments and divisions, supervisory officials, and staff aides to the central administrator in financial preparation and control and administrative and physical planning. When a fairly detailed administrative structure exists, employees are often actually hired by the department or division chief upon approval by the central administrator, unless the board expresses opposition to specific appointments.

This personnel policy is typical of the relationships of central administrators to the governing bodies of many districts of all sizes. Some district governing bodies therefore act largely as a potential vetoer of proposed actions of the appointed central administrator. In some districts the board seldom initiates policy or questions administrative practices. Over an extended period of years some of them have not disapproved or even asked for more detailed information about any proposal presented to them by the

---

[9] *Special District Governments in the United States,* U.S. Bureau of the Census, Governments Division, State and Local Government Special Studies No. 33 (Washington: 1954), pp. 2–3.

administrator. This easy acquiescence can be attributed in part to the occasional nature of service on many governing bodies and the technical character of some district operations. It is not entirely lacking in other governments, and its existence raises doubts as to whether governing bodies are exercising their proper role in the governmental process.

In many types of districts none of the employees, including the central administrator, has any tenure rights. Many districts have no formal civil service procedure and grant no contract to the administrator. This might be expected in small districts but it also prevails in some larger ones. Most of the exceptions are found among school districts, many of whose employees have job tenure after a probationary period and many of whose superintendents and administrative staff members have contracts for one to four years. In contrast, most of the more than 1,300 managers of city governments in the United States are not given contracts.

The meetings of district governing bodies are usually attended only by the members and their aides. Although such meetings are open to anyone, they are not often attended by either newspaper reporters or private citizens. The voluntary absence of the two groups is interrelated, since citizens stay away because they are not sufficiently interested, and newspapers generally report only those public affairs in which there is a reasonable amount of public interest. Most newspapers simply cannot afford to have representatives watch the activities of all the governments operating in a specific area, especially those attracting a minimum of public interest. Also, citizens do not like to make such an investment of personal time unless controversial issues are going to be aired.

The major exception in public and newspaper coverage of district board meetings is found in many school districts. Here, too, however, attendance tends to be sporadic, especially by the public but also frequently by the press. Even in some large school districts located in heavily urbanized areas, newspapers send reporters only when an important issue or decision is anticipated or has been announced in advance. In contrast, regular newspaper coverage is the general rule at the meetings of city and county governing bodies.

Complete lack of newspaper and public observance of district

governing body meetings over a sustained period of time sometimes results in strange proceedings. A pertinent illustration is the
procedure followed by the directors of a special district, important
both territorially and functionally, in the western part of the
United States. The directors first hold a closed meeting in one of
the inner offices of the headquarters building at a regularly scheduled time preceding the official meeting. There they resolve their
differences of opinion, if any exist, and then proceed to the official
meeting place at the announced time. Up to this point the procedure has not been unlike that actually followed by the governing bodies of many local governments. But once the governing
body of the district officially convenes, the board secretary merely
reads off as official acts of the directors the decisions that were
made in closed session. Neither the chairman nor any member
makes a motion for adoption or generally utters any comment during the reading by the secretary. The closed session is thus followed by an almost silent meeting.

FINANCES

Limited Revenue Methods

The revenue sources legally available to special districts for financing their services are generally quite narrow. This is true of both
school and nonschool special districts, although they differ markedly in the types of sources most important to them. School districts derive more than nine-tenths of their revenue from taxes on
property and transfers of funds from other governmental units,
largely state governments. Most of the small remainder is obtained
from service charges and other miscellaneous nontax sources with
only incidental amounts coming from other taxes. The principal
direct source of revenue for school districts is therefore the property tax, with heavy supplementation by grants and subventions
from other governments. Only occasionally, as in Pennsylvania in
recent years, do other types of taxes, like those on income and sales,
produce a significant amount of direct revenue. By contrast, property taxes and intergovernmental transfers account for only
approximately one-fourth of the revenue of nonschool districts.
Instead, nontax revenues such as service charges, special assess-

ments, rates, and rents constitute about three-fourths of the total.[10] The extremely heavy reliance of special districts on a highly restricted revenue base contrasts strongly with the diversification permitted other classes of governments, including cities, states, and the national government.

Another prominent financial characteristic of many nonschool special districts is the lack of legal authorization to levy taxes. More than one-third of them have no taxing authority. Furthermore, when the taxing power exists it is usually limited to the right to levy taxes on property. Individual and corporate income, sales and gross receipts, death and gift, and motor vehicle taxes therefore bring them no revenue. More than half of the districts that do have the power to tax property are restricted in its use. This restriction is usually stated as a maximum number of mills (frequently 2 to 5 mills), a specific number of cents on each $100 of assessed valuation (often 10 cents), or a certain per cent of the value of taxable property in the district (often 1 per cent). The power to tax property is sometimes even more limited, in that the money so derived may be used only to pay the costs of organizing the district, the interest on the retirement of bonds, or the incidental administrative expenses necessary to the functional activity of the district.

Nontax Sources and Bonds

Since many districts lack the taxing power or can use it only in a circumscribed way, where do they acquire additional money to finance their operations? Nearly one-half of the types of nonschool districts and a large number of school districts are legally empowered to obtain revenue through charges for services rendered. This is an extremely important source of public funds for special districts, particularly for many nonschool districts that lack authority to levy property taxes. Many more school districts have both revenue possibilities, but service charges are much less significant to them than to nonschool districts. This nontax revenue

---

[10] *Summary of Governmental Finances in 1955*, U.S. Bureau of the Census, Governments Division (Washington: 1956), p. 20. Relatively small amounts of revenue, derived from contributions for social insurance and retirement programs, have been excluded in determining these proportions. In 1952, 7 per cent of the nonschool special districts collected revenue of $100,000 or more, and 74 per cent obtained less than $10,000. *Special District Governments in the United States*, p. 1.

source—service charges—is used in several ways by special districts. The diversity should be explained but the illustrations should not be interpreted as necessarily exemplifying uniformity of kind or function. Special assessments are exacted in proportion to the benefits derived from operation of the district. For example, districts levy assessments for draining excess water from land, transporting water to depleted soil for irrigation, or protecting an area from inundation. They impose tolls for the use of district property, such as crossing a bridge. They collect rates and charges for furnishing various services including power, transit, gas, and water. They obtain rents for housing they own and operate, and charge fees for the facilities and staff services of a hospital or sanitarium.

Districts obtain a major share of their money through borrowing, and thus incur indebtedness. Most special districts can legally issue bonds which are often retired by using income and other non-tax sources rather than property taxation. Generally a bond proposal must gain the approval of voters eligible to participate in an election. A two-thirds popular majority is the most frequent stipulation, but a simple majority is often legally adequate; infrequently a three-fifths affirmative vote is necessary. Sometimes majorities must be obtained in different parts of the district, such as within and outside a city. The majority may vary with the nature of the bonds. For example, a two-thirds margin may be necessary for general obligation bonds and a simple majority may be sufficient for revenue bonds which are dependent for payment upon money collected by the district in performing its service. Occasionally bonds may be issued without submitting the question to the voters. This is done through action initiated and approved by the district governing body.

Most state legislatures have placed restrictions on the floating of bonds. The least common is a maximum limit on the amount of outstanding bonds, ranging from 1 per cent to 25 per cent of the assessed value of the property within the district. Much more customary limitations impose a maximum interest payable to bondholders, and a maximum period of time for the bonds to be outstanding. The legal interest ranges from 4½ to 8 per cent, with 6 per cent very common. The final maturity date may be from five to seventy-five years after issue. Requirements of twenty or forty years are frequent. It is sometimes specifically stipulated that a certain portion of the bonds shall fall due at definitely scheduled periods instead of an entire issue maturing at one time. Thus, in one kind of district, 5 per cent of the bonds are due and subject to call at the end of ten years, and 5 per cent in each following year. Another type of district is required to make payment on 10 per cent of the bonds in ten years and on an additional 10 per cent in each subsequent year.

The issuance of bonds is a major method of financing district activities. It is a financial power widely extended to districts and used extensively by them, and its broad utilization is illustrated by the amount of outstanding district debt. The indebtedness of nonschool districts is more than $5.8 billion, and that of school districts exceeds $7.2 billion. The combined debt of districts is approximately four-fifths as large as the indebtedness of cities, which rank first in indebtedness among all state and local governments. District debt is mostly long-term, and a substantial portion of it has been incurred for construction purposes. However, one-third of the long-term indebtedness of nonschool districts is nonguaranteed and therefore payable only from specific sources, rather than being of the full-faith-and-credit type which pledges the entire financial resources. Conversely, all long-term debt of school districts is of the latter category.[11]

Nonschool districts rely most heavily upon bond issues and various types of service charges for income. Direct taxes and grants and subventions from other governments occupy subsidiary positions.[12] Nonschool districts are thus the only governmental units in the United States that do not place heavy dependence upon direct taxation. Bonds are also important to the finances of school districts, but service charges are subordinate. In contrast, too, the transfer of revenue from other governments and direct tax levies, especially on property, are primary and almost equally productive sources of money to school districts. Special districts therefore

[11] *Summary of Governmental Finances in 1955*, p. 32.

[12] However, soil conservation districts in numerous states are not within the customary nonschool district financing pattern. Although they can levy charges against benefited landowners, they actually finance their activities through grants and appropriations from other governments. They lack authority to levy taxes and to issue bonds.

derive their funds from various sources, but the relative importance of the sources differs for nonschool and school districts, and
district financing is substantially unlike that of any other class of
governments in the United States.

Because of the limited functional scope of most individual special districts, they collectively show a great diversity of types or
kinds and a wide variety of characteristics, far exceeding those for
any other class of governments. In turn, this has resulted in a
greater over-all complexity of the nation's governmental pattern.
For detailed consideration and analysis in subsequent chapters, the
numerous types have been arranged in five major groups which
together make up the entire class of governments known as special
districts. Because of the great variety, not every district can be
exclusively compartmentalized into a major group. This poses no
particular problem, because some districts serve as excellent illustrations in two or more groups, whereas others are definitely more
important in one group and are considered there. The following
chapters, however, present representative and important examples
rather than complete catalogs, although each district can be placed
in one of the principal categories.

Three of the major groups of special districts are determined by
the nature of the territory served. They are metropolitan, urban
fringe, and rural. Metropolitan districts relate to areas that are
heavily urbanized and contain numerous governmental units, urban fringe districts to urbanized locales that are unincorporated,
and rural districts to territory that is not urbanized and is in either
agricultural or nonagricultural use. The fourth group is determined
on the basis of its similarity in area to a general local government;
it is designated as coterminous districts. The fifth group, consisting
of school districts, is the only one based on one of the eleven functional divisions which were presented earlier to indicate the broad
range of special district functions. Dependent districts and authorities, which are adjuncts of governmental units rather than independent governments in themselves, are considered separately in
a later chapter.

CHAPTER TWO

Metropolitan
Districts

One of the most prominent corollaries of increased urbanization in the United States is the rapid growth of metropolitan areas. A metropolitan area is a densely populated section of the country whose parts are welded together by strong economic and social relationships. This economic and social integration is not paralleled by the governmental organization, for each area contains one or more central cities as well as other governmental units. Precise definition of criteria for determining the boundaries of metropolitan areas has not yet been agreed upon by analysts of this increasingly significant phenomenon. Nevertheless, there is general recognition of their existence, importance, and approximate limits. The definition used by the United States Bureau of the Census for the decennial census of 1950 has received the widest acceptance. It says that a standard metropolitan area generally consists of an entire county containing at least one city with a minimum population of 50,000, and other contiguous counties that have important economic and social contacts with this city.[1] Only in New England are metropolitan areas not defined in terms of entire counties by the Census Bureau. There, because the town rather than the county is the primary unit for reporting purposes by the Census Bureau, metropolitan areas are based on contiguous towns and cities containing at least 150 people per square mile or, where

[1] The Bureau of the Census first recognized metropolitan areas in its *Report on Social Statistics* in 1886 and initially defined them in 1910. Its definition has been modified in most of the decennial censuses but has consistently contained the concept of a city with a certain population as the basic factor. The present definition emphasizing the central-city–entire-county basis was worked out by a number of national government agencies under the direction of the Bureau of the Budget. For the complete definition and other detailed population data, see *U.S. Census of Population: 1950*, U.S. Bureau of the Census, Population and Housing Division.

strong interrelationships are evident, at least 100 persons per square mile.

CHARACTERISTICS OF METROPOLITAN AREAS

The metropolitan areas of continental United States—numbering 168 in 1950—cover only about one-fourteenth of the land area but contain approximately 84 million people, more than one-half of the nation's population.[2] More than one of every four persons in the United States lives in one of the fourteen largest metropolitan areas, each of which has in excess of 1 million population. Furthermore, the urbanization movement in this country is largely a metropolitan movement. Sixty-four per cent of the people live in urban settings; 56 per cent reside in metropolitan areas, mostly in the urban portions.

Heavy Population Growth

Metropolitan areas are experiencing an exceptionally rapid growth. Every decennial census since 1900 has demonstrated that these areas are growing more rapidly than the nation as a whole. Their relative population increase was especially large in the decade ending in 1950. Four-fifths of the population gain during this ten-year period occurred in metropolitan areas, mainly through shifts in residence rather than by increased metropolitan birth rates. Not all metropolitan areas made approximately equal gains. A few actually lost population, and some increased less rapidly than the nation. The general result, however, was a substantial proportionate increase, and there are indications in the decade of the 1950's that the metropolitan trend is still rapidly advancing. For example, according to a sample survey by the Census Bureau of civilian population for the five-year period ending in April, 1955, the increase in metropolitan areas was approximately 11,500,000 and that for the remainder of the country was only 300,000.

Most of the population increase is occurring in metropolitan areas, but the central cities generally do not account for the major part of the growth. During the twentieth century, the trend has

[2] Since the 1950 *Census of Population*, four additional metropolitan areas have been recognized and three existing ones have been territorially enlarged through redefinition.

been for a larger proportion of the metropolitan population to live outside the central city. This trend was much in evidence during the 1940–1950 decade, when approximately three-fifths of the metropolitan population gain occurred in sections not in the central city. The suburban or outlying portions of most metropolitan areas are therefore growing more rapidly than the central cities. In the thirty-two metropolitan areas possessing at least 500,000 population in 1950, only the central city of Houston, which had doubled its size through annexation during the previous ten years, grew more rapidly than the outlying sections. Most of the central cities contain more than one-half of the population of the metropolitan area in which they are located, but in almost one-fourth of the metropolitan areas the total population outside the central city now exceeds that inside its limits. This suburban growth developed both because people moved out of the central city and because new residents of the metropolitan area settled immediately in locations outside the central city. This greater suburban population increase brings more and more people into incorporated and unincorporated communities located within the metropolitan areas but not subject to the jurisdiction and control of the central city. The spreading of a larger proportion of the metropolitan population beyond the limits of the central city divides the respons:bility for functions of area-wide significance among numerous governments.

Governmental Complexity

Another important characteristic of most metropolitan areas is the proliferation of local governmental units, usually of several different types. The number of local governments in a metropolitan area averages slightly more than ninety-six. It is customary for a metropolitan area to include cities (sometimes different in legal powers), one or more counties, and several kinds of special districts, supplemented in certain sections of the country by towns or townships. Not all of the local governments in each of twenty-four metropolitan areas are in the same state. Almost one of every seven local governments in the United States is functioning in a metropolitan area. The proportion is especially high among municipalities and nonschool special districts, with about one of every five located in a metropolitan area.

Not a single metropolitan area has only one government which performs all local governmental functions within the metropolitan limits. Instead, there usually are many separate local governments, each of them containing only a fraction of the total metropolitan territory. This governmental fractionization is particularly apparent in the most populous metropolitan areas. The New York metropolitan region leads with 1,071 local governments, and the Chicago area is close behind with 960. The fourteen metropolitan areas containing 1 million or more people average more than 400 local gov-

TABLE 2

LOCAL GOVERNMENTS IN METROPOLITAN AREAS

Type of government	Number in metropolitan areas	Per cent of U.S. total in metropolitan areas
All local governments..............................	16,210	13.9
School districts.................................	7,864	11.7
Other, total....................................	8,346	16.9
Counties......................................	256	8.4
Townships and towns...........................	2,328	13.5
Municipalities.................................	3,164	18.9
Nonschool special districts.....................	2,598	21.1

SOURCE: *Local Government in Metropolitan Areas*, U.S. Bureau of the Census, Governments Division, State and Local Government Special Studies No. 36 (Washington: 1954), p. 2.

ernments. Of these fourteen, only the Baltimore area, with eleven local units, has a governmental pattern that does not resemble a jungle.

The governmental complexity of metropolitan areas is generally related to their population size. There are thirty metropolitan areas, ranging from 50,000 to over 1,000,000 in population, which have 150 or more local governments apiece. However, the proportion of metropolitan areas having so many governments increases with the population of the class. This demonstrates that there is a general relationship between the population of the metropolitan area and the number of local governments, but not a perfect correlation that can be applied in each instance. The Madison region, for example, which does not rank among the 100 most populous areas, has the dubious distinction of ranking eleventh in the number of local governments with 292.

The complex of local governments existing in most metropolitan areas results in an incoherent jumble and crazy-quilt patchwork defying comprehension. There is no shortage of local governments in metropolitan areas, and governmental boundaries are present in profusion. Different local governments share part or all of their territory with others. In some states a city, a county, and a township all occupy part of the same land which is merely a portion of the metropolitan area. Usually their areas do not coincide, but this does not prevent all three of them from overlying parts of one another. Several kinds of special districts usually add further overlapping. One district is often superimposed upon part or all of other districts and other local governments. In the forty-one most populous cities in the United States, each containing only a portion of the metropolitan area of which it is the central municipality, there is an average of more than four layers of local governments.[3] Most of these larger cities have a separate housing authority and an independent school district. In a few cases public education is spread out among several units partly or wholly overlying the city. Proliferated government aptly describes the prevailing arrangement in most metropolitan areas.

Increased Territorial Size

In general, this governmental complexity has increased steadily during the present century. Many metropolitan areas have been expanding territorially and have therefore been encompassing more existing units. Furthermore, new governmental units have been created in both the older and newer sections of metropolitan areas. The establishment of suburban municipalities and small special districts is very noticeable. New governments of these types, which have been organized in recent years, far outnumber those which have merged with others or have gone out of legal existence in the same period of time. Then, too, the relatively few governments territorially inclusive of metropolitan areas usually find it difficult to keep pace as metropolitan areas grow in size. Instead, new governments with similar functions may spring up in the new portions of the region. Water districts in a number of metropolitan

[3] *Local Government in Metropolitan Areas,* U.S. Bureau of the Census, Governments Division, State and Local Government Special Studies No. 36 (Washington: 1954), pp. 15–24. For an earlier, more detailed listing see *Governmental Units Overlying City Areas,* U.S. Bureau of the Census, Governments Division, Governmental Organization Series No. 3 (Washington: 1947).

areas are examples of this development. The governmental landscape of many metropolitan areas is becoming increasingly cluttered.

Service and Control Problems

With increased population, intensified governmental complexity,
and enlarged territorial size, metropolitan areas face problems of
inadequate service and control which are growing in number and
aggravation. These area-wide deficiencies have become so common that they are often lumped together in the term "the metropolitan problem," or in the probably appropriate disease-implying
word "suburbanitis." Functional and regulatory shortcomings
growing out of the lack of area-wide approaches are prevalent in
metropolitan environments. What particular shortcoming is most
acute varies according to local circumstances. Since the movement
of people and material is vital to all metropolitan areas, transportation difficulties often constitute the most critical deficiency. The
problems in transportation grow out of the inadequacy or poor condition of certain related elements. Mass transit lines, traffic control,
airport and port facilities, streets, highways and freeways, and rail-
way, trucking, and private vehicular accommodations are some of
the important factors whose deficiencies contribute with varying
frequency to insufficient metropolitan transportation.

But numerous other deficiencies also afflict metropolitan areas.
They appear in connection with air and water pollution control,
law enforcement, fire prevention and protection, garbage and sewage collection and disposal, water supply and distribution, regional
park and recreation facilities, and planning and zoning. In addition, there is frequent criticism of the absence of adequate popular
control and responsibility of government, and of the continuance
of financial inequity. These problems are difficult if not impossible
to solve. Of the last one it has been said that "We have not yet
answered the question of how large an area has a justifiable claim
upon the taxable resources concentrated in the business and industrial sections of the central city, in the outlying industrial sections,
and in the wealthier suburbs."[4]

---

[4] Victor Jones, "Local Government Organization in Metropolitan Areas: Its Relation to Urban Redevelopment," in Coleman Woodbury, ed., *The Future of Cities
and Urban Redevelopment* (Chicago: University of Chicago Press, 1953), p. 521.

These problems are so prevalent that citizens become callous and apathetic about the resulting discomfort and costliness. Such attitudes stem from the belief that nothing can or will be done to eliminate the difficulties. Unfortunately, this cynicism has been supported by the evidence. An adequate, area-wide governmental mechanism, however, is needed to cope with the trouble spots of metropolitanism. There are too many governments in most metropolitan areas. Their decisions, often made within the framework of what is best for their own limited portions of the metropolitan area, nevertheless affect the general course of metropolitan development. The cumulative effect of judgments made in isolation or on a limited coöperative basis is sometimes detrimental to the well-being of the metropolitan area as a whole. Because their territorial size is limited, the preponderant number of these governments can deal only in a limited way with the numerous matters calling for coördination or integrated consideration throughout the entire metropolitan area.

WHAT ARE METROPOLITAN DISTRICTS?

In response to the need to solve these problems, metropolitan districts have been established in many metropolitan areas. However, far from all special districts in metropolitan areas are metropolitan districts. Although almost one-seventh of all special districts, including more than one-fifth of all nonschool districts, are located in metropolitan areas, most of them are not metropolitan in size. Many of them are school districts or special units providing a service in an unincorporated urban development, covering only a small fraction of a metropolitan area.

A metropolitan district is a special district whose territory covers a substantial part or all of a metropolitan area. Very few metropolitan districts coincide exactly with metropolitan areas as defined by the Census Bureau, and many of them contain less than an entire metropolitan area. Conversely, some are more extensive than metropolitan areas. The Metropolitan Water District of Southern California, for example, includes territory in three metropolitan areas. On the other hand, not all districts that are regional are necessarily metropolitan, for their territory may consist largely of rural land. Whether less or more extensive territorially than the generally accepted limits of a metropolitan area, a district can accurately be called a metropolitan district only if it performs an urban function and includes the central city (or at least one central city if there are more than one) and a major part of the remainder of the territory or population of a metropolitan area.[5]

Why have metropolitan districts been used in various metropolitan areas to deal with particular problems? Why are they being utilized increasingly in recent years? In numerous instances it is because of the outright rejection, deliberate avoidance, or insufficient use or inadequacy of other governmental approaches. A consideration of the most important alternatives will help to create a better understanding of some other principal causes and of the growing significance of metropolitan districts.

AN ALTERNATIVE TO METROPOLITAN DISTRICTS: ANNEXATION

Annexation has been the most frequently used method of bringing a larger portion of the territory and population of a metropolitan area under a single local government. However, its use dwindled in the closing years of the nineteenth century, at the very time that metropolitanism was rising in importance. Before this eclipse, many of the major cities of the United States had utilized this method of territorial enlargement. These principal urban centers would be only a fraction of their present size had it not been for annexation. For example, Chicago grew from its original size of slightly more than 10 square miles to an area of 190 square miles by 1900. Annexation activity tapered off drastically during the 1920's, and in subsequent years metropolitan expansion has outstripped annexation efforts by most of the major cities located in metropolitan areas. In the current century Chicago has made only slight area gains. Some cities, notably Los Angeles and Detroit,

---

[5] Occasionally this must be construed as a major portion of the remainder of the population rather than the territory, if the Census Bureau standard of entire counties within metropolitan areas is utilized. This is because a county that is by definition within the metropolitan area could contain a large amount of rural territory. Metropolitan districts could be defined more liberally to include special units covering a substantial part of the metropolitan area but not the central city, or encompassing only the central city but providing service outside the central city. Because the absence of the central city or the lack of formal jurisdiction beyond the central city vitiates any truly metropolitan approach, however, such district governments are not included within the definition used in this book.

did make extensive use of annexation in the early decades of the twentieth century, but they were exceptions to the pattern of decline. By the latter part of the 1930's annexation successes by central cities of metropolitan areas had become virtually nonexistent, and annexation appeared to be an outmoded method of integrating metropolitan areas. But this judgment proved to be short-lived.

Much Recent Annexation

Successful annexation efforts burst forth anew in the closing year of World War II, and the number increased with each succeeding year. In 1945 there were 152 annexing cities of 5,000 or more population, and by 1952 there were more than 400. The 1953 and 1954 figures of 434 and 410 municipalities represent the top attainments in many years. This means that in both 1953 and 1954 about one-sixth of all the cities over 5,000 annexed territory. A major part of the postwar annexation activity has been occurring in metropolitan areas, frequently involving cities of at least 50,000 population. More than two-fifths of the central cities of all metropolitan areas have annexed land during the period. Annexation activity by cities other than the central city has also been brisk in many metropolitan areas. Nevertheless, this spurt of annexation is not solving the metropolitan problem.

There have been many postwar annexations and many annexing cities, but the amount of land absorbed has not usually been large. The average in both metropolitan and nonmetropolitan areas in 1954 was about four-fifths of a square mile. There have been spectacular uses of annexation in recent years by Atlanta, Dallas, Houston, and San Antonio, each of which acquired about 80 square miles.[a] Since 1948 twenty-one other principal metropolitan centers have annexed areas measuring from 10 to 67 square miles. In total, approximately one of every eight central cities has absorbed a sizable area. Most of the central cities that have used annexation, however, have obtained merely a fraction of a square mile or at most a few square miles. Furthermore, only a few of the central cities in the fourteen metropolitan areas whose population exceeds

[a] Almost a year after the San Antonio annexation was completed, a new city council majority attempted to de-annex 65 of the almost 80 square miles. The detachment action has subsequently been declared illegal by two Texas courts, the last decision being issued in July of 1954. In November of the same year the state supreme court denied a writ of error by the city.

1 million have annexed territory and in no instance has the amount been substantial.

Reasons for Limited Usefulness

The smallness of most annexed areas can be traced largely to the stringency of annexation laws. Usually the residents or property owners in the area under consideration for annexation have the controlling voice in such attempts. Very often they are the only ones who can initiate the action and frequently they can also reject the proposition through a vote restricted to them. It is no mere coincidence that most of the large recent annexations in metropolitan areas have been accomplished through laws that do not give this preëminence to the people in the area to be annexed. Most of the large annexations have materialized within the legal framework of a council ordinance or popular vote by the annexing city, an act of the state legislature, or a decision by a court. Not only has the amount of area annexed in the postwar upsurge generally been small, but also it has almost always consisted of unincorporated territory. Incorporated suburbs, partially or completely hemming in the central city, strongly and in most instances successfully resist annexation, for strict state constitutional and statutory rules work to their advantage. Their autonomy is usually protected by legal requirements stipulating that their separate approval must be forthcoming before the annexation is allowed. It has been extremely difficult to complete annexations of sizable amounts of unincorporated land in metropolitan areas. It has been virtually impossible to annex territory that is already within the boundaries of an existing municipal government.

Although annexation has recently been used in many metropolitan areas, it has not always been sufficiently comprehensive. Even in the limited number of metropolitan areas where the central city has acquired a large amount of territory, primarily because there were liberal annexation laws and considerable adjacent unincorporated land, most of the metropolitan area still remains outside of its corporate limits. Recent annexations in metropolitan areas have primarily meant the prevention of increased governmental complexity in the areas annexed, rather than the simplification of existing complicated governmental arrangements in the entire metropolitan area. Annexation has been important mainly in preventing the creation of small cities and of small single-purpose districts in the annexed area. Its principal contribution to governmental simplification has been the abolition, in the annexed areas, of some special districts that performed functions now performed by the city.

Additional Effects

Annexation has sometimes, however, caused an increase in the number of governmental units, or a feeling of animosity among existing governments. Some annexation efforts have resulted in the immediate incorporation as separate units of small areas of land adjacent to the city using the device. New incorporations in metropolitan areas have been exceeding the number of disincorporations and annexations of existing municipalities, and annexation activities in the postwar years at times contribute to the establishment of these new, small incorporated centers. Whether the number of potential and probable incorporations avoided through successful annexations is greater than the number materializing as the result of both successful and unsuccessful efforts is difficult to appraise accurately. In any event, although annexations have forestalled new incorporations in the area absorbed, they have sometimes accelerated nearby incorporations which probably would not have materialized, at least for some time to come, without such a stimulus.

In addition, much of the annexation in metropolitan areas has been completed by cities other than the central city. Sometimes the atmosphere has been that of a highly antagonistic race between the central city and a neighboring municipality. Because this kind of competitiveness occurs, or because another city in the metropolitan area has risen in importance through territorial growth, numerous central cities have found that annexation activity by them or by other cities has reduced intergovernmental coöperation. And yet, the central cities that have been unable to bring most of the metropolitan area under their jurisdiction must depend upon some kind of coöperative working arrangement for solving or reducing area-wide problems so directly affecting them.

Whatever the balance sheet of annexation in operation in each metropolitan area may show, in the over-all view the immediate needs are not met by this slow and difficult approach. Nevertheless, the usefulness of annexation in certain metropolitan situations should not be underrated. It may be a desirable supplement in various areas which adopt a more comprehensive change. It may continue to be judged in some metropolitan areas as the best of the politically feasible alternatives, even when extremely difficult legal provisions and strong opposition require a city to undertake many annexations to obtain a very small amount of land.[7]

OTHER ALTERNATIVES: CONSOLIDATION AND FEDERATION

Types of Consolidation

Many other integration proposals involve major structural changes in the county and cities of at least the central part of the metropolitan area. Some of them call for city-county consolidation, which has several variations in meaning. The most comprehensive is the complete merging of the county and the cities within the county under a single local government. Another involves substantial mergers of these units but permits retention of the county, customarily for limited purposes, as a separate legal entity. A third stipulates the unification of some, but not all, of the cities with the county. A fourth, more accurately known as city-county separation, consists of the detachment of a city, usually after territorial enlargement, from the remainder of the county and the utilization of the separated government for both city and county purposes.[8] Occasionally city-county consolidation is broadened in one or two ways: by encompassing the territory of two or more counties and the county and municipal governments within them, or by including other governments.

These methods of city-county consolidation have been seriously and recurrently advocated in numerous metropolitan areas, but so far very few areas have adopted any form of consolidation. City-county consolidation is in operation in Baton Rouge, Boston, New Orleans, New York, and Philadelphia. City-county separation is in

[7] In the seven years from 1948 through 1954, for example, Fresno had to complete 150 annexations to gain 5½ square miles. John C. Bollens, "Metropolitan and Fringe Area Developments in 1954," *Municipal Year Book: 1955* (Chicago: International City Managers' Association, 1955), p. 45. Articles on area developments have appeared in the *Municipal Year Book* since the 1949 edition.

[8] Occasionally, as in Chicago, Detroit, and New York, there have been proposals to separate the central city and its surrounding area from the state and form a city-state.

effect in Baltimore, Denver, St. Louis, San Francisco, and several metropolitan cities in Virginia. Excluding the examples in Virginia, where the process is automatic when a city attains 5,000 population, most of the others occurred before the last quarter of the nineteenth century. Furthermore, they frequently involved only a single city before it became the principal center of an appreciable metropolitan area, and were accomplished through state legislation or through the voters' approval of a state constitutional provision. The New York consolidation took place in 1898, and the Denver separation was accepted in 1902, although court litigation delayed its installation for a number of years. Despite widespread discussion and advocacy it was not until 1947 that another area adopted a form of consolidation. This was the relatively lightly populated metropolitan area of Baton Rouge, Louisiana. Several proposals, including those in the Birmingham (1948) and Miami (1953) areas, have been submitted to a state or local vote in subsequent years, but none has been approved.

Kinds of Federation

Numerous other integration proposals involving substantial county and city change emphasize the continuance of existing municipal governments. Such plans are known as federations. The traditional and generally more comprehensive form of the proposition has two major features. One is establishment of a metropolitan government, usually paralleling the boundaries of the replaced county government, to which metropolitan-type functions are allocated. The other is retention of existing cities, sometimes territorially enlarged and called boroughs, which continue to control local functions. The key points in such a plan are the redistribution of governmental activities between a central government and strictly local governments, and the method of choosing representation on the governing body of the area-wide or metropolitan government. Recommended in the Boston region as early as 1896, rejected by the voters of such metropolitan areas as Oakland and Pittsburgh, and written into still unused sections of the charter of San Francisco, federation of this type has not yet been put into operation in any metropolitan area of the United States.

A less comprehensive form of the federation idea, which is in operation, is attained through transferring various functions, judged to be metropolitan in scope, from the cities to the existing county government without necessarily reorganizing the county government. Some counties of the United States have been advancing toward the position of central government of a federation through the relatively slow, piecemeal process of functional reallocation. The usual procedure is for the county to enter into a contractual agreement with a city to take over a function or to perform it jointly. The development has materialized chiefly in such functions as corrections, public health, and public welfare, and has occasionally reached fairly extensive proportions. The most prominent example is Los Angeles County, which has gradually accumulated individual functions from a number of cities. In some metropolitan areas the process has concerned only a single function and only a few cities (and not always the central city). An attempt to transfer six major functions from Cleveland to Cuyahoga County by one comprehensive action in a proposed 1950 county charter failed to win any of the four majorities needed for its passage. Far more functions and far more cities will have to be involved in such functional arrangements before federation is attained anywhere through this method.

Obstacles and Shortcomings

Metropolitan areas and their problems are growing, and major county and city changes in the form of city-county consolidation and federation are accepted as important approaches to the difficulty. Nevertheless, they remain largely in the discussion stage. In many instances this can be traced to the inaction of the state legislature, the difficulty of amending the state constitution, the inability to gain state-wide approval for relevant constitutional amendments, or the frequent requirement of separate majority approval by the residents of each governmental unit affected. In turn, these factors can be attributed to the dominance of rural interests in one house of most state legislatures, differences in the social characteristics of residents of the units that will be altered, or the failure (sometimes founded on fear or suspicion) of legislators and citizens to face up to the reality of the metropolitan problem.

In most metropolitan areas there are a number—and sometimes a large number—of cities other than the central city, a situation much more complex than when most consolidations were accomplished. The residents and officials of these cities, in addition to those of the noncity areas of the county, often fear that the central city is proposing a consolidation or federation as a thinly disguised method of obtaining control over them. Often, too, the rallying point of the opposition is the proportion of representation on the governing body of the new metropolitan central government to be allotted to the central city. The suggested distribution of functions between the metropolitan central government and the local governments is also frequently attacked. Existing county governments usually do not enjoy sufficient public confidence within the metropolitan area, and would have to undergo substantial internal reorganization, to be considered seriously for the role of central government in a federation. The evolution of county government through functional transfers is perceptible but slow.

The failure to acquire popular approval of a consolidation or federation proposal is sometimes the responsibility of residents of the central city who have exhibited inertia, lack of organizational ability, or ineptitude in dramatizing the interrelatedness of all the people within the county. This is most noticeable when only a single majority vote of the entire county is required.[9]

City-county consolidation or federation as usually proposed and infrequently achieved has severe limitations. The plan normally pertains only to governments within one county. Furthermore, it has been extremely difficult to enlarge the boundaries of existing consolidated governments when they need to expand. Directly related to these territorial limitations is the fact that approximately one-third of all metropolitan areas currently contain two or more counties. Limitation of the proposals to a single county may therefore restrict their usefulness to part of the metropolitan territory. In addition, the rigidity of the boundaries of established governmental consolidations should serve as fair warning to metropolitan areas that are currently contained wholly within one county but are experiencing continued population growth. Even less useful is city-county separation, since it confines the separated government to a small amount of land, a portion of the original county. In practice, the four principal cities separated through this process have found expansion slow or impossible, and two of them, St.

---

[9] See, for example, the observations of John Willmott on the consolidation effort in the Miami area in 1947 in *GRA Reporter*, 4 (Sept., 1948), 2–3.

Louis and San Francisco, have sought unsuccessfully to merge with the respective counties to which they initially belonged.[10]

TURNING TO METROPOLITAN DISTRICTS:
THE ST. LOUIS EXPERIENCE

Annexation and Separation

The St. Louis metropolitan area furnishes an excellent case study of efforts, both accepted and rejected, to use other integration methods before turning to the metropolitan district mechanism.[11] Incorporated in the eighteenth century, the city of St. Louis annexed both unincorporated and incorporated territory until the 1870's through state legislative acts enlarging its boundaries. In each instance, the city established new wards in the annexed area for the purpose of furnishing representation on the city council. Toward the end of this period of annexation, the city became highly critical of the county government, calling it extravagant and incompetent and charging it with exploiting the city of St. Louis for the benefit of out-of-city residents in the county.

In 1875, St. Louis civic leaders succeeded in having a section permitting city-county separation added to the new state constitution. The wording of the amendment was advantageous to the city. The elected board of thirteen city freeholders, charged with drafting a separation plan and a city charter, was to decide how much of the county should be included within the enlarged separated city. The amendment stipulated that the separation plan be submitted to a single combined vote of the city and the county electorate. Possessing the right of unilateral decision on the matter of territorial enlargement, the freeholders more than tripled the

---

[10] As currently utilized, devices such as extraterritorial jurisdiction and services by cities, coöperation among several governments, and metropolitan planning without a metropolitan government are less significant and are therefore omitted from consideration here. Also omitted are the extension of state administration and the extension of federal activities, which have been largely along individual functional lines. These latter exclusions are not meant to imply that the state and national governments should not furnish increased general leadership in metropolitan areas. On the latter point, see Daniel R. Grant, "Federal-Municipal Relationships and Metropolitan Integration," *Public Administration Review*, 14 (Autumn, 1954), 259–267 and *The States and the Metropolitan Problem*, Council of State Governments (Chicago, 1956), prepared under the directorship of John C. Bollens.

[11] The outstanding analysis is William N. Cassella, Jr., "Governing the Saint Louis Metropolitan Area" (unpublished Ph.D. dissertation, Harvard University, Cambridge, 1952).

area of St. Louis. Since less than one-half of the land of the enlarged city was urbanized, it was felt that no further extension of
the city's boundaries would ever be necessary. As might be anticipated, the combined vote on the separation proposition weighed in
favor of the city, which contained a large proportion of the voters
of the county, and in August of 1876 separation was approved by
a slim twelve-to-eleven margin.

After obtaining separation and a charter, the newly enlarged
city seemed to be in the enviable position of having permanently
eliminated its area problems. But those who plan governmental
action cannot always anticipate the effects of later technological
developments. Within thirty years suburban areas in St. Louis
County, the county from which the city of St. Louis had been separated, were growing rapidly. The city was faced with increasing
area problems, but could not through its own action satisfy its desire for further territorial expansion. Successful adoption of the
two techniques of annexation and city-county separation had failed
to supply long-range answers. Other area proposals were not
adopted for many years.

Problems stemming from the population growth both inside and
outside the city of St. Louis continued to multiply during the early
part of the twentieth century, but the city's efforts to enlarge its
boundaries through state legislative action met with defeat after
defeat. In the early 1920's the voters of the state rejected proposed
constitutional amendments that would have enabled St. Louis to
expand. Thus, during almost fifty years after city-county separation, there was no popular sanction of any area changes.

The Consolidation Defeat

Hope within St. Louis was revived in 1924 with the adoption of a
state constitutional amendment authorizing establishment of a
board of freeholders, consisting of nine members each from St.
Louis and St. Louis County, to consider readjustments in city-
county relations. The freeholders were given three alternatives:
city-county consolidation under the city government, reëntry of
the city into the county, and annexation of part of the county by
the city. The city-county consolidation plan, finally agreed upon
by a narrow majority vote of the board, called for the outright

absorption of the county by the city. The consolidated government would cover more than 500 square miles (as compared to the 61 square miles the city then included), and St. Louis County and the cities within the county would cease to exist as separate legal entities. Unlike the city-county separation of 1876, this plan required separate majority approval by St. Louis and St. Louis County voters; with such uncompromising terms, it was destined to meet strong opposition in the county. In a special election in October, 1926, the voters of St. Louis favored the proposal by more than six to one, with less than one-fourth of the registered voters going to the polls, and the county voters opposed it by more than two to one, with two-thirds of those eligible taking part. A metropolitan solution had been rejected, but the metropolitan problems continued.

The Federation Rejection

Four years later, in 1930, a state constitutional amendment permitting the county and the city of St. Louis to draft a federation charter was proposed. The proposition envisioned a metropolitan government encompassing the territory of both county and city, the abolition of the county, and the continuing independence of the municipalities in the county in respect to strictly local services. But the amendment, attempting to provide for a metropolitan government while preserving a degree of local autonomy, was turned down in a state-wide vote. Thus another metropolitan approach had been defeated before it could be considered in specific detail in a charter.

The government of the St. Louis metropolitan area was gradually becoming more complicated through the creation of small special districts and small incorporated suburbs. In the 1930's, for example, twenty-three new incorporations were added to the previous total of fifteen in St. Louis County. By 1950 there were ninety cities in St. Louis County.[12] At this time the metropolitan area contained more than 1.5 million people, embraced four counties in Missouri

---

[12] By 1952, four more incorporations had occurred, and the St. Louis County Planning Commission significantly titled a report *Let's Get Together: A Report on the Advantages of an Integrated Community* (Clayton: 1952). According to the Census Bureau only Cook County, Illinois, had more municipalities than St. Louis County in 1952.

and Illinois in addition to the city of St. Louis, and had 420 units of local government.

Creation of Two Metropolitan Districts

Favorable action on two integration proposals for the St. Louis area finally materialized near the middle of the present century. Stimulated by the efforts of the privately sponsored Metropolitan Plan Association, established in 1944 to promote coördinated development of the metropolitan area, the Missouri State Legislature in 1949 authorized an interstate compact with Illinois to create the Bi-State Development District. After the Illinois Legislature passed a similar law, a compact was made by the two states and was subsequently approved by Congress. Including three counties in Illinois on one side of the Mississippi River, and three counties and St. Louis in Missouri on the other side, the district is governed by ten directors, five appointed by each governor. The directors can charge fees but cannot levy taxes. Furthermore, they can issue bonds without referral to the voters of the district. The district is authorized to construct and operate airports, bridges, tunnels, and terminal facilities, and to make plans and policy recommendations for sewage and drainage facilities. A degree of integration has finally been achieved by establishing a metropolitan district through state legislative action rather than through direct approval by the voters of the area.

The second proposal, also featuring a metropolitan district, was submitted to the local electorate and received approval in 1954, nine years after legal permission to create the district had been granted. Missouri's new state constitution, adopted in 1945, provided an additional technique for dealing with relations between St. Louis and St. Louis County by permitting the establishment, by petition, of a joint city-county commission to draw up a charter for one or more metropolitan districts to satisfy area service needs. The sewage problem of St. Louis and parts of St. Louis County was especially critical; after studies had been made by a joint city-county interim committee and the Bi-State Development District, petitions asking for a commission to prepare a charter for a metropolitan sewer district were successfully circulated in 1953. The commission, which had nineteen members, drew up a plan for a special district consisting of the city of St. Louis and the densely populated adjacent one-third of St. Louis County. The charter provided that the district could acquire, operate, build, and maintain all sewer facilities within its territory, and could furnish any additional service authorized by the district voters through amendment of the charter.

The metropolitan sewer district was established in February, 1954, through separate approval of the charter by three-to-one margins of the voters of the city and the entire county. Its governing body consists of three trustees appointed by the mayor of St. Louis with the approval of a majority of the judges of the circuit court in the city, and three selected by the single county supervisor of St. Louis County with similar approval by the local district court. The district can levy taxes up to 10 cents for each $100 of assessed valuation, collect special assessments, issue bonds after voter approval, and make service charges. Territory can also be added to the district through petition of a majority of the landowners possessing more than one-half of the land to be annexed, followed by board ordinance, or through petition of at least 100 owners of land to be annexed and approval by a majority of voters in the area. Unlike the Bi-State Development District, the sewer district can undertake the function of sewage disposal and can use the taxing power.

The sequence of integration efforts in the St. Louis metropolitan area is clear. The failure of annexation and city-county separation to serve as lasting solutions to area problems was followed by the inability to gain acceptance of consolidation and federation. These developments led ultimately to the installation, through different methods, of two metropolitan district governments. Will many metropolitan districts now spring up in the St. Louis area, or will the multifunctional authorization in the charter of the metropolitan sewer district be used? The first subsequent effort was in the direction of the former, but the proposed metropolitan transit district was rejected by both the city and county voters in February, 1955.

OTHER CAUSES OF METROPOLITAN DISTRICTS

As in the St. Louis metropolitan area, the relatively low number of adoptions of other proposals for metropolitan organization is often a principal reason for the creation of metropolitan districts. After diligent but fruitless efforts to gain approval of one or more devices, numerous metropolitan areas have turned, sometimes in desperation, to the district mechanism as a means of solving serious metropolitan problems. A metropolitan district is frequently a last resort, for which new state legislation must sometimes be sought.

In a number of instances, however, the avoidance of other methods of integration is the result rather than the cause of the increase in the number of metropolitan districts. If the district device is regarded as coequal or superior to the alternatives, it is deliberately chosen in preference to them. It is often easier to secure state enabling laws or permissive constitutional provisions for metropolitan districts. Also, legal requirements for establishing metropolitan districts, particularly when only a single over-all popular vote is required or when no voter approval is necessary, are frequently more liberal than those for other techniques. A third reason for preferring districts, which may become increasingly important, is the narrow geographical framework in which the other devices are conceived, sometimes because of legal restrictions. For example, practically all consolidation and federation proposals have been for intrastate (and most for intracounty) organization. Twenty-four metropolitan areas, however, cross state lines and twenty-nine others border them. Together they account for more than one-half of the total metropolitan population. In contrast to the area limitations imposed on other devices, several metropolitan districts are in operation in more than one state. The reliance on metropolitan districts can be lessened if there is sufficient interest in eliminating legal obstacles to other possibilities.

But there are more basic and deep-seated reasons for both the disinterest in changing the legal provisions of other options and the frequent preference for metropolitan districts. Extensive use of such alternatives as annexation by cities, city-county consolidation, and federation means the immediate displacement or substantial modification of existing governments. On the other hand, a metropolitan district with its limited functions merely adds another government to the present array and does not immediately, and in fact may never, curtail most of the services of other units. Its lack of comprehensiveness is therefore very attractive to many public officials, both elected officeholders and appointed administrators, who feel that the metropolitan district is not a potential threat to their positions, as another governmental innovation might be. The metropolitan district also appeals to many citizens who for selfish or unselfish reasons become highly emotional over suggestions for changing the area of the general local government in which they reside. Some officials and laymen find it attractive for another reason. This is because they apply a restricted view to the general metropolitan problem; their exclusive concern is to remedy a single deficiency despite the existence of many others that differ only in intensity. The district form is a convenient means of attacking some of the metropolitan area difficulties without disturbing many governmental relationships and without facing the total problem.

It is also sometimes preferred to milder types of integration, such as intergovernmental contracts. Here suspicion of one unit by another is revealed, for there is competition as well as coöperation between governments. At times officials are more willing to establish a new governmental unit, a metropolitan district, than they are to transfer a function to an existing government. Concealed or open expressions of self-protection, fear, and suspicion can thus transform individuals and groups who oppose other types of change into ardent supporters of metropolitan districts. Such thinking, which is hard to dispel, contributes to the legal complexities of some of the other methods and prompts the utilization of metropolitan districts.

IMPORTANT FEATURES OF METROPOLITAN DISTRICTS

Geographical and Functional Extensiveness

The use of metropolitan districts in the metropolitan areas of the United States is increasing. In operation in more than one-fourth of such areas, they are proportionately most prevalent in concentrations of 500,000 or more people. Approximately three-fourths of the thirty-three most populous areas have at least one metropolitan district, and it is not unusual for them to have more than one. Geographical location has constituted no barrier, for these districts are found in metropolitan areas in all sections of the United States. Although appearing in Philadelphia as early as 1790 and in such areas as Chicago and Portland, Oregon, in the latter part of the nineteenth century, metropolitan districts are largely a post–World War I development.[13] Once established, most of them have given indications of being permanent or long-lived. In contrast to many other types of districts, few of them have become inactive or been abolished or merged.

Collectively, metropolitan districts are concerned with a wide range of activities and have eliminated or mitigated some of the most important problems of specific metropolitan areas. Although their most frequent services have to do with port facilities, sewage disposal, water supply, and parks, they also own and operate bridges, tunnels, airports, housing, libraries, and mass transit facilities; furnish public health services, regional planning, power, ice, gas, and coke; regulate navigation channels; and control water to prevent disasters. They emphasize service rather than regulatory functions. Certain functions considered by many people to be metropolitan are not provided by any metropolitan district. The most notable omissions are fire protection and law enforcement.

Mostly Single-Purpose

An overwhelming majority of these districts are legally limited to supplying a single service. Prominent examples among the relatively few districts that perform more than one function are the Port of New York Authority, the Hartford County (Connecticut) Metropolitan District, the Bi-State Development District (St. Louis metropolitan area), and the East Bay Municipal Utility District (San Francisco-Oakland metropolitan area). Although it has happened that one or more functions of these districts were authorized after their establishment, generally neither metropolitan districts nor their residents have shown much interest in assuming new obligations. Very few metropolitan districts have therefore increased functionally through subsequent authorization by the state legislature, or through the exercise of other powers originally granted them. The usual pattern has been to have one metropolitan district carry out one function, and to establish other metropolitan districts for additional single purposes if sufficient concern

---

[13] For details on early metropolitan districts, see Paul Studenski, *The Government of Metropolitan Areas in the United States* (New York: National Municipal League, 1930), pp. 256–265. Several districts discussed by Mr. Studenski are not independent or are less than metropolitan in jurisdiction.

develops. As a result, no metropolitan district is presently serving as a comprehensive multifunctional metropolitan government. Instead, all of them are operating as limited governments of metropolitan jurisdiction.

Large and Flexible Areas

Metropolitan districts have large areas, and on the average are larger than any other kind of special district. Some districts in rural sections, for example, are very extensive, but others contain only a fraction of a square mile or a few square miles. On the other hand, the territory of metropolitan districts is consistently measured in tens or hundreds of square miles and in some instances exceeds a thousand square miles. Then, too, since metropolitan districts have jurisdiction in densely settled areas, they usually encompass a large number of general and special district governments. Furthermore, the territory of some of them crosses state boundaries, a feature foreign to most special districts and to all general governments except the national government. Some metropolitan districts have grown substantially through annexation. An illustration is the Metropolitan Sanitary District of Greater Chicago which has almost tripled its original size of 185 square miles. Thousands, sometimes millions, of people reside within each metropolitan district and use or benefit from its service. In addition, many nondistrict residents benefit from the operations of certain functional kinds of metropolitan districts, such as those operating parks, mass transit, and ports.

Sometimes Big Government

Although performing only one or a few functions, some metropolitan districts are very large governmental operations, and may even be larger than state governments in some respects. The Chicago Transit Authority, for example, outranked seventeen states in number of employees and twelve states in annual revenue in the fiscal year 1952. At the same time, the Port of New York Authority had more long-term outstanding debt than each of thirty-nine individual states.[14] Metropolitan districts with the most extensive

---

[14] *Special District Governments in the United States,* U.S. Bureau of the Census, Governments Division, State and Local Government Special Studies No. 33 (Washington: 1954), p. 3.

TABLE 3

The Largest Nonschool Districts

District	Number of employees, October, 1952	Revenue for fiscal year 1952 ($ thousands)	Total long-term outstanding debt, 1952 ($ thousands)
Metropolitan Districts			
Chicago Transit Authority...........	17,472	119,064	137,400
Metropolitan Transit Authority (Boston)........................	7,652	50,004	131,054
Port of New York Authority.........	3,745	57,097	241,688
Metropolitan Sanitary District of Greater Chicago..................	1,882	29,246	141,164
Indianapolis Utilities District........	1,230	21,828	11,785
East Bay Municipal Utility District (eastern section of San Francisco Bay area)........................	1,208	17,708	69,530
Omaha Public Power District........	1,116	17,942	71,528
Omaha Metropolitan Utility District.	1,007	10,515	....
Other Districts			
Chicago Park District..............	3,935	27,497	66,230
Washington Suburban Sanitary District (Maryland)..............	1,398	8,550	75,032
Consumers Public Power District (Nebraska)....................	1,193	13,775	40,698
Imperial Irrigation District (California)........................	1,040	10,946	62,412
Totals.........................	42,878	384,172	1,048,521
Per cent of nonschool district totals	35	38	28

Source: *Special District Governments in the United States,* U.S. Bureau of the Census, Governments Division, State and Local Government Special Studies No. 33 (Washington: 1954), p. 3. The Chicago Park District is coterminous with the city limits of Chicago; the Washington Suburban District operates in part of the Washington metropolitan area; and the Consumers Public Power District is state-wide. Of the twelve districts, only the Imperial Irrigation District operates entirely outside a metropolitan area.

operations also stand out in comparison with other districts. Of the twelve largest nonschool districts, eight are metropolitan and three others are located in metropolitan areas but are less than metropolitan territorially (see table 3). These are the most important metropolitan districts in terms of operations, but in addition there are a number of others that are significant in one or more of the categories of personnel, revenue, and debt. These others similarly demonstrate the high relative operational importance of metropolitan districts, especially among nonschool special units.

The significance of metropolitan districts in general is emphasized by these data on the three major aspects of their operations: personnel, revenue, and debt. An even fuller understanding, however, is derived from several case studies.[15] These examples reveal the basic importance of many metropolitan districts to the people they serve, furnish additional specific illustrations of features discussed earlier, and reveal the diversity and frequent complexity of other characteristics, several of which deserve subsequent comment and appraisal.

CLEVELAND METROPOLITAN PARK DISTRICT

The present metropolitan park district in the Cleveland metropolitan area was established in 1917 to replace a county park board, whose members, as county officials, had to be elected. But advocates of the park program felt strongly that greater progress would be made if the directors were not made subject to the electoral process. They reasoned that appointment by the common pleas court would be preferable to popular election, since the judge could appeal to outstanding citizens to accept membership on the board of directors.

Court Formation and Appointment

The state enabling legislation which stipulated formation of a metropolitan park district in the Cleveland area through a nonvoting procedure was enacted in 1917 and promptly used. Several local governments in Cuyahoga County, which contains the central city of Cleveland, felt that the Cleveland park system was insuf-

---

[15] Each of the metropolitan districts selected is an important (sometimes the most important) one in a heavily populated metropolitan area. The Metropolitan St. Louis Sewer District and the Bi-State Development District, discussed earlier in this chapter, are appropriate for reconsideration with these case studies. Although functionally larger, the Port of New York Authority is organizationally similar to the Bi-State Development District and is omitted as a case study because the examples are chosen mainly to show diversity of characteristics. Furthermore, the Port of New York Authority, which has territory in New York and New Jersey, is not as clear-cut an example of metropolitan district government as those considered in the following pages. One major distinction is that the actions of its governing body can be vetoed by the governors of New York and New Jersey. The Port of New York Authority is classified as an independent government by the Census Bureau largely because it is not assignable as a whole to either New York or New Jersey, nor can its operations be accurately apportioned to the two states. If it were entirely within one state, it would according to Census Bureau criteria be considered an agency of the state government.

ficient for metropolitan area needs. They adopted favorable resolutions and upon affirmative action by the probate court the district came into legal existence. Initially all of Cuyahoga County was included with the exception of one township. This was done deliberately so that it could not be claimed that the district governing board members were in fact county officials. Within a few years the district annexed the remaining township, as well as territory in another county which contained unusually scenic areas, one of which was developed into a sizable inland lake.

The desires of the park proponents for a nonelective governing body were incorporated in the state enabling law and again, as in the formation proceedings, a part of the judiciary was endowed with the responsibility. The three board members are appointed for three-year staggered terms by the probate judge who is nominated at a partisan primary and elected on a judicial ballot devoid of party designations. The judge has the power to remove board members if complaints against them are upheld in a formal hearing. The directors receive no compensation. The district now contains within its boundaries approximately 480 square miles and more than 1.5 million people. It owns slightly less than 14,000 acres of land, some of which are outside the district territory in two adjoining counties. The basic purpose of the program has been to obtain and to preserve or restore naturally scenic areas. In addition, a wide range of recreational opportunities has been provided. Included are park drives, foot trails, bridle paths, bicycle trails, camping centers, swimming pools, softball and baseball diamonds, playfields, picnic grounds, bathing beaches, golf courses, and ice-skating rinks.

Financing the Services

A large portion of the expenses of the district are financed through money acquired from a direct property tax which cannot legally exceed .5 mill for each dollar of assessed property valuation, and which normally runs about one-tenth of this amount. An additional tax levy limited to .3 mill may be imposed if approved by 55 per cent of the district electorate voting on the issue. Such levies can be collected for one or more years, and most of them have been used for capital purposes like land acquisition and permanent improvements. Special assessments for improving and developing a park area may be made upon adjacent or otherwise specifically benefited land, but so far this power has not been used. In addition, money is obtained from the use of golf courses and clubhouses and from rents, concessions, and nursery stock sales. The county treasurer and the county auditor function as the financial officers of the district. No charge is made for their services.

Annexation and Service Rejections

Two powers of the Cleveland Metropolitan Park District have remained relatively or completely dormant. One is its ability to annex territory. Despite the absence of limits on the territory that can be absorbed, the district has not experienced large-scale area growth. Petitions requesting the annexation of several townships in two counties adjoining the central county have been presented to the governing body, but were turned down. At the time of the presentation, the directors concluded that the district lacked sufficient money to carry out its contemplated program within the existing district territory and that the general burden would simply be increased through territorial enlargement.

The second and completely inactive power is the authority to assume administration and operation of municipal parks in cities within the district. In a recent year the park director of Cleveland suggested that the metropolitan park district take over the city parks, but the governing body did not react favorably, chiefly because of financial considerations. Since the district was unable to finance the metropolitan park system adequately, it could hardly assume the additional burden of a municipal park system. Furthermore, although the city administration agreed to give the district the amount appropriated for city parks and playgrounds, the district had no legal assurance that succeeding administrations would follow this practice.

Two other considerations influenced the decision not to take over the municipal system. First, the directors feared a court ruling that certain activities in a municipal park and playground program were not legitimate functions of the metropolitan park district. Second, they felt that the creation of a complete metropolitan park system was of primary importance and that attainment of this objective might be delayed by entering into municipal park activities. The primary objective, they reasoned, could be accomplished only by the metropolitan park district, but each city had authority to carry out a local park program. Many over-all gains might well be derived from the metropolitan park district's assumption of the local parks of Cleveland and other cities, but this development seems unlikely to occur in the foreseeable future.

METROPOLITAN SANITARY DISTRICT OF GREATER CHICAGO

The desire to protect the water supply derived from Lake Michigan by removing the major pollutant, sewage, promoted the early establishment of a sanitary district in the Chicago area. In 1889 the state legislature passed a law which really amounted to special legislation, for it contained, in addition to general provisions, specific references to this single district. The people were quick to make use of the act. Petitions were signed by more than the requisite 5,000 residents in the proposed district territory, which had to contain at least two cities in the same county needing a common sewage outlet. With the approval of the voters of the area delineated in the petitions filed in the county court, the Sanitary District of Chicago was established in the same year that the enabling legislation was passed. In 1955 the state legislature altered the title of the district, renaming it the Metropolitan Sanitary District of Greater Chicago. The first sanitary district to be organized in Illinois, it is now the oldest active independent metropolitan district government in the United States.

Growth of Restricted Area

The original boundaries of the district included about 185 square miles consisting of the entire area of Chicago and parts of the municipalities of Cicero, Riverside, and Lyons. Through thirty subsequent legislative acts the district territory has been enlarged to embrace almost 500 square miles. In general, neither the district residents nor its governing body has had a vote in these boundary decisions, nor has the electorate in any area to be annexed ever exercised its right to petition for an election. Still legally restricted to land within Cook County, the district presently includes about 50 per cent of the territory of the county and about 95 per cent of its population and assessed valuation. It now has authority to make its limits coterminous with the boundaries of Cook County upon gaining majority approval of the residents of the areas to be annexed. Its channels and outlets extend into adjacent Will County at Lockport.

Change in Disposal Method

Emphasizing sewage dilution in its early operations, the district in 1900 completed construction of a 30-mile sanitary and ship canal connecting two rivers, diverted sufficient water from Lake Michigan to dilute the sewage, and reversed the flow of the Chicago River to carry the sewage downstream and away from the lake which was the source of the water supply. Opposition to this method of sewage purification soon mounted, as other states and shipping and iron ore interests protested the diversion of substantial water from Lake Michigan, and residents objected to passage of the sewage effluent through the Illinois Valley. Unfavorable decisions by the United States Supreme Court prompted legal authorization in 1925 for the district to build sewage treatment plants to supplement the dilution process. This was undertaken during the 1930's, with the stimulus of major financial aid from the United States Public Works Administration.

Still permitted to divert some lake water, the district has as its main activity disposal of the sewage of the heavily urbanized portions, including more than seventy incorporated centers, of the Cook County section of the Chicago metropolitan area. In addition, since 1935 it has been permitted to make special provision and special charges for industrial waste disposal, a power which has not yet been exercised. Its incidental functions include the utilization of its channels, with the operation of necessary docks, for navigation; the control and use of water and power incidentally generated; and the production and sale of fertilizer from heat-dried, activated sludge. The district may also provide storm drainage and is currently studying possible methods of financing such service. There are important developments in some of these subordinate functions. The Chicago Regional Port District, another independent special district created in 1951, is very much inter-

ested in the improvement of the Calumet-Sag Channel, built by
the sanitary district. In 1953 the sanitary district discontinued its
commercial power operations and began to use all of the power it
generated. Furthermore, the district anticipates a doubling of its
annual fertilizer sales to a total of $3 million.

Trustees and Finance

The governing body of the district consists of nine trustees, three
of whom are elected from the district at large for six-year terms
at each regular biennial county election. The trustees receive an
annual salary of $7,500. There have been lengthy periods, such as
that from 1932 to 1946, when all nine representatives belonged
to the same political party. The trustees choose one of their members as president, and he has the power to veto ordinances passed
by them. Under provisions of an unsuccessful legislative bill of
the 1953 session, the governor would have appointed the governing
body members on a bipartisan basis with the approval of a majority
of Cook County's circuit court judges.

Activities have been financed in various and sometimes unusual
ways. In addition to the power to levy taxes for debt service and
operating costs up to a prescribed limit, the district has the authority to issue bonds with the approval of the district voters. In 1929,
as the result of urgent need, the district was granted the right to
issue bonds without referral to the district electorate. By 1953 the
district had floated $178 million in bonds, and needed $30 million
more for construction work.[16] In the same year the district trustees
proposed to eliminate nonreferendum bonds and to substitute the
power to levy a special nonreferendum tax for construction designed to bring in approximately $6 million annually for a six-year
period ending in 1959. The legislature approved the plan. The
district has given little attention to the revenue possibilities of
special assessments and special service charges which are familiar
practices in a number of sewage operations in other metropolitan
areas. In the past, the district has also received money through a

---

[16] Bonds have already financed a program originally estimated to cost $45,000,000.
Gilbert Y. Steiner, *Chicago Sanitary District* (Springfield: Illinois Legislative Council, 1953), p. 23. The district has been charged with wasteful expenditure a number
of times. See, for example, Charles E. Merriam, *Scrambled Government: Who Rules
What in Chicagoland* (Chicago: League for Industrial Democracy, 1934), p. 4.

grant-in-aid from the national government, which partially defrayed labor and material costs in initial construction work, and through income from power sales, although the latter was uneconomic in several of the years before its abandonment. As mentioned previously, fertilizer sales are expected to be an increasingly important source of revenue.

The Water Concession

An original sanitary district legislation provision, which is still operative, imposed a highly unusual requirement on the city of Chicago. This provision compels the city to sell water through connecting mains at its limits to municipalities within the district at a rate not higher than the rate to Chicago consumers for similar quantities. This stipulation was made in order to compensate municipalities benefiting only indirectly from the main purpose of the district legislation, which was to protect the Chicago water system. Because of later appreciable territorial extensions of the district, Chicago supplies water directly to thirty-seven suburban municipalities and indirectly to eleven others. These municipalities resell the water to consumers at rates averaging three times the price that Chicago is allowed to charge. The supreme court of the state upheld the constitutionality of this compulsory arrangement as early as 1904, and Chicago has since been unable to persuade the legislature to eliminate the provision or to permit a differential rate. Yet only portions of three of the recipient municipalities were members of the district when it was formed in 1889, and all of them currently gain from disposal of sewage through district facilities. The operations and territory of this sanitary district therefore have a direct and important effect upon the water system separately established and operated by the government of the most populous city in the district.

HURON-CLINTON METROPOLITAN AUTHORITY

Private Stimulation

The rapid increase in the population of the Detroit metropolitan area during the first part of the twentieth century created a great need for recreational areas. By the 1930's there was a serious lack of adequate facilities within a reasonable distance of the residences of many inhabitants. Mushrooming growth was continuing but if concerted action could be generated there was still fine acreage available, largely in the four counties surrounding Wayne County and Detroit. In 1937 a privately sponsored park and parkways organization was established with the objectives of utilizing the Huron and Clinton river valleys for recreational purposes under the administration of a special district. The group made a survey of recreational facilities and outlined plans for a parkway along the river valleys. A special act was passed by the state legislature in 1939 over the opposition of the Wayne County legislative delegation, which felt that taxpayers of its county would pay an unfair proportion of the cost and that the bulk of the development would take place outside the county.[17] Here was a situation, therefore, in which the hub county of the metropolitan area unsuccessfully fought state enabling legislation to facilitate an area-wide approach to a metropolitan problem.

The special law provided for the establishment of the Huron-Clinton Metropolitan Authority and defined its area as consisting of Wayne County and four surrounding counties. It endowed this metropolitan district with the power to provide parks, connecting drives, and limited access highways inside and outside its territorial limits. To bring the district into legal existence required separate approval by the voters of the five counties, and these sanctions were forthcoming in the following year by decisive majorities.

After court decisions upholding the legality of the governmental unit and determining that the state-equalized valuation was the proper basis for its tax levy, the authority began operation in 1942. The maximum limit of its tax rate, which must be uniform throughout the district, is .25 mill on the total assessed valuation of the district. The district can also issue revenue bonds and collect fees and charges for the use of its facilities. About nine-tenths of its revenue comes from property taxation, levied by the various counties for the district, and the remainder from project operations. The bond issuing power has not been used. The governing body consists of seven commissioners chosen by six different appointing

---

[17] Betty Tableman, *Governmental Organization in Metropolitan Areas* (Ann Arbor: University of Michigan Press, 1951), p. 110.

authorities. Each board of supervisors of the five counties selects one county resident for a six-year term, and the governor appoints two commissioners from the district at large for four-year terms. The commissioners receive no compensation. The 1944 session of the state legislature appropriated $1 million to the authority for land acquisition on a matching basis of dollar for dollar. By 1949, all of the money had been spent and the park land total had reached 6,300 acres.

Parks and Parkways

In the sixth year of operation of the Huron-Clinton Metropolitan Authority, the following forecast was made: "In the very near future the metropolitan area of Detroit will no longer be at the bottom of the list of highly populated areas in providing accessible recreational facilities for its citizens but on the contrary will take its place high among the leaders."[18] The district is working toward the fulfillment of this prediction. Aiming at preserving and developing recreational facilities in two river valleys and making them, as well as other recreational opportunities, readily accessible to a five-county population, the authority has constructed or is constructing a beach site, numerous parks, and an extensive connecting parkway 160 miles long. Furthermore, with its broad territorial jurisdiction, it can coöperate effectively with other park- and road-building agencies that are parts of smaller governments in the area.

GOLDEN GATE BRIDGE AND HIGHWAY DISTRICT

A long-time, widespread desire to facilitate the movement of people and goods between San Francisco and the area to its north materialized in 1937 with the completion of the Golden Gate Bridge, the longest single-span bridge in the world. This development materially lessened the geographical isolation of San Francisco, which covers 42 square miles at the tip of the peninsula bordering the entrance to San Francisco Bay, and which before 1936 lacked major northern or eastern bridge facilities.[19] The first

---

[18] *The Huron-Clinton Metropolitan Authority,* American Public Works Association (Chicago: 1948), p. 9.

[19] The California Toll Bridge Authority, a state agency, finished the San Francisco–Oakland Bay Bridge from San Francisco to the East Bay section of the metropolitan area several months earlier, in 1936.

official action toward attainment of the Golden Gate Bridge was
the passage of a resolution by the San Francisco governing body
in 1919 calling for state enabling legislation. Four years later a
newly formed citizen group, known as the Bridging the Golden
Gate Association, succeeded in getting a law passed which authorized the establishment of bridge and highway districts. The War
Department granted a provisional construction permit for a northern span from San Francisco in the following year.

Involved and Contested Initiation

Under the complex provisions of the state law, the boards of supervisors of six counties, including the City-County of San Francisco,
initially passed ordinances stating that they wished to have all or
part of their territory within the proposed district. Petitions were
then circulated and signed by a minimum of 10 per cent of the
qualified voters in each county. After review of the petitions and
protests in the superior court of each county, the California Secretary of State declared the district incorporated and notified the
supervisors of each participating county to appoint directors for
the district. This final legal step was delayed for a substantial
period of time.

The decision to use the district mechanism was rooted in the
beliefs that it would expedite bridge construction and that the
financial burden properly belonged to those most benefited rather
than to all the people of the state.[20] The latter conviction was
strongly doubted by a number of district residents, and for almost
six years taxpayers' suits made the proposed district a matter of
acrimonious court litigation. During this time one county and
part of a second withdrew from the district, after which the state
legislation was amended to permit noncontiguous territory to join.
The county to the north of the withdrawing county then went
through the legal process of becoming part of the district. The
Golden Gate Bridge and Highway District, composed of San Francisco, four entire counties, and a portion of another county, came
into legal existence in late 1928. Its first governing body members
were promptly installed a month later.

[20] *The Golden Gate Bridge: Report of the Chief Engineer,* Golden Gate Bridge
and Highway District (San Francisco: 1930), I, 22.

Complex Governing Body Composition

Like the legal procedure for establishing the district, the method
of constituting its governing body is also complicated. The members are selected for four-year terms by the boards of supervisors
of the participating counties, the number from each county depending upon its population. A city-county of more than 500,000
population, however, is entitled to half of the membership. San
Francisco, a city-county, therefore selects seven of the fourteen directors and each of the other counties selects one or two. The district can issue bonds up to 15 per cent of the assessed property valuation with approval of two-thirds of the district electorate, and can
levy taxes if its toll charge revenues are inadequate. However,
except for tax levies in 1929 and 1939 for preliminary organizational and engineering expenses and a $35 million bond issue for
actual construction, the district has operated entirely out of revenues derived from tolls. More than $1.5 million were collected by
the district during its first year of operation. By mid-1946, the end
of its eighth year of service, the revenue had more than doubled.
Numerous bills have been introduced in the state legislature since
1941 to have the state government operate the Golden Gate Bridge,
but none has mustered sufficient support.

METROPOLITAN WATER DISTRICT OF
SOUTHERN CALIFORNIA

Communities in the semiarid southern California coastal plain,
heavily dependent upon a substantial water supply to sustain
themselves and continue their development, faced a critical shortage during the drought of 1924–1926. Los Angeles had completed
in 1913, and fully utilized five years later, an aqueduct more than
200 miles long; it was extended in the early 1930's after the passage
of a municipal bond issue. This major construction project used the
Owens River on the eastern slope of the Sierra Nevada to supplement increasingly depleted sources, but the city soon needed additional water. Although neighboring localities were in even worse
straits, Los Angeles assumed the initiative in trying to solve this
vital problem, and turned to the possibility of transporting Colorado River water by means of another aqueduct. Possessing the

major share of assessed valuation and population of the area, Los Angeles nevertheless decided that the project should be undertaken in conjunction with other local governments.

Joining Forces

The preference for combined action was based on several factors. The city had recently been engaged in bitter and at times violent conflict over efforts to acquire more water rights in the Owens Valley, where its first aqueduct had been built. There was widespread resentment by numerous adjacent municipalities which opposed the efforts of Los Angeles to use the inducement of water in attempts to bring about territorial absorption. Furthermore, controversy over possible public power development at Boulder Canyon, in which Los Angeles wished to participate, was sufficiently large to make the city's officials desirous of avoiding a disagreement of similar magnitude over water acquisition. Finally, the Los Angeles city administration realized that a united effort would be more persuasive in perfecting adequate water rights through the state and national governments and in securing congressional approval of the construction by the national government of the Boulder Canyon Project on the Colorado River.[21]

A committee of the newly established Colorado River Aqueduct Association, formed by representatives of thirty-eight communities in southern California to promote construction of the aqueduct, drafted a bill providing for the metropolitan water district. After its defeat in the 1925 state legislative session, the bill and the Colorado River development became the chief issues in the Los Angeles municipal election of the same year. An advisory referendum was favorable by almost a seven-to-one margin and the mayoralty and council candidates committed to the program were elected. The bill, largely the same as initially submitted except for reductions in the district's power of eminent domain, decisively passed both houses of the California Legislature at the regular biennial session of 1927.

Under the general state enabling act, a metropolitan water district can be formed by two or more cities to develop, store, and

---

[21] Vincent Ostrom, *Water Supply*, monograph No. 8 in *Metropolitan Los Angeles: A Study in Integration* (Los Angeles: Haynes Foundation, 1953), pp. 20, 136.

distribute water. Notwithstanding the simplicity of this basic requirement, the Metropolitan Water District of Southern California is the only one that has been established under its provisions. In February, 1928, acting under the formation section of the enabling law, the governing body of Pasadena adopted an ordinance which declared that public necessity and convenience required the establishment of the Metropolitan Water District of Southern California. Of the twenty-one cities in four counties proposed for inclusion by the ordinance, thirteen subsequently took favorable action. Following a State Supreme Court decision upholding the constitutionality of the law, Pasadena called a special election in the thirteen cities on the inclusion question. The proposition received majority approval in eleven of the cities, including Burbank, Glendale, Los Angeles, Pasadena, Santa Ana, and Santa Monica. The district began its legal existence in December, 1928, with eleven member cities, not all of them contiguous, in three counties. This occurred two weeks before Congress and the President approved construction of the Boulder Canyon Project.

The Great Aqueduct

Bringing water across the complete width of California from the distant Colorado River via an aqueduct was the tremendous engineering project undertaken by the newly formed district. A bond issue of $220 million was authorized and early in 1933 construction was started on the most economical of fifty-four routes surveyed. By building the aqueduct at less than full capacity, the initial outlay was considerably lessened. Through a series of loans the Reconstruction Finance Corporation became committed to purchase a major share of the authorized bonds. In addition, the Public Works Administration, also an agency of the national government, made a loan and grant of more than $2 million.

The aqueduct diverts water from a lake reservoir behind Parker Dam on the Colorado River. The water is lifted in several separate actions more than 1,300 feet above the intake level, flows by gravity through lined and open canals and conduit and siphon pipelines, and proceeds through mountain tunnels and valleys to Lake Mathews, a distance of 242 miles. This is the terminal reservoir of the Colorado River Aqueduct from which the distribution takes place. Completed after more than six years, the aqueduct made its first deliveries for domestic consumption in 1941.

The district handles water entirely as a wholesale distributor. It transmits water to its constituent members, and they either distribute it retail to the consumer or make arrangements for public or private systems to do so. The district prohibits the sale of water to areas outside its territorial limits, except in extreme emergencies such as the need of nearby military installations at the beginning of World War II. The total length of the aqueduct, including main, distribution, and branch lines, exceeds 450 miles, the longest water supply facility in the United States. Since 1942 surplus power, derived by the district from sources at Hoover and Parker dams, has been sold to the city of Los Angeles and to a major privately owned electric company. The district retains sufficient power for its own pumping operations.[22]

Annexation Conditions

The district has experienced substantial area growth. Before construction bonds were authorized in 1931, four cities were annexed by the district and two of the original member cities withdrew, the only deannexing actions in the district's history. Detachment is possible through the decision of local voters, but the property remains subject to taxation for indebtedness incurred during the time it was part of the district. There was no further change in district territory until 1942. Meanwhile the anticipation that original member cities would complete sizable annexations was not materializing, and in 1938 the district laid down a new annexation policy. Units seeking to be included in the district must henceforth be of such size and water requirements as to make water delivery economically feasible. In addition, they should preferably contain sufficient territory to control the entire production of water from affected underground basins. The policy was therefore aimed at reducing the number of future individual members and encouraging water conservation. As a result, annexations of new units as constituent members of the district since 1942 include nine municipal water districts and one county water authority. These in turn

[22] Vincent Ostrom, *Water and Politics* (Los Angeles: Haynes Foundation, 1953), p. 182.

are composed of cities and unincorporated areas, some of which are within smaller water districts.

Annexations to member cities of the district, which automatically bring the territory within the district, receive more advantageous treatment than other annexations. An annexation to a member water district or as a proposed constituent member of the metropolitan water district must be submitted to the directors of the Metropolitan Water District of Southern California, who specify the terms and conditions. This precedes the popular vote in the local area on joining the metropolitan water district. It follows voter decision to organize a local water district and to elect five directors. In addition to stipulations on matters such as supply-line location and connection facilities, the principal and always present condition is the payment of back taxes in the amount that the area would have paid if it had joined the metropolitan water district at its inauguration, plus 4 per cent delinquency charges. At the option of the area desiring annexation the payment may be amortized over a maximum of thirty years; since 1950, 3 to 4 per cent interest has been added to the unpaid balance. No back taxes, however, are levied against an area annexing to a member city. The territorial size of the metropolitan water district has increased somewhat through annexations to member cities, but in spite of the tax obligation most of the area growth has occurred by annexation of water districts. The metropolitan water district, more than quadrupling its size since it began operation in 1941, contains approximately 2,700 square miles and serves about 6 million people in five counties which are located in three metropolitan areas. Most of the sixty-six cities in the district are members of municipal water districts or of the county water authority, and these in turn are member units of the metropolitan water district. No cities have become member units since 1931.

Directors and Voting Power

Each member city and each member water district or authority of the metropolitan water district has at least one representative on the governing body, called the board of directors. The representative is selected by the chief executive of the member unit with the approval of its legislative body. A member unit can also appoint one representative for each $300 million of assessed property valuation taxable for district purposes located within its territory. The thirty-six directors constitute an unwieldy number and much of the board's work is done by subcommittees.

Voting power is determined on a different basis. Each member unit has one vote for each $10 million of assessed property valuation. Each is entitled to a minimum of one vote, but no one may have more votes than the combined total of all the others. Most decisions require a simple majority of the votes. Although at the inception of the district the city of Los Angeles had a preponderance of the assessed valuation, it could never legally have more than 50 per cent of the votes. With the annexation by the metropolitan district of a large municipal water district in 1954, the voting strength of Los Angeles dropped for the first time below one-half of the total. Representatives of a unit must vote as a bloc, after arriving at a majority decision. Directors serve without compensation and presumably at the pleasure of the appointing official, though the enabling law is silent on the latter point. Several directors have been on the board for twenty years or more. There is evidence that municipal water districts which are member units tend more and more to select their representatives from their own governing bodies or professional staffs rather than from the lay residents.

The district has a diversity of financing means. It may issue general obligation bonds for acquisition and construction upon majority rather than two-thirds popular approval. This course of action was followed in 1931. The district also levies property taxes to pay bonded indebtedness and additional expenditures not absorbed by other revenues. Another source of income is the sale of water to district members and of power to several suppliers. Taxation has been used primarily for bond redemption and interest payments, with the peak of indebtedness occurring in the fiscal year 1952–1953, and water sales have provided money for the maintenance and operation of the aqueduct and the distribution system. A relatively heavy burden has been placed upon property taxation in order to keep the price of water at a competitive level. As debt charges decrease and the revenue from water sales increases, the money to be raised annually from taxes will lessen.

It is anticipated that all expenditures will eventually be paid from operating revenues. A final important source of funds is the collec-tion of back taxes from late entrants into the district. The major part of future construction is to be financed with these funds.

OTHER GENERAL METROPOLITAN DISTRICT FEATURES

Variations and Limitations

These illustrations reëmphasize several characteristics of metro-politan districts discussed earlier, such as their vital importance in specific situations, their frequent post–World War I origin, and their functional range. They also help to point up other aspects of metropolitan district development. For example, there is wide variation in the features of metropolitan districts despite their relatively limited number. This can be seen by recalling the forma-tion, governing board composition, and financing characteristics of the districts presented as case studies. Even functionally similar districts operating in metropolitan areas in the same state may have marked differences. The Metropolitan Water District of Southern California and the East Bay Municipal Utility District supply water to residents of different California metropolitan areas. The former is largely financed by property taxation, the latter depends upon service charges. There are frequently great differences be-tween two metropolitan districts in the same metropolitan area. For example, the formation procedure and the method of selecting the governing body of the Metropolitan Sanitary District of Greater Chicago and the Chicago Transit Authority contrast sharply.

Metropolitan districts differ appreciably in the proportion of the metropolitan area or population which they include, although all of them encompass at least a major part of one or the other. Beyond this, however, there is frequently little similarity. Some districts, such as the Huron-Clinton Metropolitan Authority, extend outside the metropolitan area into nonmetropolitan land, whereas the Metropolitan Water District of Southern California contains most of one metropolitan area and parts of two others. By contrast, the Metropolitan Sanitary District of Greater Chicago includes about one-half the territory and most of the population of only the core county of a metropolitan area. This district, as a result of territorial limitations, cannot prevent sewage dumping in the portion of the metropolitan area which is outside district boundaries. Its geographical limits lessen its functional effectiveness. Most metropolitan districts contain less than the entire metropolitan area.

Although metropolitan districts collectively engage in many functions, in no metropolitan area are all or even nearly all metropolitan functions handled by metropolitan districts. Such units are therefore solving only part of the over-all metropolitan problem. As noted previously, most metropolitan districts have not increased their functions since their establishment. Generally when they have grown in this manner they have taken on functions closely related to their initial functions. For example, the Port of New York Authority has enlarged its operations, but within the original field of transportation, and the East Bay Municipal Utility District, which started by supplying water, has added sewage disposal.

Control and Complexity

One of the most striking features of metropolitan districts is the fact that metropolitan residents lack determination of and control over certain important aspects of the districts. This situation is not an isolated one, but appears with some frequency, especially in metropolitan districts containing territory in two states. Establishing a district by state legislative or judicial action, permitting the district directors to issue bonds on their own decision, effectuating annexations through state laws, and having members of the governing body chosen by a governor or a judge whose constituency is wider than that of the metropolitan area are important examples of the remoteness of some districts from the voters of metropolitan areas. A number of metropolitan districts utilize one or two of these procedures, but interstate metropolitan districts use all of them. Metropolitan districts with territory in two states are created by the adoption of similar laws by two state legislatures, approval by Congress, and the completion of an interstate compact. The members of the governing body are appointed by the respective governors and occasionally some of them are ex officio state officials. The governing body may issue bonds through its own unilateral action. The district area can be enlarged by amendment of the

interstate compact. How can such districts, which operate in metropolitan areas and materially affect the local people, be held sufficiently accountable by the metropolitan population? The only
possible regular channel of control is through the legislature or the
governor, but such a route is often too circuitous to be effective.

With a substantial number of metropolitan areas already territorially interstate and more about to become so, district government is likely to be used more frequently. So far the uniform district pattern in interstate situations has been detachment from
responsibility to the people most intimately affected by such governments. There is of course no logical reason why districts in
these circumstances cannot be organized under a system calling
for direct metropolitan determination and control. Such a procedure would, however, require a reshaping of the established
mold.

These interstate metropolitan districts, and certain other metropolitan districts subject to repeated amendment by state law,
seem to represent a hybrid level of government, neither truly local
nor state. They are local governments principally in the sense that
they function in a local area. At the same time they are operationally separated from the area they serve, or are affected by major
changes initiated by the state legislature, which may or may not
be directly responsive to the desires of the metropolitan people.
These districts are very close to being adjuncts of the state government, a matter of concern to persons who want the approaches
to metropolitan difficulties to be locally determined and locally
accountable.

Another prominent feature of metropolitan districts is the complexity of their composition or functioning. This handicap, found
in more than a few of these districts, renders metropolitan determination and control less effective. The Metropolitan Water District of Southern California is a prominent example, for the composition of its governing body, the distribution of voting power,
the requirement of bloc voting, and the methods of annexing territory combine to make it an extremely complicated system.
Furthermore, there is a stratification of governments within governments as major parts and subordinate parts of this metropolitan
operation. For example, in San Diego County the Crest Public

Utility District and the cities of La Mesa and El Cajon are part of the La Mesa, Lemon Grove, and Spring Valley Irrigation District, which in turn is a constituent member of the Metropolitan Water District of Southern California. A similar intricate pyramiding exists in Orange County, and numerous other areas within the metropolitan district are only slightly less involved. There is no question that metropolitan determination and control were conceived as being part of the original arrangement, but the intricacies that have developed severely dilute the possibilities of their full and consistent attainment.

The complexity usually centers around the composition of the governing body. In the Chicago Transit Authority three of the seven members are appointed by the governor with the consent of the state senate and the approval of the mayor of Chicago. One of these three must reside outside the Chicago city limits. The remaining four are appointed by the mayor of Chicago with the consent of the city council and the sanction of the governor. The Milwaukee Metropolitan Sewerage District has two governing bodies, a city commission and a metropolitan commission. The city commission, consisting of five appointees of the mayor of Milwaukee, builds and operates intercepting sewers and the sewage plant inside Milwaukee and operates sewers outside the city in the district. The metropolitan commission, whose three members are selected by the governor, is responsible for the building of main sewers outside Milwaukee. Special districts should not be so complicated as to negate the worthy objectives of understanding and interest by metropolitan residents.

Criticism and Potentialities

Strong objections to metropolitan districts are frequently raised, but some of them, of course, are based on specific situations and hence do not apply to all districts. Two of the most common criticisms are that districts are too remote from public influence and regulation, and that they have substituted control by a professional administrative guild of experts and an allied interest group for public control.[23] Also often stated are complaints about the limita-

---

[23] The latter point is stressed by Victor Jones in his talk, "Methodology in the Study of Metropolitan Areas," which appears in *The Study of the Metropolitan Region of Chicago: Objectives and Methodology* (Evanston: Northwestern University Department of Political Science, 1952), p. 10.

tions on types of district activities which result from mandatory reliance on nontax sources for financing, and about the lack of intergovernmental coöperation and coördinated planning. A more general objection to districts focuses on the effects of restricting their functional scope. It is argued that this type of functional consolidation, without any alteration of existing governmental areas, is simply a makeshift or expedient and lacks sufficient comprehensiveness to meet the many difficulties of the metropolitan problem. Putting the argument in the form of a medical analogy, a long-time analyst observed that "If a patient were suffering from cataracts, heart disease, diabetes and an infected toe, amputating the toe might enable him to walk around for awhile but it could not be considered a really important step toward restoring him to health. Just so with [metropolitan] districts and the metropolitan problem."[24] The limited scope of each district therefore leads to further profusion of governmental units which increases the confusion of citizens. In addition, utilization of the metropolitan district device in a restricted manner takes the impetus and interest away from more thorough approaches by alleviating the most pressing difficulties.

In view of this general censure of metropolitan districts, it is significant that for a long time there have been expressions of interest in a remedial measure. This is the idea of broadening the range of functions so as to make metropolitan districts multipurpose operations. So far, however, districts of limited purpose have shown little inclination to seek authorization for additional services. Furthermore, in the relatively few district laws that allow the performance of several functions, most districts undertake only one. The same is true of the even rarer districts which may legally perform numerous diversified functions. Nevertheless, interest in creating new multipurpose metropolitan districts continues, as does optimism that some of the established districts will evolve into such governments.[25]

---

[24] Thomas H. Reed, "The Metropolitan Problem—1941," *National Municipal Review*, 30 (July, 1941), 407.

[25] For two examples of advocacy of multipurpose metropolitan districts see Ralph F. Fuchs, "Regional Agencies for Metropolitan Areas," *Washington University Law Quarterly*, 22 (Dec., 1936), 64–78, and Coleman Woodbury, "The Background and Prospects of Urban Redevelopment in the United States," in Woodbury, *op. cit.*, p. 632. A recent illustration of anticipating the transformation of a single-purpose metropolitan district into a multipurpose one is found in Cassella, *op. cit.*, chap. 5.

The ease of establishing metropolitan districts, in contrast to the difficulty of achieving other types of metropolitan integration, makes this approach extremely inviting. In addition, public acceptance of the district idea does not seem to lessen with the granting of more than one function, probably because most metropolitan districts vested with multiple functions perform only one at the outset. This technique, unconsciously used for the most part, may well be a key strategy which advocates of multipurpose metropolitan districts should deliberately use. Will this transformation of the metropolitan district mechanism be attempted in efforts to accomplish metropolitan integration? An affirmative answer seemingly has broad implications for the future.

The apparent political feasibility of establishing multipurpose metropolitan districts, and the attractiveness of forming some type of metropolitan government, should not cause important parts of the plan to be overlooked. There should be metropolitan determination and control of metropolitan districts. There should also be an adequate and equitable financial base. Many metropolitan districts of limited functional scope do not adequately meet these standards. The question of success or failure in adoption of a plan should not overshadow the careful formulation of its proper elements, for governments tend to be permanent, and original provisions are sometimes difficult to change. Therefore, although the idea of multipurpose metropolitan districts may be very applicable in specific situations, the details of such proposals are highly important and should not be neglected in the early stages.

If the future possibility of functional enlargement and other changes is put aside, what is the current status of metropolitan districts? As has been shown, they are subject to substantial criticism, often by observers who oppose fragmentary government wherever it exists. Some individual districts receive mild praise or tacit commendation from people living within their jurisdictions. In general, however, critical judgment is far more prevalent than approbation. Nevertheless, metropolitan districts are usually effective in the performance of their responsibilities. Furthermore, in spite of their limited functional scope and their frequent deficiencies in formation, structure, or finances, metropolitan districts represent the nearest existing approximation to area-wide government in many metropolitan areas.

CHAPTER THREE

Urban
Fringe
Districts

Increased urbanization has meant the growth not only of metropolitan areas but also of unincorporated urban fringe areas in both
metropolitan and nonmetropolitan situations. In turn fringe
growth has often caused extensive utilization of special district
governments to cope with the resulting conditions. At this point
it must be emphasized that urban fringe areas and urban fringe
districts located in metropolitan areas are part of the metropolitan
area problem and should be considered in relation to the subject
matter of the previous chapter, and that comprehensive approaches to the problems of metropolitan areas would solve the
local fringe difficulties. It seems preferable, however, to consider
urban fringe districts in a separate chapter for two reasons. First,
the urban fringe area problem has generally been attacked, not in
the context of broad metropolitan solutions, but rather in terms of
unincorporated urban territory alone or in association with an
adjoining city. Second, the urban fringe difficulty is significant in
nonmetropolitan as well as in metropolitan environments.

Briefly defined, an unincorporated urban fringe is substantially
populated land located at the border but outside the legal boundaries of an existing city. It has urban needs but lacks comprehensive urban government. Some urban fringes adjoin cities that are
within metropolitan areas, others adjoin municipalities that are not
in metropolitan areas. But whatever their location, they are very
prevalent, for an extremely large proportion of cities in the United

States which are not completely surrounded by other cities have adjoining unincorporated urban fringes.[1]

THE GROWTH OF THE URBAN FRINGE

Technological and Human Forces

The rise and rapid growth of urban fringes can be attributed to many reasons, of varying importance in different localities. An extensive inquiry into these causes could be carried back to the factors that led to urbanization in general, such as the agricultural revolution which freed many people from the soil and medical and health advances which made living close together possible. But a detailed review of these contributing forces hardly seems necessary here. Specifically, urban fringe growth has been possible because the greater freedom of movement resulting from the increased supply of automobiles and the major improvements in roads has enabled people to live farther away from their jobs. Of course, technological improvements aiding urbanization and fringe growth had to be accompanied by human desires and wishes. Granted the existence of physical means, who do people want to live in urban fringes? Sometimes the answer is predominantly economic. It is the availability of homes, and frequently of home ownership, at prices within reach of more families. Builders are often attracted to residential and commercial construction in the fringe because of the high asking price for remaining city lots, the added cost of demolishing buildings in the city, and the absence of building and zoning controls in the fringe comparable to city standards.

People move to fringe areas not only because of financial considerations but also because they desire openness or open country, a feeling traceable in some instances to the influence of earlier residence in rural areas. Many fringe dwellers, regardless of their economic status, want to get away from the noise, dirt, and congestion of the city to pleasanter neighborhoods which are quieter, cleaner, and less crowded. The desire for physical escape from the city does not, however, necessarily mean a desire to leave city con-

---

[1] Officials of only three of 177 cities, who were interrogated by the author, stated that there was no urban fringe locally. In the three exceptions, the fringe had recently been absorbed by the city, or the city had been completely circumscribed by other incorporated centers.

veniences and attractions. Furthermore, the longing for openness
is often not realized permanently, for many of these newly developed areas later become noisy, dirty, and congested. What about
the lower taxes in a fringe when it is first settled? They are considered by prospective home buyers but do not usually constitute
a decisive factor in the decision to purchase in the fringe.

Rapid Population Gains

Urban fringes are in an expansionist phase which in various geographical locations has attained spectacular proportions. The
population increase is most noticeable in metropolitan areas, where
the portions lying beyond the central city and consisting of unincorporated urban fringes and suburban municipalities grew more
than two and one-half times as fast as the central cities during the
decade of the 1940's. There are many specific illustrations of the
rapid increase of fringe populations. For example, during the sev-
enteen-year period ending in 1947, the central city of the Flint
metropolitan area remained practically stationary in population,
while its unincorporated urban fringe was doubling its number of
inhabitants. Fringe population increase is similarly noticeable in
numerous nonmetropolitan situations where no city in the county
has as many as 50,000 people.[2]

THE NATURE OF THE URBAN FRINGE

Population Range

The total population residing in urban areas that are near but not
within cities is numerically impressive. In 1950 the United States
Census Bureau defined 157 urbanized areas, each including one or
more cities of at least 50,000 population, all neighboring incorporated centers with at least 2,500 people, and all nearby closely
settled but less populous incorporated places and unincorporated
urban territory. The bureau then calculated that almost 8 million
people were residing in the incorporated centers of less than 2,500
and the unincorporated urban territory of the 157 urbanized areas.

[2] For illustrations see Walter T. Martin's study of the Eugene-Springfield area,
The Rural-Urban Fringe (Eugene: University of Oregon Press, 1953), and Noel P.
Gist's article about Columbia, Missouri, "Direction in Urban Decentralization,"
Social Forces, 30 (Mar., 1952), 257–267.

No further breakdown of population between these two categories was made. Additional fringe population lives in settlements that are not within these urbanized areas. This evidence indicates that at least several million people currently live in urban fringes.[3]

Although these areas are found throughout the United States, their population range is wide, extending from a few hundred to tens of thousands. Many of them are one-fourth to one-half as large as the adjoining city, a ratio that applies to some populous cities as well as to numerous smaller ones. About one-third of the population of the Nashville metropolitan area, for example, lives in the urban fringe. Furthermore, in some states several urban fringes are more populous than the average city, and some approximate the population of the neighboring municipality. Recent illustrations of the latter have been the urban fringes of The Dalles, Oregon; Benton Harbor, Michigan; Danville, Virginia; Grand Junction, Colorado; Daytona Beach, Florida; and Salinas, California.

Inferior Standards and Services

Most urban fringes are actual or potential problem areas because their standards and services are inferior to those maintained by the cities they border. Such areas frequently represent the conflict that inevitably results from the mingling of urban conditions with the instruments and attitudes of more rural-oriented governments, such as counties within whose jurisdiction they are located. Many county governments have inadequate zoning and subdivision laws. Others have no legislation at all in these fields, or lack the power to enact any. Moreover, although cities in some states have the authority to regulate such matters beyond their limits, it is often limited to a portion of the fringe. Many entire fringes and major sections of others are therefore not subject to basic urban zoning and subdivision standards; at least some of the ill effects of urban fringes can be traced to these inadequacies. Poor land use and deficient subdivision layout are costly to rectify as an area becomes more thickly populated, and values can rapidly depreciate. But

[3] For a discussion of urbanized areas by the Census Bureau's Population and Housing Division chief, see Howard G. Brunsman, "Urban Places and Population," *Municipal Year Book: 1952* (Chicago: International City Managers' Association, 1952), pp. 21–22.

these deficiencies can have far more than local repercussions. For example, they can adversely affect the health and safety of not only fringe residents but also inhabitants of the neighboring city. The sufficiency of zoning and subdividing regulations is important to the adequacy of an urban development, especially on a long-range basis. Mistakes become embedded, and inertia and costliness work in favor of their continuance.

More directly and more promptly felt is the absence or inadequacy of public services in urban fringes. An urban area, whether or not incorporated, needs a certain minimum of service in order to survive. Most urban fringes suffer significant deficiencies in this respect, although their residents and property owners usually manage to obtain some services from public or private agencies. The most prevalent difficulties are the inferior condition or nonexistence of sewage, sanitation, and drainage.[4] Other services that are often entirely ignored or only partially satisfied include street construction and maintenance, street lighting, paving, water, fire protection, law enforcement, recreation, and public health.

Inadequate or nonexistent standards and services turn some urban fringes into cheap and unsubstantial developments. These fringes have unsanitary conditions, unpaved and sometimes impassable streets in unfinished subdivisions, and incongruous mixtures of industrial, commercial, and residential land uses. Other fringes are asylums for vice and gambling. Still others represent major fire hazards. Many have less apparent weaknesses which are nevertheless dangerous. The various shortcomings have detrimental results both within and beyond the fringe. Many of the defects, especially in fire protection, health, law enforcement, and sanitation, spill over into and harass the adjacent city. Cities are often powerless to eradicate the undesirable conditions that are geographically so close at hand. Most municipalities cannot compel the fringe to improve or to become a part of a municipal government. In addition, they cannot maintain continual vigilance at their borders to eliminate problems emanating from the fringe. Because of the free movement of people throughout an entire urban area, such action would be unrealistic as well as costly.

---

[4] John C. Bollens, "Fringe Area Conditions and Relations," *Public Management*, 32 (Mar., 1950), 50–51.

THE GROWTH OF URBAN FRINGE DISTRICTS

One response to the needs growing out of the rise and development
of urban fringes has been the establishment of special district governments. Although some of these districts are used in nonfringe
or only partial fringe situations, such as unincorporated urban
areas geographically separated from any incorporated community
or territory embracing both a city and a fringe, they are mainly
located wholly in fringes and can be appropriately designated as
urban fringe districts. There are several thousand urban fringe
districts functioning in the unincorporated urban territory adjacent
to cities.[5]

Urban fringe districts are geographically widespread but are not
evenly distributed throughout the United States. They exist in all
of the major geographic regions of the United States, and are important in such widely scattered states as Connecticut, South Carolina, Texas, Colorado, and Washington. On the other hand, urban
fringe districts are of little or no consequence in states such as
Alabama, Michigan, and New York. The unevenness of their geographical distribution is attributable in part to differences in the
intensity of urban fringe needs and in the success of other governments in meeting those needs. In New York, for example, numerous fringe demands are satisfied by dependent districts which are
part of the town government, a solution which obviates the necessity of creating separate and independent urban fringe districts.

Metropolitan and Nonmetropolitan Use

Numerous urban fringe districts operate in the unincorporated
portions of metropolitan areas. Slightly less than 2,600 nonschool
special districts are functioning in metropolitan areas, and a sub-

---

[5] Their restriction to unincorporated urban areas therefore clearly distinguishes
urban fringe districts from other major groups of districts. Metropolitan districts
often serve both incorporated and unincorporated areas. Coterminous districts,
which are special districts whose areas coincide exactly or approximately with those
of general local governments, function principally in incorporated territory and unincorporated nonfringe land. Rural districts mainly include unincorporated non-
urban territory within their limits. Some school districts are technically urban fringe
districts since they function entirely in unincorporated urban land. In this study,
however, school districts are treated as a separate group regardless of geographical
location.

stantial part of the total are urban fringe districts.[6] In the state of Washington, for example, there are heavy concentrations of these districts in the Seattle, Spokane, and Tacoma metropolitan areas. Such districts are also common in the outskirts of cities not within metropolitan areas.

A rapid growth of urban fringe districts has been occurring in many parts of the United States, noticeably since the decade of the 1940's and mostly in metropolitan areas and in unincorporated areas bordering nonmetropolitan cities that have been undergoing heavy urbanization. Exact comparisons with the early decades of the twentieth century are impossible because of the lack of comprehensive data. Illustrations from two states, however, demonstrate the existence of this trend in recent years. In the period from 1940 through 1955 four types of special districts in California (fire protection, street lighting, sanitation, and water), functioning largely in urban fringes, approximately doubled in number. In 1943 a university research agency in Oregon could speak of a relatively new trend in the state involving two new types of districts, water and fire protection, which were largely being formed in thickly populated unincorporated areas. In 1954, the same organization noted that urban fringe districts were assuming increasing importance in Oregon local government and that the legislature had recently passed laws authorizing the establishment of many new functional types of urban fringe districts. In this eleven-year period, the number of fire protection districts, many of which are urban fringe districts, increased more than sixfold.[7]

Fastest Growing Units

Numerically exceeding only metropolitan and coterminous districts among the five major groups of special district governments, urban fringe districts are growing faster than any other category

---

[6] *Local Government in Metropolitan Areas,* U.S. Bureau of the Census, Governments Division, State and Local Government Special Studies No. 36 (Washington: 1954), p. 2.

[7] The California information is based on *Summary of Taxing Jurisdictions,* California State Board of Equalization (Sacramento: 1940–1955). The Oregon reports are *The Units of Government in Oregon: 1941* and *The Units of Government in Oregon: 1951,* published in 1943 and 1954, respectively, by the Bureau of Municipal Research and Service of the University of Oregon at Eugene.

of governmental units in the United States.[8] Some urban fringe districts have existed for many years, but the great proliferation of them is recent. What is the setting in which urban fringe districts have become numerous and continue to grow? A major element is the conviction of many urban fringe dwellers that they need, or at least are willing to finance, only a few public services. They hold fast to this conviction despite the heavy urbanization ultimately experienced in most urban fringes. Even when their areas are densely settled, urban fringe dwellers are likely to resist the traditional processes of incorporation and annexation, which could give them comprehensive local government, and turn instead, when absolutely necessary, to special district governments. Neither incorporation nor annexation is being utilized sufficiently to cope with the urban fringe problem in a period of rapid urban fringe growth.

Incorporation Lag

The device of incorporation was conceived for the express purpose of enabling urban dwellers to obtain public services directly. Its utilization, however, is usually based on initiation and consent by the people most immediately concerned. If these local actions do not materialize—and they often have not in recent years—incorporation does not take place. In the period of heavy urbanization from 1942 to 1952, the number of municipalities in the United States increased by less than 3.5 per cent. Meanwhile nonschool special districts increased almost 50 per cent. In California, the number of incorporations in the thirty years after 1920 was less than one-half the number in the previous twenty years, in spite of the largest influx of urban population in the history of the state. Many people settled in cities which had incorporated earlier, but many located in adjacent urbanized areas which did not incorporate. Incorporation is not keeping pace with fringe area expansion, principally because of negative decisions or inaction by urban fringe residents.

---

[8] Compilations based on Bureau of the Census data may give the impression that agricultural districts are experiencing the greatest growth. Most of the almost 2,000 soil conservation districts enumerated in 1952, however, were not considered governmental units in 1942. Governments in the United States in 1952, U.S. Bureau of the Census, Governments Division, State and Local Government Special Studies No. 31 (Washington: 1953), p. 9.

Moderate Success of Annexation

Annexation, which is a supplement to incorporation, has experienced a somewhat similar development. At the beginning of urban local government in the United States it was recognized that many incorporated centers would need to expand territorially and that a method of accomplishing such adjustments was necessary. Although annexation has been more useful in absorbing fringe areas than in integrating entire metropolitan areas, its utilization is often restricted by the same requirements of fringe initiation and approval which have drastically curtailed the use of incorporation. No matter how obviously the fringe territory is a part of the adjoining city in terms of economic and social realities and of the necessity for orderly growth, the judgment of the people living in the unincorporated fringe sector is frequently the controlling factor. Acting within the framework of the annexation policy in effect in numerous states, the neighboring city can do little so long as its urban fringe does not wish to join with it. At times, too, the city does not want to annex the fringe, especially if there has been substantial development at a substandard level. Too few cities have assumed leadership and responsibility in trying to solve the problems of the urban community that includes the city and the fringe. And finally, some noncity general local governments which are antagonistic toward cities urge fringe dwellers to establish independent special districts instead of becoming part of existing municipal governments.

There has been a burst of annexations in the post–World War II years, but the over-all development as related to urban fringe areas has been more significant in the number of participating cities than in the proportion of urban fringes that have been annexed. Furthermore, most municipalities that have completed sizable annexations in recent years find themselves already plagued by new bordering fringes. It may well be that the technological forces which have made possible the spreading of urbanization over a broader geographical area have also appreciably reduced the usefulness of annexation. Extensive recent attempts to use annexation, the usual method of attack on the urban fringe problem, suggest that this approach is not the final answer but is utilized only for want of a better device.

General Governmental Inadequacy and Disinterest

Often the urban fringe is successful in staying outside the jurisdiction of an adjoining city and refuses to become a separate city even when it meets the minimum population requirement. Nevertheless, it is still within the territory of a larger local unit, such as the county in most states or the township or town in a number of Midwestern and New England states. Why don't these units furnish services to the urban fringe, charging additionally for new or more intensified functions that are not supplied throughout the entire territory of the general government? Some of them, such as those in Kansas and New York, do create special taxing or assessment areas which remain under their control, thereby avoiding the creation of separate special district governments. The idea has been discussed and advocated in states like Illinois and Rhode Island. A private state-wide research group in Rhode Island, for example, urged that, as a substitute for independent fringe districts, towns be empowered to add the cost of extended service to individual tax bills in localized areas within the town. With the installation of this plan, it was stressed, "most of the special districts would be unnecessary and might be discontinued."[9]

Most general local units encompassing the urban fringe, however, lack the legal authority to create subareas that can be charged directly for new or additional services. They are usually confined to providing area-wide services for which a uniform area-wide charge must be made. Furthermore, many of them are disinclined to expand functionally (sometimes because they would need new types of equipment and additional personnel), to seek permission to create subordinate areas, or to use the authorization when it exists. The legal inability or the disinclination of such units to use a financing mechanism that would force urban fringes to pay for certain added services has prompted numerous fringes to establish special district governments to handle particular needs which could have been fulfilled by the general units. In reality, some of these general units provide additional service at no extra charge to the fringe, which then has no need to establish special districts to supply the services. This practice, however, causes cities to com-

---

[9] *A Study of State and Local Relationships,* Rhode Island Public Expenditure Council (Providence: 1946), p. 63.

plain of financial injustice, since the higher level of service or the new service is financed disproportionately out of money collected by the general unit from cities within its jurisdiction.

Stimulation by General Governments

The granting of services by county or other local units and by cities is stimulating the use of urban fringe districts. Many counties, townships, towns, and cities provide a variety of services to urban fringes and thus enable these fringes to fulfill some but not all of their public needs. However, services furnished by general governments can be supplemented by others obtained through the establishment of urban fringe districts. This complementary, piecemeal approach is a fringe substitute for incorporation or annexation, or for seeking to have a general local unit granted legal authority to designate the fringe as a subarea for financing needed services.

Abundance of Enabling Laws

The growth of urban fringe districts has been facilitated by the ease with which enabling legislation has been passed in numerous states. Without permissive laws, more urban fringes would have to turn to incorporation, annexation, or designation by a general local government as a special service area in order to obtain a sufficient quantity of service. But local residents desiring to have a district government provide a service, or specialists of the state government concerned about the need for a particular function, have usually found little opposition to their suggestions for legislation authorizing a specific type of district. A large amount of district legislation usable in urban fringes has been enacted in numerous states, especially since the 1940's. Furthermore, much of it has been designed exclusively for urban fringes. This is evident by its provisions, which endow the district with urban functions but limit its area to unincorporated territory, and sometimes even restrict the district territory to a certain radial distance from the legal city limits or require it to be adjacent to a city. At times, too, the formation of urban fringe districts is fostered through advisory and financial help from the national and state governments.

In summary, several elements stand out prominently as contributing to the growth of urban fringe districts. First is the determined opposition by many urban fringe residents to using the power, vested exclusively or chiefly in them, of making their area subject to general local government either through annexation or incorporation. Next is the usual lack of an adequate financing mechanism by general local units having fringes within their boundaries. Then there is the practice by numerous general local governments of providing some services to urban fringes. And, finally, the availability of appropriate legislation and encouragement by other governments are reasons for the growth of urban fringe districts.

URBAN FRINGE DISTRICT CHARACTERISTICS

Limited Areas

Most urban fringe districts can be well characterized as dwarf-sized governmental units, but collectively they are important because they are so numerous. Moreover, their significance as a group is ordinarily overlooked because of the paucity of information about them. Most urban fringe districts are small, commonly extending from a fraction of a square mile to several square miles. What might not be expected is that such a district frequently is smaller than the fringe area in which it exists. A fringe district may be organized at various stages in the development of the urban fringe. Some of the earlier districts annex territory as the fringe area grows, but others do not expand territorially. This is often because residents of the newer portions, disliking the officials of an existing district or the idea of assuming a share of its financial obligations, desire separate, highly localized control of a function. The financial reason partially accounts for many of the small sanitation districts in the urban fringe of Denver, none of which is large enough to finance an adequate sewage plant. Resistance to annexation to an active district, or disinterest by the district in increasing its size, means that at least two districts will be performing a similar function in different parts of the same urban fringe, and that together they will serve perhaps only several hundred or a few thousand people.

Confusing and Pyramiding Boundaries

When used extensively in an urban fringe, special districts generally present a bewildering crisscross of boundaries. Because they were originally established with dissimilar limits, and did not annex at all or did not annex the same amount of land, no two urban fringe districts are coterminous in many areas. Furthermore, there is frequently no logic to their boundaries, and their territorial smallness makes it impossible to use other governmental areas to identify at least part of the district territory. Urban fringe districts, unlike numerous metropolitan districts, do not include entire areas of existing general governments within their limits.

At the time of establishment, urban fringe districts are located immediately outside a city. Later, after the fringe area incorporates, or is annexed by an existing city, some of the districts fall within city limits, for they are not always automatically dissolved under such circumstances or easy to abolish. Most urban fringe districts are situated within one county, either because of the location of the fringe they serve or because of legislative restrictions. An urban fringe district almost always pyramids over part of a county and sometimes occupies a portion of a township or town, but the greatest overlapping is with other districts functioning in the fringe. The existence of several urban fringe districts in the same fringe makes the governmental pattern highly complicated and diffused. Urban fringes containing numerous urban fringe districts support more independent governments than does any other type of land development in a comparable amount of area.

Structure, Finance, and Functions

Urban fringe districts are usually small operations with skeletal staffs. The work is frequently administered directly by the governing board members alone or in conjunction with a part-time or full-time secretary or engineer-administrator. The number of employees is usually limited and sometimes, as in numerous fire protection districts, consists partly of volunteers. An illustration from Jefferson County, Colorado, demonstrates how small an urban fringe district can be and still constitute an active independent unit of government. In 1952 the Miller Heights Water District obtained $71 in revenue and its total assessed property valuation was $7,180.[10] Most urban fringe districts rely upon property taxation or assessment, often in combination with the issuance of bonds. There is much diversity in the composition of the governing body, but a customary arrangement is direct election of three to five local residents to serve as directors, usually for a term of two years. Most urban fringe districts are highly localized and personalized governments.

The functions of these districts reflect many of the past and present problems of urban fringes. The districts, however, seldom handle all the functional needs of fringe areas, and indeed do not operate at all in some of them. Most urban fringe districts perform one function, a smaller number provide two related services, and a few are multipurpose. Their emphasis is almost entirely upon services, to the exclusion of control or regulatory activities. The major exception is in the field of law enforcement. The four most prevalent services of urban fringe districts are water, sewerage, fire protection, and garbage collection.[11] These functions are similar to those provided by general local governments, particularly cities, and make urban fringe districts direct competitors of the older, established units.

THE JUNIOR CITY URBAN FRINGE DISTRICT

Multipurpose urban fringe districts are potentially the most important functional competitors of general governmental units. Although the idea of multipurpose districts has not yet been widely adopted, the utilization of laws permitting its implementation is increasing. Enabling laws have been enacted in Connecticut, South Carolina, Michigan, Colorado, and California, and there has been serious discussion of the idea in Oregon and Washington. Such laws do not merely authorize districts to have two or three related functions instead of the customary one, but call for an assortment of functions, generally varying from six to twelve. The objective is to establish governmental units limited to fewer powers than a

---

[10] *Forty-First Annual Report,* Colorado Tax Commission (Denver: 1952), p. 144.
[11] John C. Bollens, "Controls and Services in Unincorporated Urban Fringes," *Municipal Year Book: 1954* (Chicago: International City Managers' Association, 1954), p. 58.

general government, such as a city, but functionally much broader than the usual single-purpose special district. These multipurpose units may therefore appropriately be designated as junior city districts.

The focus here is upon deliberate efforts to create multipurpose district governments that would really be junior cities. This intent can often, but not always, be determined from the inclusion of words such as community, metropolitan, or municipal in the title of the district legislation. Although attention is centered on districts falling in this category, there are other districts with limited functional titles which were initially multipurpose or have become so through later legislative amendments and can be used in urban fringe situations. Sanitary districts in North Carolina and sanitation and water districts in Colorado are illustrations.

Utilization in Five States

An examination of junior city districts in five states will illustrate this development and the direction it is taking. Connecticut is the only one of the five in which there has been legislation authorizing two kinds of junior city districts. The first, based largely on general law and applicable only to the noncity and nonborough portions of a town, is the municipal district which may undertake many activities. The permissible functions are street lighting; street sprinkling; fire protection; tree planting and care; sidewalk, drain, and sewer construction and maintenance; police protection; garbage and refuse collection and disposal; and building-line control. District officers, elected at regular annual meetings, may levy taxes and assessments. The second kind of Connecticut junior city district is the improvement association. Located mainly in summer resorts near ocean or lake, these associations are all founded on individual special legislative acts and differ considerably in the powers allotted to them. Many are authorized to carry out a broad range of functions. Included are nuisance control, police protection, fire protection, street lighting, business regulation, dock and breakwater construction, harbor dredging, and water-front, pier, and bathhouse regulation. Furthermore, several of the associations are empowered to pass zoning ordinances. These associations, governed by directors usually elected by landowners, may tax and

make special assessments, but most of them do not have the power
to issue bonds.

The junior city district governments of South Carolina are
legally known as public service districts. Each is created by a special legislative act, but there is nevertheless considerable uniformity in their legal provisions. The functional range of these districts
is very broad and the state legislature has frequently passed
amendments to the original law increasing the permissible areas
of activity. These public service districts may engage in fire protection, sewage disposal, sanitary regulation, drainage, street lighting, street cleaning, garbage collection and disposal, water supply,
and recreation. At least one of them can enact and enforce zoning
regulations. Usually their governing board members are appointed
by the governor on recommendation of the legislative delegation
from the county in which the district is to be located. The districts
have power to levy taxes and collect service charges, and to issue
bonds after voter sanction.

Junior city districts can be established in Michigan under provisions of the metropolitan district law, which is also usable in
larger areas. Metropolitan districts functioning solely within the
urban fringe can own and operate parks, dispose of sewage, provide drainage, supply water, and furnish transportation. In addition, they can provide housing facilities, garbage and rubbish
disposal systems, stadiums, auditoriums, hospitals, public buildings, recreation, and aeronautic facilities. The method of selecting
the directors is left to the judgment of the local voters at the time
the district is established. Districts in operation have decided upon
directors elected from township areas. Taxes, service charges, and
bond issues are permitted.

Similarly named legislation has been enacted in Colorado. Unlike Michigan, however, Colorado specifically designed its metropolitan district law for use in urban fringes in order to reduce the
present number of single-purpose special districts and to discour-
age the creation of more. A metropolitan district in Colorado is
entitled to exercise all the powers of water, sanitation, fire protection, and police protection districts. In addition, it can license, tax,
regulate, or prohibit hucksters, pawnbrokers, amusement places,

junk dealers, and the transportation or storage of inflammable or dangerous materials. It can also provide public libraries and parks and adopt a master plan for physical development. Elected directors can levy taxes, impose service charges, and float bonds. Indebtedness proposals of more than $5,000 or 1 per cent of assessed valuation must first gain popular consent.

The community services district is the junior city district in California. Such a district may embrace territory in the unincorporated portions of more than one county. It is permitted to handle water supply, sewage disposal, garbage collection and disposal, drainage, fire protection, recreation, police protection, street lighting, and mosquito abatement. Possessing elected directors, the community services district can tax, determine rates and charges, accept contributions, and issue bonds after popular approval.

Junior city districts in these five states all possess numerous powers, but they vary widely as to specific functions. In spite of this diversity, each of them has the legal authority to perform a group of functions which, if substantially utilized, guarantees that the junior city district will have a noticeable governmental impact on the area it serves. Significantly, too, some of these districts may exercise land-use controls in the form of planning and zoning regulations to guide the growth of the community. But these vital powers are lacking in junior city districts in the populous states of California and Michigan. The functional variety of junior city districts is not matched by comparable organizational and financial dissimilarities. All of them, except those in South Carolina, have elected governing board members and only in Connecticut are they generally prohibited from issuing bonds. In all five states they possess the power of taxation.

Recent Increased Interest

The greatest amount of interest in junior city districts has developed since the 1940's. In this recent period serious consideration has been given to the idea in Washington and Oregon and enabling laws have been passed in Colorado and California. Actual use of the concept antedates this time, and in the example of improvement associations in Connecticut goes back into the latter years of the nineteenth century. The South Carolina public service district made its first appearance in 1928, and a year later the metropolitan district law passed the Michigan Legislature, although it was not used for nine years. Originally conceived before the most recent era of intensely rapid urbanization, the junior city district idea has become the object of enthusiastic advocacy as well as of increased hostility.

Moderate Development

In general, the junior city district concept has not been extensively utilized. Among the three states adopting permissive legislation before 1940, only Connecticut has numerous junior city districts in operation. Michigan and South Carolina together have less than ten. Only one such district has been established under the enabling legislation passed in Colorado in 1949. On the other hand, California, with the most recent permissive law, had fourteen districts become operative in the first three years and ranks next to Connecticut which is far ahead in number of active junior city districts. The development has been moderate not only in total number of junior city districts established but also in the extent to which legally available functional powers have been used. By no means should it be concluded that all active districts organized under junior city district legislation are performing numerous public services. In fact, there is strong evidence that in practice many of them functionally resemble single-purpose special districts more closely than modified city government operations. In other words, numerous districts functioning under multipurpose legislation are actually using merely one or two of many permissive powers. Authorization is present but implementation has often not materialized, a condition now virtually unknown in other classes of governments that possess numerous functions.

Community Services Districts in California

The experience in California demonstrates the frequency of the limited-purpose approach of junior city districts. Nineteen community services districts have been legally established since the enabling law became effective in late 1951, and California, unlike

Colorado, Michigan, and South Carolina, is apparently on its way toward wide application of the junior city district idea.[12] Five of the districts, however, have never been activated and five others are very small. The most significant feature of the fourteen active community services districts is that none of them is performing more than a single function. It might be contended that they are all new governments and as such have not had time to undertake additional services. This argument can be dispelled for two reasons. First, at the activation stage only five districts expected eventually to take on as many as three types of activity. Second, only three districts now feel that they will later undertake additional services.

Only three of the nine kinds of services available to community services districts are presently being performed. One district is providing police protection, three are disposing of sewage, and ten are supplying water. None is engaged in garbage collection and disposal, drainage, fire protection, recreation, street lighting, or mosquito abatement, although at least one organized district initially expressed interest in each of these functions. In not one instance has a community services district been established in order to merge the activities of several single-purpose districts. These districts can actually become junior cities, but none approaches this status. All the functions of these community services districts could have been provided through existing special district laws. Some areas did originally intend to perform a combination of functions found only in the community services district act, but most of them utilized the enabling legislation simply because it was as convenient as any other and because the publicity regarding its recent passage made it better known. In terms of theory and legal permission, California community services districts are junior city districts, but in practice they have so far been merely typical limited-purpose special district governments.

---

[12] The increasing interest of city officials in the development is apparent in Robert O. Bailey, "Summary of the Use of the Community Services District Law and the County Service Area Law" (speech at annual conference of the League of California Cities, Los Angeles, Oct. 18, 1954), pp. 1–6. As noted earlier, districts known as urban fringe districts because of their importance in urban fringe areas also at times function in other locations, such as unincorporated urban areas that are outside the fringe of a city. This is true of some community services districts as well as of a number of junior city districts elsewhere.

Two South Carolina Public Service Districts

The gap between the potentialities and the actualities of junior
city districts in California is not characteristic of all states possessing relevant enabling legislation. Connecticut provides various
comprehensive examples which could be discussed as a group, but
the contrast is most graphically shown by the two public service
districts operating in the urban fringe of Charleston, South Carolina.[13] Directly north of the city of Charleston is the St. Phillip's
and St. Michael's Public Service District which, since its establishment in 1928, has grown substantially in area until it now
exceeds 10 square miles. It supplies numerous services to its population of approximately 40,000. Included are water supply (obtained from Charleston), fire protection, drainage, sewage disposal,
sanitation, street lighting, street marking, and zoning. Immediately
beyond this district is another, the North Charleston Public Service
District, organized in 1935. Somewhat smaller in area than the
earlier one, this public service district contains more than 20,000
residents and also performs many services. It provides street lighting, supplies water (obtained from Charleston), disposes of sewage, removes debris and trash from streets, furnishes fire protection,
collects and disposes of garbage, names streets, and issues sanitary
regulations. As demonstrated by their functional range, these public service districts are actually the equivalent of modified city
operations or junior cities.

Opposition to the Idea

Despite the relatively small number of junior city districts in existence and their generally limited use of authorized powers, the idea
has been encountering strong opposition. The hostility has come
largely from cities in states where such districts are operating or
where the proposal has been seriously discussed. Cities regard
these districts as competitors threatening their own position and
status. They are caught in a dilemma when it becomes apparent
that the enabling legislation is going to be enacted. Some city offi-

---

[13] For a discussion of the two districts, see Christian L. Larsen and Robert H.
Stoudemire, *Metropolitan Charleston* (Columbia: University of South Carolina
Bureau of Public Administration, 1949), pp. 5–12.

cials and organizations hold that their best defense is to insist that
regulatory and land-use control authorizations be legally withheld
from these potentially multipurpose districts. Otherwise, they
argue, there is little inducement for an area to be annexed or to
incorporate.

Others feel that so long as the state laws give urban fringes a
controlling voice in annexation or incorporation decisions, the
most intelligent approach is to endow junior city districts with
these powers. The reasoning is that the absence of such powers in
urban fringes is a very serious aspect of the fringe problem. Therefore, the policy of deliberately denying them to an area preferring
to establish a junior city district instead of becoming a separate
city or part of an existing one is shortsighted. Land-use control has
usually been omitted from junior city district legislation, but regulatory authority, especially as related to health or safety, has often
been included.

The junior city district idea is controversial in part because it
lies outside the usual concept of special district governments.
Nevertheless, thorough utilization of this approach can substantially reduce the number of separate limited-function district governments in many urbanized areas. Although this objective has not
yet been attained, its accomplishment would be hailed as a vast
improvement over the superabundance of single-purpose districts
in some areas. Furthermore, the potentialities of the junior city
district idea for governmental simplification in many urban fringes
are enhanced by the difficulty of using many of the annexation
laws.

Without land-use powers, junior city districts can simplify the
governmental pattern of urban fringes by performing a range of
functions through a single government. With land-use powers,
they can not only supply these services but can also help to eradicate urban fringe problems arising from inadequate control of land
development. Junior city districts are thus approximations of
smaller cities in states where different ranges of functions are
authorized for different classes of cities. Utilization of this district
concept can bring into being a modified but general government
capable of meeting many of the major service and control inade-

quacies of urban fringes. Individual states should weigh the possible value of junior city districts against the present and foreseeable future adequacy of other solutions to urban fringe problems.

CRITICISM OF URBAN FRINGE DISTRICTS

The division of opinion over junior city urban fringe districts is not found in connection with limited-purpose urban fringe districts, which constitute the vast majority of the total. There is much more agreement, and the consensus is largely negative. Several overlapping urban fringe districts in an area usually constitute a web of small, costly operations, lacking adequate land-use and regulatory authority as well as recognizable boundaries. Many fringe residents argue erroneously that the condition of their area is solely their own business or concern. What is particularly ironic is their frequent failure to realize that the gradual accretion of special districts eventually results in uneconomic government. The comparative cost of the same amount of service in the fringe and in the nearby city generally favors the city. Furthermore, fringe costs based on total taxes, higher insurance rates, and possibly higher utility charges sometimes exceed comparable outlays in the neighboring city, even when the city provides more and better services. In a recent year, for example, the fringe of Eugene, Oregon, discovered this to be true and promptly requested annexation.

Limited-purpose urban fringe districts are uneconomic in another way that has more far-reaching effects. Emphasizing one service without coördinating it with others and without exercising needed regulation and controls, they foster poor fringe development which is expensive to undo in the future. They are also criticized for splintering governmental functions into so many partially overlapping compartments that the individual district, unobserved and unnoticed by the public, may become irresponsive and irresponsible. A recent appraisal of limited-purpose urban fringe districts in a single locale has wide applicability. The investigator concluded that "Under these costly jurisdictions the area suffers from too much government and yet has no real government. . . . The community is a groping, headless organism that operates under conditions approaching anarchy."[14] Most of the arguments

---

[14] Harry Erlich, "San Francisco's Bed Room Communities," *Western City*, 29 (June, 1953), 29, 30.

about the size of governments concern the relative merits of big-
ness. At the bottom of the scale, a government can be too small,
and numerous urban fringe districts stand out as glaring examples.
Condemning them, however, does not eliminate the causes that
have been rapidly increasing their number. As viewed by an experienced governmental observer, "The multiplication of overlapping
special districts will continue unless steps are taken to equip our
traditional units of local government with greater flexibility and
authority to meet the service needs of suburban [fringe] areas.
This has become the number one problem of governmental organization in this state [of Oregon]."[15]

[15] Herman Kehrli, "Letter of Transmittal" (Apr. 5, 1954) to University of Oregon
Bureau of Municipal Research and Service study, *The Units of Government in
Oregon: 1951* (Eugene: 1954).

CHAPTER FOUR

Coterminous
Districts

Numerous special districts are readily identifiable by their approximate or exact coextensiveness in area with an earlier established general government. For simplicity of terminology, they are all called coterminous districts. The outstanding examples are local housing authorities, most of which are independent districts. School districts are often nearly or completely coterminous with other units, but are treated as a separate major group of special districts and are discussed in a later chapter.

Local housing authorities are functioning in forty-one states, as dependent agencies of other local governments in five of them and as independent special district governments in the other thirty-six. This was not always the ratio. According to the *Census of Governments*, all local housing authorities were independent governments in 1942. By ten years later, local housing authorities in Arizona, Kentucky, Michigan, New York, and New Mexico had been reclassified by the Census Bureau as dependent agencies of general local governments. This study is concerned only with independent coterminous districts. Moreover, because the activities, extensiveness, and intergovernmental relations of local housing authorities are so conspicuous, most of the chapter is devoted to them.

COTERMINOUS DISTRICTS:
LOCAL HOUSING AUTHORITIES

Not only are local housing authorities the most important illustration of coterminous districts, but the extent of their operations is very significant in comparison with other nonschool special dis-

116

tricts. Although constituting slightly less than one-fourteenth of all such units, they account for approximately two-fifths of the total expenditures and three-tenths of the total long-term debt.[1] Also, in view of the broad diversity of nonschool functional types, housing authorities are impressive both in number and geographical extensiveness; there are about 850 of them in three-fourths of the states. Moreover, they have additional significance because of the impact of other governments, especially the national government, upon their establishment and development.

EARLY NATIONAL-LOCAL HOUSING RELATIONS

The First Years of General Public Housing

The legislative and administrative activities of the national government in the field of public housing have had direct, prompt, and important effects upon local housing authorities, particularly in their formation and continuance. State governments, except for the passage of necessary legislation, have had a less significant effect upon local housing authorities, though some of them have furnished grants and loans, guaranteed bond issues, and acted in an advisory or supervisory capacity.

The actual beginning of major public housing activities in the United States is generally regarded as stemming from provisions of the National Industrial Recovery Act of 1933, which authorized the use of federal funds to finance low-cost and slum-clearance housing and subsistence homesteads. To carry out these objectives, the housing division in the Public Works Administration of the Department of the Interior was established. Dissatisfied with the results of its early efforts to furnish grants and loans to legally constituted public bodies and loans to private corporations, the agency turned to building and operating housing projects of its own. Fifty projects containing 21,600 units in thirty-seven cities were subsequently built on cleared slum locations and vacant land. Meanwhile, several states, including Ohio, Illinois, and West Virginia, had enacted legislation permitting the creation of local housing authorities. The first such authority was organized in Cleveland

[1] *Special District Governments in the United States*, U.S. Bureau of the Census, Governments Division, State and Local Government Special Studies No. 33 (Washington: 1954), p. 2.

in 1933, the same year the national housing legislation was passed. Once the Public Works Administration had decided to function as builder and landlord, however, it preferred to continue this highly centralized operation and to utilize local authorities merely as advisory organizations. In 1937, the last year of PWA housing activity, a lower federal court decided that the national government did not have power to condemn land for housing purposes.

By November of 1937, of the forty-six local housing authorities in existence, only the one in New York City was sponsoring a sizable housing program. The others were limited in their operations because of inadequate funds, although some of them were doing useful research and preparatory work. But in the main they were paper organizations without real working programs and with small financial resources and only skeletal staffs. Because their activities were so inconsequential, local housing authorities had little governmental importance at that time. A drastic alteration occurred in the closing months of 1937, when new national housing legislation became effective.

A Change in Emphasis

The United States Housing Act of 1937 supplanted public housing construction and operation by the national government with federal financial assistance to local governments that were prepared to undertake housing projects. It called for local responsibility in planning, constructing, and managing projects, and for the disposal to the local agencies of existing projects built by the national government. It provided, furthermore, that the newly created national housing agency could make loans at low interest up to a maximum of sixty years to cover as much as 90 per cent of the capital cost of the projects. The remainder was to be furnished locally. In addition, the agency was authorized to provide an annual subsidy to bring the project rents within the reach of low-income families, if local subsidies amounting to at least one-fifth of the national contribution were forthcoming. Local subsidies have consistently taken the form of real property tax exemptions and reductions. Congress initially authorized $500 million in loans and $20 million in subsidies, and subsequently made substantial additions to these amounts. The legislation imposed several requirements that had to be met locally, in addition to the financial stipulation. Local agencies had to establish a maximum construction cost for each room and each dwelling unit, eliminate (except during housing shortages) substandard dwellings equivalent in number to the new dwellings constructed, and restrict project housing to families in the lowest income group.

This congressional action served as a catalytic agent for local housing authorities. Additional states passed laws permitting the creation of authorities; others revised their original acts, sometimes by incorporating tax-exemption provisions or by increasing the number of localities eligible to undertake housing activities. In the single year of 1938 the number of local housing authorities quadrupled. Their growth in number and extent of activity was remarkably rapid, unmistakably a direct effect of the action of the national government. Vitalization of a new governmental unit had materialized through the device of financial aid from the national government.

REASONS FOR CREATION

At this point in the discussion of the first large-scale utilization of local housing authorities it is appropriate to raise two questions. What were the reasons for establishing a new governmental unit rather than using an existing one to engage in housing activities? Did the national government play a significant role, other than supplying financial aid, in fostering its creation? The most important reason for forming new units was the financial inability of general local governments, especially cities, to undertake the function. This was a period of economic depression and local taxation curtailment, and debt limitations on local governments were prevalent in the form of state constitutional and legislative provisions. It was therefore legally impossible for many of them to undertake a new function requiring bond issues, and impossible as a practical matter for them to impose and collect additional taxes to finance part of a housing program. Furthermore, existing restrictions on their financial power definitely or seemingly excluded a purpose such as housing.[2] Individuals and groups primarily interested in

---

[2] Morris B. Schnapper, "Our New Municipal Landlords," *National Municipal Review*, 28 (June, 1939), 423. At the time of this article Mr. Schnapper was a staff member of the national housing agency.

housing reacted as many others who are concerned about one particular function have done in other situations. Instead of trying to remove the obstacles to performance of the activity by general governments, they took the line of less political resistance and urged establishment of a new governmental unit that was free of such barriers. It should be noted here that this was a time of trying to stimulate the national economy and to get public housing construction under way. Housing advocates therefore thought it inappropriate or useless to defer housing activities until financial changes could be made in general local units. Furthermore, the desire to make the function independent sometimes grew out of the apathy of local government officials, and their fear and dislike of public housing.

Other arguments were advanced to support the establishment of local housing authorities. One was the requirement, applicable to most general governments, that bond issues had to gain local voter approval, often by a large majority. This provision, it was feared, might seriously interfere with the inauguration and expansion of housing programs. Another argument, frequently used to justify the formation of other types of special districts, was that the function should be kept "out of politics." Placing the housing function within the jurisdiction of general local governments, it was felt, would create problems of insuring continuity of management and of keeping the housing operation out of the political arena. By implication, these dangers would be avoided or lessened if housing were given independent governmental status.[3] These frequently stated arguments had a positive effect on the development of local housing authorities.

Promotion by the National Government

In addition, the national government has influenced the development of local housing authorities through both financial devices and direct advocacy and promotion of the idea. The nonfinancial stimulation has sometimes come as part of the official actions of

---

[3] *State Laws for Public Housing: A Memorandum on the Drafting of Enabling Acts for Public Housing Agencies*, National Association of Housing Officials (Chicago: 1934), p. 6. This publication, issued soon after the national housing legislation of 1933, mentions debt limitation, voter sanction of bond issues, and political entanglements as supporting reasons for the establishment of local housing authori-

housing administrators. For example, during the mid-1930's, when the Public Works Administration was in charge of national housing activity, its legal division sent out drafts of suggested local housing authority laws to state governors. What was the effect of such recommendations? In 1940, several years after the model bills had first been distributed, it was reported that "The Housing Division of the Public Works Administration long recommended general housing laws and marked the path to the present semi-uniform state public housing [local authority] legislation."[4] The national government's direct advocacy and strong financial support of local housing authorities have proved a potent combination of forces in the development of this type of special district government.

RECENT NATIONAL-LOCAL HOUSING RELATIONS

The Defense and War Impetus

The local housing authority movement, first stimulated by the national government through the housing legislation of 1937, soon received further invigoration. The new contributor to the numerical growth and functional expansion of these authorities was the defense and war public housing program fostered by the national government. Two actions by Congress in 1940 were very significant. The first, an amendment to the 1937 housing law, permitted the previous loan and subsidy provisions and the projects completed or under construction to be used for the housing of defense workers and military personnel. It also waived the requirements for local contributions to capital costs and for the elimination of substandard dwellings. Furthermore, the amendment authorized priorities in the delivery of materials for national defense. By 1949, the time of the national legislative extension of public housing, approximately 170,000 dwelling units in more than 260 localities had been built and were being operated by local housing authori-

---

ties as special districts. The National Association of Housing Officials, an unofficial organization composed principally of administrators, governing body members, and functional specialists concerned with housing, clearly urged as early as 1934 the utilization of separate local housing authorities.

[4] *State Enabling Legislation for Public Housing*, National Association of Housing Officials, Legal Committee (Chicago: 1940), p. 5.

ties. This total included 51,300 units constructed under the defense amendment to the original legislation, almost all of which had been converted to low-rent use by this date.[5]

The second important congressional housing action of 1940 was the Lanham Act which, as subsequently amended, became the public war-housing law. Initially $150 million was provided for defense housing, an amount substantially increased during the war years. Under this newly created program, it was possible for the national government to build and operate developments without depending upon local initiative and action. Local housing authorities, however, played a central role in the management and construction activities resulting from this program, for the national government realized the benefits to be derived from the knowledge, experience, and facilities of these units. Furthermore, numerous new authorities were established through local decision for the specific purpose of participating in the Lanham Act program. Functioning under the supervision of an administrative division of the national housing agency, many local housing authorities performed the delegated responsibilities of selecting architects, preparing and adapting plans and specifications, and awarding construction contracts. During the defense and war period, these authorities handled 47 per cent of the war housing construction program and 58 per cent of management responsibilities.[6] In localities where local housing authorities did not exist or had not been established through local determination to participate in the program, the national government supervised construction directly and employed its own administrators. Under the Lanham Act, with its amendments and related laws, 945,000 public war-housing accommodations, many of a temporary nature, were furnished, including the veterans' emergency housing built after World War II. Many were later disposed of by sale, removal, transfer, or lease cancellation.

The Postwar Housing Act

The next major impetus to the development of local housing authorities was the Housing Act of 1949, which Congress enacted

[5] *Federal Housing Programs*, U.S. Senate, Committee on Banking and Currency, 81st Cong., 2d sess. (Washington: 1950), p. 34.

[6] *Public Housing: The Work of the Federal Public Housing Authority*, National Housing Agency, Federal Public Housing Authority (Washington: 1946), p. 9.

only after strong opposition lasting for several years had been overcome. The number of local housing authorities, which had remained relatively unchanged for several years, spurted forward. Some of them had been organized in anticipation of passage of the act, and many others were established soon after the bill became a law. Two provisions of the act in particular had important effects on local housing authorities. Title III of the Housing Act of 1949 increased federal financial assistance as established in 1937. It authorized over a six-year period the expenditure of $1,500 million for loans and a maximum of $308 million for annual contributions to local housing authorities for 810,000 new low-rent dwelling units. It also facilitated 100 per cent private capital financing by the local housing authorities, diminished the maximum period of annual contributions by the national government from sixty to forty years, increased the limits on construction costs, and furnished added assurance that low-rent public housing would not compete with adequate private housing.

Title I of the 1949 housing legislation authorized $1,000 million in loans and $500 million in capital grants by the national government over a five-year period to properly authorized local public agencies for assistance in slum clearance and redevelopment programs. Specifically, this section of the act was designed to enable local agencies to obtain, clear, and prepare slum and blighted land which would then be sold or leased to private or public organizations for sound rebuilding. Included were both temporary loans to be repaid within ten years and long-term loans to be paid back in not more than forty years and to be used only where part or all of the land in the project area was leased for redevelopment. The grants were made available so that local agencies could pay for the loss resulting from the difference between the cost of purchasing and clearing a site and the price obtained from a developer. In this way the national government took care of two-thirds of the loss, and local agencies the remainder.

This portion of the Housing Act of 1949 provided local communities with a stimulus for a comprehensive attack upon slums and blighted areas. In the earlier years of the decade, urban redevelopment legislation had been adopted by half of the states and some pioneering work had been started. Until the 1949 congressional action, however, actual redevelopment at the local level had been limited by the seemingly insurmountable problems of large capital outlays, high write-down costs in selling or leasing cleared land, and rehousing the people displaced by such projects. The redevelopment provisions of the 1949 legislation were of considerable importance to local housing authorities. Redevelopment laws, which exist in a substantial majority of the states, generally authorize one of three types of local public agencies to undertake the function: local housing authorities, redevelopment agencies, or city governments. More than half of the local public organizations that have undertaken redevelopment are housing authorities. Three states permit the use of any of the three alternatives, and two allow a choice between the housing authority and the redevelopment agency. Redevelopment agencies are adjuncts of general local governments; they lack sufficient autonomy to be classified as special districts.[7]

Moderate Progress

The congressional authorization in 1949 for increased public housing was not implemented without difficulty. There had been hostility to such a program since its inauguration in the 1930's, but concerted opposition, spearheaded by organized realtors and home builders, crystallized during the late 1940's. This opposition centered on the prevention of further federal aid to public housing. After passage of the law it shifted much effort to local communities. Recommendations were made to city councils not to sign the requisite tax-exemption agreements, to refuse city services to authority projects, and to reject requests for building permits or zoning waivers. Although most of these suggestions were turned down, they caused a great deal of misunderstanding. There were demands for local referenda on the question of whether or not the program should proceed. In 1950 slightly more than half of thirty local referenda were unfavorable to the housing program, and in the following year seven of eleven votes were rejections. Bills were introduced in numerous state legislatures to require local referenda on many phases of public housing programs, but they passed in

[7] For a well-reasoned discussion of the redevelopment laws, see Philip H. Hill, "Recent Slum Clearance and Urban Redevelopment Laws," *Washington and Lee Law Review*, 9 (1952), 173–188.

only a few states, such as Nebraska and Montana. Efforts made under the banner of defense economy to have Congress curtail its appropriations for public housing were at least partly responsible for severe cutbacks from the annual total of 135,000 units authorized by the 1949 legislation for a six-year period.[8] By the end of August, 1954, for example, approximately 345,000 dwelling units had been completed or were under construction under the public housing provisions of the Housing Act of 1949. National housing legislation in 1954 limited the number of additional dwelling units to 35,000 for the 1955 fiscal year. It also restricted new contracts to communities carrying out slum-clearance and urban redevelopment projects under Title I of the Housing Act of 1949 and needing aid to fulfill relocation requirements.

Urban redevelopment, also bolstered by the national government, has encountered less opposition. Nevertheless, accomplishments thus far have not been especially plentiful, although recently both attainments and serious activity have increased. In the twelve months after passage of the 1949 legislation, more than 200 localities attempted to qualify for national financial aid. Some received funds, but relatively few moved into the active planning stage. The requirement of relocation housing for persons displaced from cleared areas as a condition of federal financial assistance retarded progress in urban redevelopment. It was difficult to find adequate housing within the financial means of these people, particularly when tight housing market conditions prevailed. Another deterrent has been the public's lack of understanding of this new governmental activity. This has necessitated the exercise of extraordinary care in proceeding with the various steps and in prefacing them with information and explanations to the public. The constitutionality of various state redevelopment laws has been tested in court, with most of the cases resulting in favorable judgments. This symptom of the newness of an activity often slows down action until the court renders an affirmative decision.

The pace of activity quickened in 1952. Increasingly detailed plans were being formulated, sites approved, and projects under-

[8] The articles on housing developments beginning in the 1951 edition of the *Municipal Year Book*, published by the International City Managers' Association, contain additional details on activities since 1950.

taken. The next year witnessed substantial accomplishments. By the end of 1953 tenants were occupying completed redevelopment projects in five cities, demolition was in progress in twenty-five localities, twenty-one communities had obtained federal approval for land acquisition and clearance, and seventy-nine local areas were preparing final plans. Under the Housing Act of 1954 the national government continued its financial assistance to localities for the phases of urban redevelopment supported in the 1949 legislation, but in addition it extended aid for neighborhood rehabilitation and conservation. Thus federal participation in the urban renewal program was expanded beyond loans and grants for acquisition and demolition of slums and partial absorption of write-down costs to include financial help for rehabilitation and conservation.[9]

CHARACTERISTICS

Local housing authorities have many similarities, even though they operate in thirty-six states. Their frequently identical or only slightly different characteristics, set within the same broad framework, reveal the influence of suggestions by the national government for provisions in the state public housing laws. In some states, however, variations exist largely because of particular legislative preferences. Although there are several types of local housing authorities, the most prevalent by far are city housing authorities and county housing authorities. The official titles of these housing units often include the word "city" or "county," as well as the name of the geographical location. Examples are the Housing Authority of the City of Caldwell (Idaho) and the Housing Authority of Adams County (Illinois). Since an appellation like "City of Caldwell" suggests the city government, many people are led to the erroneous belief that the housing authority is part of the city government. Other types, variously known as regional, metropolitan, and consolidated authorities, combine the areas of two or more

[9] William L. Slayton, "The States and Urban Renewal," *State Government,* 27 (Oct., 1954), 203–204, 215–217, analyzes some aspects of the legislation. Also noteworthy is the provision of the law which authorizes federal grants on an equal matching basis to facilitate planning in smaller communities and in metropolitan and regional areas.

cities or counties. The discussion here is limited to the two most numerous kinds, city and county authorities.

Overlapping Territory

City housing authorities are the most common, since the laws of many states allow the creation of these agencies only in cities. Usually the cities permitted to have housing authorities must belong to a certain class or contain a specific minimum population. In a number of states, however, all cities are eligible to have housing authorities. Counties (and, in several New England states, towns) are the second most common locations where it is permissible to establish these governmental units.[10] Although state laws sometimes restrict housing authorities to certain classes of cities, they usually grant all counties or New England towns, irrespective of their classification or population size, permission to set up authorities. Only rarely is permission granted to part of a county, such as a township.

The areas of city and county housing authorities generally approximate or exactly coincide with those of city and county governments, and some state laws specify coterminous boundaries. More of them, however, stipulate that the city housing authority shall include the city and a certain number of miles beyond its official limits. This extension of the authority beyond city limits is often specified because land near cities is available for public housing at a relatively low price, and because slums have often developed in suburban areas. The number of additional miles varies from three to ten; sometimes it depends upon the kind of government in the territory beyond the city boundaries. Territory occupied by other city housing authorities or by other cities, especially those eligible to create housing authorities, is frequently excluded. Although many city housing authorities are coterminous, or nearly so, with city governments, most county housing authorities are territorially smaller than county governments. Customarily the county housing authority includes all of the county except the cities or city housing authorities which lie within its borders.

[10] Housing authorities are usually located in towns rather than counties in the New England states. Much of the discussion of the legal features of housing authorities in counties is applicable also to New England towns.

Simple Creation Procedure

The process of creating a city or a county housing authority is relatively simple and does not involve direct consent of the electorate. In some states the governing body of a city (which sometimes includes the mayor as a voting member) or a county government can establish an authority by its own majority vote. In others the governing body is empowered to act after petition by a small number of residents, normally twenty-five. Some state laws create housing authorities in all or in specified classes of cities and counties, but the agencies are latent until local action materializes. Thus the number of housing authorities existing in law may differ substantially from the number in actual operation. The responsibility of justifying the creation of an authority frequently rests on the governmental officials legally able to establish it.

Similarity in Governing Body Features

There is much uniformity in the method of selection, eligibility, compensation, and removal of the members of the governing bodies of city and county housing authorities. Usually the mayor of a city or the governing body of a county or New England town appoints five persons for staggered five-year terms or, less frequently, for four-year terms. The staggering and length of the terms are particularly meaningful to the independence of the governing boards of city housing authorities, for many mayors are elected for two years and do not serve consecutive terms. In rather rare instances a governor or a judge participates in choosing part of the membership. Usually no official, and sometimes even no employee, of the city or county may serve as a member of the governing body of a housing authority. Those serving in a governing capacity in a city or a county housing authority seldom receive compensation other than reimbursement for necessary expenditures, including required travel expenses. Usually any one of them can be removed by the person or group that appointed him, after he receives a copy of the charges against him and is given the opportunity to be heard in person or to be represented by counsel. The reasons for removal, however, are normally limited by state law to inefficiency, neglect of duty, or misconduct in office, so that authority members enjoy considerable freedom from officials who appoint them.

Housing and Redevelopment Functions

The principal function of local housing authorities is to develop and manage public housing facilities for occupancy by families with low incomes. To realize this objective and to meet a requirement for federal financial assistance, they are vested with the power of eminent domain to obtain real property for low-rent housing and slum clearance. They also possess legal authorization to issue bonds and assume other financial obligations to finance housing projects, and to make agreements necessary for guaranteeing low rents and for securing their bonds and other commitments. In general, the property and bonds of local housing authorities, judged to be for public purposes, are exempt from taxation by other governments, but the authorities may make in-lieu payments for improvements, services, and facilities furnished by a general local government. They collect property rentals. They do not, however, have the power of taxation. Although city and county housing authorities both engage in public housing, their geographical differences often cause a differentiation in their respective activities. City housing authorities provide housing in incorporated urban centers, often in only the more populous communities. County housing authorities furnish housing in more rural sections and frequently in the less populous cities. Unincorporated urban fringes are within the jurisdiction of one or the other, depending upon whether a city housing authority has been established and possesses authorization to operate beyond the city limits. Since 1945 the activities of local housing authorities have been legally expanded to include more than the original functions of public housing development and slum clearance. More than one-half of the states that have public housing laws have given housing authorities legal permission to undertake urban redevelopment.

OPPOSITION TO INDEPENDENCE

The public housing function is carried out largely by local housing authorities which are special district governments. Less often, but still in a majority of instances, urban redevelopment is also handled by local housing authorities. The independence of these authorities, especially in connection with their public housing activities, is strongly embedded in the local governmental pattern and is staunchly defended by many public housing advocates. Nevertheless, their autonomous position has not stood unchallenged by responsible groups and individuals who oppose, not public housing in itself, but the independent status of the operations.

A Research Study

Three illustrations, one early and two more recent, indicate the reasoning of the opposition. In 1941, soon after the establishment of local housing authorities had been accelerated, an intensive research study of these units in certain communities was completed. Noting at the outset that the forty-year struggle for integration of local government had been opened on the new front of housing, the analysis reached the conclusion, to recur in later evaluations, that the independence of housing operations created serious problems in the area of governmental coördination. The researcher directed her anti-independence argument specifically at city housing authorities, and to support it stated that public housing programs touch practically every phase of municipal government, including health, safety, recreation, public works, finance, and planning. And, furthermore, they produce substantial changes in the city pattern without adequate guidance and control by the city government.[11]

A Consulting Survey

The other two examples of opposition to the independence of local housing authorities appeared in 1952. The first was a report on housing and redevelopment in Chicago financed by the city government and undertaken by Public Administration Service, a widely known and long-established consulting organization. Its principal recommendation was the integration of housing and redevelopment functions carried on by five separate independent,

[11] Annette Baker Fox, "The Local Housing Authority and the Municipal Government," *Journal of Land and Public Utility Economics*, 17 (Aug., 1941), 280, 284. The same author presents more data in "Coordination of Local Housing Authority with the Municipal Government" (unpublished Ph.D. dissertation, University of Chicago, 1941).

semi-independent, and dependent organizations into a single department of the city government. The proposal was supported by a number of reasons. The plan gave the mayor and city council full control of currently scattered housing and redevelopment activities, thereby coördinating the attack on housing problems and enabling citizens to place the responsibility for both achievements and failures on the proper officials. The proposal was also expected to aid appreciably in coördinating housing and redevelopment with related fields such as planning, streets, building regulation, and health. Finally, it combined a refutation of the belief that independence of action means independence from political influence with an advocacy of strengthening the units of general local government. The report found that local autonomous and semiautonomous agencies had not necessarily been unaffected by strong political pressures, and stated the conviction that a municipal government does not progress toward responsible, clean, and efficient government by removing (or keeping removed) important functions from its elected chief executive and governing body.[12]

A Public Official's Speech

In 1952, the same year the Chicago report was issued, a speech was made opposing independent governmental status for local housing authorities. At first thought a speech might be viewed as of less significance than, for example, an independent report financed by a local government. In this instance, however, the oral remarks were important because of the individual who uttered them and the group before which they were presented. The occasion was the annual conference of the National Association of Housing Officials, which was widely attended by governing body members and professional staff personnel of local housing authorities. The speaker was B. T. Fitzpatrick, the deputy administrator and general counsel of the United States Housing and Home Finance Agency, a man of almost two decades of experience in federal housing affairs.

---

[12] *Government Organization for Redevelopment and Housing in the City of Chicago*, Public Administration Service (Chicago: 1952), especially pp. 8–15. The report also presented some persuasive arguments that housing and redevelopment should be carried out by one city department instead of two. A summary of the study appeared in the same year under the title, *Reorganizing Chicago's Redevelopment and Housing*.

In diagnosing the marked decline in public knowledge and acceptance of public housing between 1949 and 1952, Fitzpatrick concluded that one of the most significant factors was the independence of the local housing authority. The difficulty was, he said, "the rather impractical notion that a local housing authority should operate as an entirely autonomous political subdivision of the state and completely independent from the government of the city in which it operates."[13] He noted that unfortunately the only point of contact between the local housing authority and the city government was sometimes the legal requirement that the latter approve the application of the former for a preliminary loan from the national government and enter into the necessary coöperative agreement. Fitzpatrick observed that the compelling reasons for the original independence of local housing authorities were financial, and were not based on concern for the most effective city governmental organization. And then, in a statement reminiscent of the 1941 study, the veteran housing official of the national government urged that those financial reasons offer "no sensible basis for a belief that a housing authority should not be fitted in as an integral part of city governmental organization—especially since public housing cuts across the whole pattern of the administration of the modern community."[14] Local housing programs, he concluded, should of course be kept out of city partisan politics, but they should be in city governmental politics in the sense of being a part of the city government, which is responsible and directly accountable to all its citizens for civic welfare.

COTERMINOUS DISTRICTS: CHICAGO PARK DISTRICT

Most special district governments that now have exactly or approximately the same boundaries as a general local governmental unit possessed the same area limits when they were originally established. This has been true of most local housing authorities

---

[13] "Remarks of B. T. Fitzpatrick before the Annual Conference of the National Association of Housing Officials, Buffalo, October 15, 1952," p. 4. The speech of Mr. Fitzpatrick, who had observed early in his remarks that he did not think his views would win him any popularity contests, proved to be unpopular with most of the conference delegates. On the day after Fitzpatrick spoke, Louis H. Pink,

in numerous states and of other functional types of districts in individual localities. There are important exceptions, however, the most significant of which is the Chicago Park District, one of the twelve largest nonschool special districts in number of employees, annual revenue, and long-term indebtedness. Although the geographical overlapping of the city of Chicago and the independent Chicago Park District is confusing, the district has nevertheless greatly simplified a bewildering situation that had existed for many decades.

INCREASING NUMBER OF PARK DISTRICTS

State Legislative Actions

The antecedents of the current park district are found deep in the nineteenth century. In 1866 the Illinois State Legislature passed a bill authorizing the establishment of a park district to include the southern part of Chicago and three suburban towns upon the approval of the voters of the affected areas. The proposal was rejected at the polls in the following year, but in 1869 an almost identical bill was passed and popular sanction soon followed. Almost simultaneously the state legislature passed another law setting up a park district encompassing the northern section of Chicago and the adjoining territory, but this time omitted the provision for voter approval. During the same legislative session a committee of the city council of Chicago was sent to the state capitol to urge enactment of a bill establishing a park and boulevard program throughout the entire city, but discovered that bills had already been submitted for south and north park districts. It then urged passage of a bill for a park district on the west side of the city. This proposition was also enacted and gained the required voter approval. All three special acts were passed in the same month. All three park districts were authorized to carry out not only park and recreational activities but also the construction, maintenance, and policing of pleasure drives, boulevards, and parkways. Initially all

former chairman of the New York State Housing Board and member of the New York City Housing Authority, delivered a speech that was in part a rebuttal to Mr. Fitzpatrick. He concluded that the success and public backing of local housing authorities were attributable to their freedom of action.

[14] "Remarks of B. T. Fitzpatrick . . . , October 15, 1952," p. 5.

three included territory that was partly outside of Chicago, but later annexations by the city brought all of their territory within the Chicago corporate boundaries.[15] Special state legislation, both with and without the stipulation of local consent, had directly caused the virtually simultaneous creation of three separate park operations.

Later legislative action endowed the three park districts with broader taxing and bonding powers and authorized more intensive development of facilities. The total area of the districts did not at any time include all of Chicago, and as population increased there were greater and more numerous demands by unserved portions of the city. The state legislature responded in 1895, but its decision did not enlarge the existing districts. Instead, it permitted additional park districts to be established through the initiating action of a small number of local voters followed by majority voter approval. The law received prompt use within the Chicago limits. One new district appeared in 1896, five others in the first decade of the twentieth century, and a seventh in 1911.

Strong Criticism

The year 1911 witnessed both the creation of the tenth park district and the issuance of a scathing criticism of the organization and operations of the park district system by a private research organization, the Chicago Bureau of Public Efficiency. The report strongly urged the integration of the numerous park districts with the city government to bring about a more equitable community-wide distribution of benefits and revenues, and appraised the existing diffused arrangements. It first evaluated the three largest districts. The South Park District was judged to have high standards of public service but to be wasteful, a practice encouraged by its abundance of funds. The building of its own steam-driven electric plant a few years earlier was cited as an obvious example of waste. The report denounced the West Park District for its pronounced political and extremely inefficient operations. Only the Lincoln (North) Park District fared well under the scrutiny of the investigation. Its operations were considered conservative, careful, and

---

[15] *Local Governments in Chicago and Cook County,* Illinois Legislative Reference Bureau, Constitutional Convention Bulletin No. 11 (Springfield: 1920), p. 931.

generally creditable. The seven smaller districts collectively received unfavorable comment. The emphasis was upon the difficulty of gathering the main facts about these units, whose governing boards were termed "sequestered bodies of which the taxpayers know little."[16]

The Bureau of Public Efficiency also made general charges
against all of the park districts, noting especially the misuse of
automobiles, the excessively costly police service, and the duplication of work by park and city policemen on boulevard duty. In
addition, the failure of the districts to delegate sufficient responsibility to department heads impaired operating efficiency. Board
meetings were held in unannounced places, their proceedings were
not published, and proposed ordinances were not available before
adoption. Adherence to a definite financial plan and utilization of
centralized purchasing were unknown. The most startling statement in the survey was the estimate that unification of park activities under the city government would mean a savings of $500,000 a
year.

Despite the charges and evidence of wastefulness, inefficiency,
and impropriety, and the urgings of the advantages of integration
with the city, the park districts were neither immediately abolished
nor halted at the stage of development then attained. In fact, the
number of park districts containing territory within the city of
Chicago continued to increase for more than two decades. By 1930,
park activities within the city limits of Chicago were being carried
out by twenty-two separate park district governments. They consisted of the original three large park districts, each of which had
been functioning for approximately sixty years, and nineteen
smaller park units created under the state enabling legislation of
1895.

Another Appraisal

In 1933 an inquiry into the governmental organization of the Chicago metropolitan area was completed by three University of
Chicago faculty and research members. Their decidedly unfavorable observations about the many park districts operating within

---

[16] *The Park Governments of Chicago: An Inquiry into Their Organization and
Methods of Administration*, Chicago Bureau of Public Efficiency (Chicago: 1911),
p. 21.

Chicago were reminiscent of the civic group investigation made earlier in the century. The great inequalities in financial resources, park acreage, and population among the three large park districts were pointed out. For example, the district in the southern part of the city had disproportionately extensive financial resources and park acreage relative to its population. At the other extreme, the district on the west side of the city had inadequate funds and facilities for the heaviest park needs in the Chicago area. The main conclusion about the three largest park units was that their presence in the city "causes disintegration of control, results in gross inequalities in the distribution of park facilities, and fails to strike a balance between park resources and recreational requirements."[17] Furthermore, although the governing body members of the South Park District were selected by the county circuit court and those of the northern and western districts by the governor, all three were regarded as political prizes subject to partisan manipulation by the appointing authorities. The appraisal of the smaller park districts was also negative. Each of them, it was decided, was too small to perform the authorized services adequately.

THE CONSOLIDATION

The Legislative Remedy

In the same depression year of 1933, when this comprehensive research study was published, the state legislature began to remedy the park district fragmentation which it had made possible sixty-four years before. It passed a special act—the same legal device used for the original formation of the three large park districts—stipulating that a new governmental unit, the Chicago Park District, be the successor to all park districts within its proposed territorial limits. The new district was also to exercise supervision and control over the operation of all parks, boulevards, and other public property of the abolished districts. Although originally its area was to consist of the city and of the land outside which was in any park district lying partly within and partly beyond Chicago, subse-

---

[17] Charles E. Merriam, Spencer D. Parratt, and Albert Lepawsky, *The Government of the Metropolitan Region of Chicago* (Chicago: University of Chicago Press, 1933), p. 46.

quent legislation disconnected all area outside Chicago. This made
the park district exactly coterminous in area with the city. The
legislation provided that the integration proposal must be submitted to the voters, and in April, 1934, a majority of the electorate
within the proposed district approved the measure.

The Difficulties of Transition

Governing body members of the supplanted park districts either
had been appointed by the county circuit court judges or the governor or they had been popularly elected. None of these three
methods was utilized in the legal provisions pertaining to the
Chicago Park District. Its first five governing body members, called
commissioners, were appointed for staggered terms by the mayor
of Chicago, with the approval of the city council, soon after voters
had sanctioned the district. They took office on the first day of
May. However, court litigation over the constitutionality of the
consolidation arose immediately after the appointment of the commissioners. To avoid serious confusion, should the court find the
merger unconstitutional, a period of dual jurisdiction was inaugurated. During this time the separate governing bodies of the
twenty-two districts continued to function and their actions were
reviewed and approved by the commissioners of the new Chicago
Park District.

The difficulties of integrating twenty-two separate governments
into one park district did not terminate with the favorable settling
of the legal question five and one-half months later. There were no
legal precedents to guide the new government in its efforts to solve
the administrative problems growing out of consolidation. Almost
all of the replaced units were in serious financial straits at the time
of their abolition. Most of them were defaulting on the principal or
interest of their bonded indebtedness. Many were delinquent in
the payment of salaries to employees. Some were behind in paying
for materials and supplies. The Chicago Park District had to
remedy these and other financial difficulties, establish a reorganized personnel system, shape a new administrative organization,
and promptly handle many administrative details, some of which
could not have been fully anticipated.

Continued Independence

In subsequent years the Chicago Park District has continued to function as a separate governmental unit under the provisions of the consolidation act. Since 1935, as the result of an amendment to the state law, it has had the same boundaries as the city of Chicago. This coterminous special district government operates and maintains 165 parks containing more than 6,000 acres and 205 miles of boulevards and park driveways. It maintains its own police force.[18] It also pays for lighting, engineering, traffic control, maintenance, and improvements in its boulevards and parks as well as on the twenty-eight miles of Lake Michigan shore line under its authority, including the famed Outer Drive. The district levies a general tax on all property in the city of Chicago, and collects fees, licenses, and other miscellaneous revenues. It issues bonds for park acquisition and improvement upon approval of the electorate.

In 1947 a bill was introduced in the lower house of the Illinois State Legislature to consolidate the park district with the city of Chicago. Such action had been urged by resolution of the city council in the closing days of the previous year. During the same period a committee of the Chicago City Club, a privately supported research organization, urged that both significant economies and better city-wide service would result from the consolidation. The bill did not pass. The merger of many park districts into one in the 1930's was a major accomplishment and the first important step in the simplification of government in the metropolitan area. Nevertheless, there is seemingly no logical reason for the continuance of the park function apart from the city government, but logic does not always prevail in human situations.

[18] The importance of this activity is noticeable in the issuance of a report by the district titled *The Police and Minority Groups: A Manual Prepared for Use in the Chicago Park District Training School* (Chicago: 1947).

CHAPTER FIVE

Rural
Districts

Nonschool special districts are most numerous in rural areas, and many of them are highly important to the people they serve. There are three major categories of districts active in nonagricultural and agricultural rural territory. Those in the first category serve rural communities of less than 2,500 people situated outside the densely settled urban fringe. They often provide functions identical with those supplied in urban fringes by districts organized under the same laws. Since most types of districts which can operate in either nonagricultural rural communities or urban fringes are more consequential to the latter, they have been discussed in a previous chapter. This does not mean, however, that they are insignificant in rural areas. Districts in the second category are concerned with people both in rural communities and on agricultural land; their relative importance to rural community dwellers and to farmers and ranchers varies among states and sometimes within the same state. In the third group are the numerous districts that perform services designed to improve agricultural lands and to increase the well-being of their residents and owners. Since districts in the last two categories are the most important nonschool districts functioning in rural environments, much of the discussion in this chapter focuses on them.

THE GENERAL DEVELOPMENT

Many Causes

In numerous states these governments in rural settings were among the first districts to be authorized, sometimes second only in date of origin to school districts. Furthermore, such units have

grown over the years in total number and in number of types, as
new reasons for their creation have been added to the original
ones.[1] From an early time, specific rural public needs and resources
for satisfying them have not coincided with the boundaries of
established general governments. The areas to be served are often
either larger or smaller than a county or a township, for example,
and adequate functional and organizational adaptations of existing
governments to meet the demands are not always possible. As for
needs transcending the boundaries of regular units, intergovernmental contracts for joint performance of a function or for performance by one of the two parties have not been common among rural
governments. When the area in which a service is desired is territorially smaller than an existing government, and the need is not
met through incorporation, the existing government usually lacks
authorization to set up a subarea for the purpose of adding charges
for added services. Even where present such authority has seldom
been used, if at all. Elected rural governing bodies hesitate to
exercise previously authorized functions or to seek legal permission
for new ones, for fear that the resulting increased costs will jeopard-
ize their tenure in office.[2] The high degree of inelasticity of certain
governments has therefore contributed substantially to the establishment of special district governments in rural areas.

There have been other causes contributing to the growth of
rural districts. In some instances, rural districts have been created
because city residents objected to helping to pay for a function
they were already enjoying, like library service. In others, as in
the example of soil conservation districts which currently number
almost 2,000, the promotional activity of the national government
has been the prompting force. And finally, an important and sometimes compelling influence is the desire of rural inhabitants for the
independent handling of a function in which they are much interested because of its intimate effect upon them. Acting singly or in

[1] Occasionally, however, there have been drastic numerical reductions in a particular kind of rural district. During the 1930's, for example, large numbers of rural
road and bridge districts in Arkansas and of rural road districts in Illinois were
eliminated. In this connection it should be noted that the two largest groups of
special districts, rural and school, have lost the largest number of districts through
abolishment.

[2] This statement was made to the author in various forms by numerous observers
and officials during field research for this study. Although reluctant to assume additional functions, the incumbents strongly oppose the abdication of any present
powers.

combination, these causes largely account for the widespread utilization of rural districts, which sometimes furnish examples of both the largest and smallest governmental areas in a state.

Many Functions

As a result of these circumstances, rural districts perform a wide range of functions.[3] They dispose of sewage, protect persons and property, and fight fires. They supply library service and roads. Many of them operating under a variety of names, such as irrigation, water conservation, reclamation, drainage, and levee, are concerned with uses and controls of water. These districts are engaged in bringing in adequate water, getting rid of excess water, or keeping unwanted water away. Some furnish drainage or water for both agricultural and community activities. Rural districts provide services that conserve and improve agricultural soil. They eradicate weeds and pests harmful to fruits, vegetables, and animals. They supply electric power. In these important aspects of life, special district governments are vital to the welfare of rural inhabitants.

The characteristics of rural districts are so varied that generalizations are not very meaningful. A better understanding of this major group of special district governments can be obtained from a study of several individual types. A few words of explanation about those selected as illustrations are appropriate. Irrigation and soil conservation districts have an important effect on agricultural developments and show the influence of the national government. Drainage districts perform a diversity of functions, each of which is important in itself. Rural fire protection districts, especially those in Illinois, are significant to both rural communities and agricultural lands. Weed eradication districts illustrate the use of the district government mechanism to satisfy a particularized need.

IRRIGATION DISTRICTS

Irrigation farming contributes appreciably to the well-being of the western half of the United States and consequently to the total agricultural economy of the country. Governments usually known as irrigation districts, but sometimes as water improvement, water

---

[3] Some districts that cover predominantly rural land are not primarily used by rural people. Navigation and airport districts are illustrations.

conservation, and reclamation districts, play an important role in this type of farming. Designated here as irrigation districts, their primary purpose is to apply water by artificial means to lands used for agricultural purposes.' In addition, some irrigation districts furnish services such as drainage, power development, flood control, and water for domestic use.

Irrigation, an Expanding Activity

Irrigation is most important to the seventeen states ranging from the Pacific Coast to the tier from North Dakota southward to Texas. More than 99 per cent of the irrigation activity in progress in the United States takes place in these western states, with the addition of Arkansas, Florida, and Louisiana. The last three, however, account for less than 6 per cent of the total. Irrigation districts are functioning in most of these states as a significant enterprise, but they are not the only agencies active in irrigation. Their status can be best understood by taking an over-all view of irrigation and of the various organizations involved.

The amount of land benefited by irrigation has increased phenomenally over a relatively short period of time. There were about 3½ million acres of irrigated land in 1889. Sixty years later, the total acreage approximated 26 million, with the greatest increase occurring in the most recent ten-year period. In addition, it is estimated that in the seventeen western states there are approximately 17 million more potentially irrigable acres. Another indication of the growing importance of irrigation is the relative capital investment in such activities at the beginning and at the end of this same period. The investment grew from somewhat less than $30 million to nearly $2 billion. Irrigation is a big and expanding activity.

One of Many Organizations

Irrigation work is divided among almost 124,000 organized enterprises in the twenty states consisting of the seventeen western states, Arkansas, Florida, and Louisiana. The number increased

---

' This grouping follows that used in the *U.S. Census of Agriculture: 1950*, Vol. III, *Irrigation of Agricultural Lands*, U.S. Bureau of the Census, Agriculture Division (Washington: 1952), p. 3. Data relating to irrigation have been included in each decennial census of agriculture since 1890. Beginning in 1910, in addition to the

by nearly one-third in the 1940–1950 period. Less than 1 per cent
of all the enterprises are irrigation districts, which totaled 489 in
1950, a 10 per cent gain in ten years.[5] Nine-tenths of all irrigation
operations are conducted by individual farmers on single farms
who operate supply works or equipment to obtain irrigation water
for their own lands. There are also two types of mutual or coöperative irrigation companies, incorporated and unincorporated; they
are private, voluntary associations of farmers which provide irrigation water at cost, generally for members only. The final major
type of organization operating in this field is the commercial irrigation company, organized for profit by investors and selling its
services to customers who need them. Less important in number
of organizations and in acreage directly irrigated are enterprises
conducted by the United States Bureau of Reclamation, the United
States Bureau of Indian Affairs, states, and cities.

In spite of the broad diversity of organizational activity, irrigation districts occupy a key position in this development, which is
so significant to agriculture. Although constituting only a very
small fraction of the total number of enterprises, special district
governments provide for the irrigation of almost 5 million acres
of land. This marks a sizable recent increase, for the total was 3½
million acres in 1940. Furthermore, special districts irrigate almost
one-fifth of the total irrigated by all the various enterprises. The
prominence of the districts is even more apparent in individual
states. In Nebraska, North Dakota, South Dakota, and Washington
they exceed all other types of enterprises in number of acres irrigated, and in California, Nevada, Oregon, and Texas they are second in this respect only to single-farm endeavors.

Early Development and Growth

The initial translation of the irrigation district idea into state legislation occurred in California, which enacted the first generally

---

regular decennial agricultural census, a special census of irrigation has been taken
in the states where irrigation has been most intensive. The 1950 census included
the seventeen western states plus Arkansas, Florida, and Louisiana. Substantial
portions of the early part of this section are based on this report.

[5] This is the figure given in *U.S. Census of Agriculture: 1950*, Vol. III, *Irrigation
of Agricultural Lands*, p. 13. It is somewhat lower than the number determined by
the Governments Division of the same agency in 1952. The exact number is not
especially important. More significant is the low proportion of irrigation districts in
the total of all irrigation enterprises.

applicable and widely utilized law in 1887.⁶ It was passed largely
at the urging of Central Valley farmers who, suffering from decreasing yields of grain, wanted to establish a public irrigation
organization to which an obstructive minority, whose lands were
essential to the undertaking, would have to contribute. The rail-
roads also favored the act as a boost to the further development of
the state. In 1896, after much litigation over formation attempts
and bond issues, the United States Supreme Court finally upheld
the constitutionality of the law. The decision paved the way for
more widespread acceptance of the idea in other states, especially
in the western half of the United States. In the closing years of
the nineteenth century only California and Washington had active irrigation districts, although Kansas, Nevada, Oregon, and
Nebraska had adopted irrigation district laws before the Supreme
Court verdict.

The compelling need for irrigation districts outweighed their
own mistakes and the economic adversities that beset many of
them. Although many of the early ones were well planned and had
legitimate objectives, others were unsound speculative and promotional ventures. Sometimes inadequate consideration was given
to the water source, agricultural potentialities, and means of financing. The panic of 1893 worked to the detriment of a number of
irrigation districts, as it did to other phases of the economy. Because of these factors, the California Legislature amended the
pioneer law in 1897 by tightening the provisions for district formation and bond issues.

Irrigation district activity was accelerated, most noticeably in
Nebraska, Idaho, Colorado, and Oregon, during the early years of
the new century. Districts, especially in Colorado, soon engaged
in highly speculative promotion which reached its peak about 1910
and resulted in a substantial amount of defaulting. Although irrigation securities were widely discredited, the movement survived
and in 1917 entered upon a period of extensive growth. The economic depression after 1929 brought on another severe test and
caused much financial delinquency and bond defaulting. After
thorough financial reorganization, fostered by federal loans, the

⁶ Wells A. Hutchins, *Irrigation Districts: Their Organization, Operation and
Financing*, Technical Bulletin No. 254 (Washington: U.S. Department of Agriculture, 1931), pp. 70–71.

irrigation district development has proceeded on a much smoother course. Irrigation districts now exist in seventeen of the twenty states undertaking more than 99 per cent of all irrigation activity. The only exceptions are Kansas, Louisiana, and Oklahoma.

Area Flexibility

Proponents of establishing an irrigation district have great latitude in laying out the territory proposed for inclusion. They are never confined, for example, to suggesting boundaries that are wholly within a single county. In fact, the enabling laws anticipated the intercounty possibility by stipulating that petitions be sent to the governing body of the county containing the greater or greatest amount of land in the proposed district. Actually very few territorial restrictions are placed upon these districts, which are frequently intercounty. Irrigation districts, when authorized by an interstate compact, can even include territory situated in more than one state. Five interstate irrigation districts exist, two containing portions of Montana and North Dakota, two more involving Nebraska and Wyoming, and one including parts of Nevada and California. In practice, therefore, state boundaries have not been an insurmountable barrier. The most common restriction is that an irrigation district cannot overlap any part of a similar district, but even this can be circumvented if the directors of the district first including the land consent. Occasionally the legislation specifies that the land must be susceptible of irrigation from one or more sources and by one or more systems. In some instances noncontiguous lands may be included. The areas of these special district governments vary widely, from less than 1 square mile to almost 1,400 square miles. All the land within the districts is benefited by irrigation, although it is not always directly irrigated. These districts are also empowered to annex lands, to consolidate with one another, and to dissolve. When dissolving, they must make sufficient provision for the liquidation of outstanding indebtedness.

Landowner and State Government Roles

The landowners, whether or not they are local residents, usually make the decision to initiate the formation of an irrigation district.

One of the few exceptions is in Utah, where the governor may start proceedings upon recommendation of the state engineer. There is often the legal requirement that a majority of the landowners, representing a specified portion—ranging from one-fourth to three-fifths—of the acreage proposed for inclusion, must petition for a district. Landowners are therefore necessary parties to the creation of the district. In most states the petition is presented to the county governing body which considers the proposal. At this point in most proceedings, the state government plays a significant role. Before the county board holds a hearing and determines the final boundaries, the state engineer or a state department or board investigates and reports on the sufficiency of the proposed water supply and the feasibility of the irrigation plan. In some states the recommendation on forming a district is simply advisory, but in others it can be overridden only by a petition signed by a large majority of the landowners. A majority of votes cast in the affirmative at the formation election is usually sufficient to create the district.

Voting power in the district is generally based on landowner-ship, rather than on the more customary criteria in the United States of citizenship and local residence.[7] Frequently neither local nor state residence is required. The landownership voting require-ment is applicable in all regular and special elections relating to the choosing of governing board members and the approval of bond proposals. In several states the number of votes possessed by each landowner is determined by the amount of acreage owned by him or acre-feet of water allocated to his land. There is a sharp difference of opinion over the justice of plural voting based on prop-erty ownership. Advocates argue that the district resembles a business corporation and should be conducted in the same way, that is, the majority in interest should have control. Antagonists counter by pointing out that small landowners are vitally affected by district activities, and that proportionate voting permits a few large landowning interests to make the ultimate decisions in dis-trict affairs.[8] The conflict is not concerned with substituting a simple local residence requirement for the property qualification,

---

[7] A major deviation is in the important irrigation state of California, where the electorate consists of resident voters.

[8] Hutchins, *op. cit.*, pp. 16–17.

but rather with the question of single or multiple votes for property owners.

In addition to checking on the advisability of organizing an irrigation district, state governments often participate when a district is considering a bond issue. Many states require that the plans and estimates for such bond proposals be submitted for review to a state official, department, or board in the engineering, banking, or legal fields. This official or agency, though usually acting in only an advisory capacity, is occasionally required to give consent to any changes made after initial state approval. In considering plans and estimates, the state makes a detailed study of costs which were analyzed only in a summary manner when the question of organization was being investigated. Some states supervise certain aspects of actual construction work by the district.

A state organization exercising comprehensive authority over numerous irrigation district activities is the California Districts Securities Commission. This agency, established in 1931, grew out of a legislative investigation conducted in the previous year because districts were experiencing financial difficulties in a period of growing economic depression. The commission has many responsibilities after a district is created. It investigates and reports on the sufficiency of water supply, soil fertility, feasibility of proposed works, and economic soundness of the project for which bonds are to be issued. When appropriate, it recommends project modifications. The commission must approve the issuance of bonds and expenditures from bond sales. It passes upon contracts that increase indebtedness, oversees refinancing propositions, keeps records on the financial and physical conditions of the units, and examines district books and affairs. Since the establishment of the commission in 1931, bonds issued and contracts executed have involved capital amounts exceeding $125 million, and not a single irrigation district has defaulted in the payment of principal or interest when due.[9]

Substantial District Discretion

Irrigation districts have substantial independence within the framework of state organizational and financial guidance or con-

---

[9] *Report on Irrigation Districts in California, 1944–50,* California Department of Public Works, Division of Water Resources, Bulletin No. 21-P (Sacramento: n.d.), p. 22.

trol. Directors or commissioners are usually elected directly to serve as the governing body. The directors must generally be resident voters and frequently must also be owners of land within the district. A common election requirement is that directors be selected from separate divisions consisting of approximately equal amounts of territory. The governing board has from three to seven members, with the exact number sometimes dependent upon the decision of the organizational petitioners or the district electorate. A three-year term is customary and is sometimes utilized in combination with overlapping tenure. In a few states directors may be recalled from office.

Although the county treasurer usually handles the custody and distribution of district funds, elected district officials and their appointees are responsible for policy decisions and many internal affairs. Occasionally, instead of relying upon other governmental units for assistance, districts elect or appoint their own officers to perform financial and other tasks. The board of directors or commissioners has considerable authority, including the power to appoint and remove district officers and employees. The major appointee of the board is the chief engineer or, in some large irrigation districts, the general manager, who is sometimes chosen because of appropriate administrative training and experience rather than engineering background. The chief engineer or general manager (and at times the two titles are combined) is responsible to the governing body for supervision and direction of district activities.

The governing bodies of irrigation districts have other important responsibilities. Their main job is the procurement and distribution of water for agricultural uses. In the early years most districts were formed in order to construct new facilities. Subsequently they have been organized not only for this original purpose but also to supplement existing developments and to obtain, complete, or rehabilitate privately owned works. Directors must reach decisions on this basic question of the nature of the district irrigation operations. They must also make and formalize judgments regarding the acquisition of a water supply, water rights, and other property, and the construction and operation of distribution systems.

Districts apportion water in different ways, and governing body members have significant responsibilities in all of them. In some districts the board formulates equitable rules founded on beneficial use. In others it administers state enabling law provisions basing allocation on assessed property valuation or allotting an equal amount to each acre. The governing body applies federal regulations when water is obtained through contract with the national government. Furnishing water to agricultural lands is the primary purpose of irrigation districts, but some may legally perform other functions. These are providing water for domestic purposes, at times including land outside the district limits; participating in flood control; building drainage works; and generating and transmitting electric power. Relatively few irrigation districts engage in the power function, but in some states this activity accounts for a sizable part of the total income of irrigation districts.[10]

Finances

Unlike many nonspecial district governments, irrigation districts usually lack the power of taxation. Instead, their two principal sources of funds are assessments and bond issues.[11] Assessments do not have to be uniform nor to be applied throughout the entire territory of a government. They are collected to pay for the principal and interest on outstanding bonded indebtedness and for water contract obligations, and to finance the operational and maintenance expenses of delivering water to district lands and of keeping the system in efficient condition. Decisions about the areas subject to assessment and about the total amount of money needed from this source rest with the district, regardless of whether or not it collects its own funds. Assessments are liens upon the land and collection is enforced through refusal to deliver water, sale of

[10] In Nebraska, the only complete public power state, all electric facilities are owned and operated by numerous special district governments, some of which are authorized to supply both irrigation and power. A lucid explanation of these districts and the public power development is contained in Clarence A. Davis, *Nebraska's Public Power Explained* (Lincoln: privately printed, 1949).

[11] There is some difference of opinion among writers on irrigation as to what is a tax and what is an assessment. Hutchins, *op. cit.*, p. 20, notes that "the words tax and assessment are often used indiscriminately to denote charges against land. However, court decisions involving the nature of this charge usually distinguish clearly between tax and assessment and in most cases have held the district charge to be an assessment."

delinquent lands, or favorable judgments in lawsuits. Interest and penalties are usually charged when payments, sometimes due on a semiannual installment basis, are not forthcoming by the deadline.

The sale of bonds is the principal source of capital to be invested in facilities designed for developing or diverting, and then storing and carrying water to the users. Funds from bond sales therefore pay for irrigation system construction or acquisition, water rights, and needed lands or rights of way, and often for office and shop land and buildings. The consent of the district voters to the proposed bond issue, usually by majority decision, is a customary requirement. In addition to requiring the state government's appraisal of the bond proposal, the state law often sets a maximum limit on the interest rate to be paid to bondholders and on the period of years over which the bonds can be outstanding. Six per cent is the most usual interest rate. There is much diversity as to maturity date. Twenty- to forty-year limits are most common, but the range extends from five to fifty years. Security for the bonds is customarily the power and duty of the district to levy assessments sufficient to meet interest and principal. If the district is negligent or recalcitrant about the levy, the bondholders may compel action through a court order. The power to issue bonds has been a major impetus to the formation of irrigation districts, and most districts have used this type of financing.

There are several other less important sources of funds. Tolls or charges for the use of water may often be imposed to supplement or substitute for assessments. This power has been widely used in California. Many districts may also sell or lease excess water inside or outside their boundaries. Furthermore, districts that perform a corollary function, such as drainage or power, may make a separate charge for such service.

The lack of taxing power has not handicapped the activities and growth of irrigation districts. One of them, the Imperial Irrigation District of California, is among the twelve largest nonschool special districts in the United States. The exclusive supplier of water and power to the Imperial Valley and of power to the Coachella Valley, and the operator of the All-American Canal, the district has more than 1,000 employees and recently had a gross annual revenue of more than $10 million from its irrigation and electric power divisions and its Mexican subsidiary. It also has approximately $60 million in both outstanding debt and total assets.

National Government Efforts

The national government has had substantial impact on the creation, activities, and existence of numerous irrigation districts. In total, its efforts have played a major role in the development of irrigation districts over a long period of years. The Reclamation Act of 1902 authorized large-scale participation by the national government in irrigation matters, and close relations have developed between the Bureau of Reclamation, originally known as the Reclamation Service, and irrigation districts.[12]

Initially, in administering its program, the Bureau of Reclamation dealt with settlers on each project whose applications for water rights it had accepted. Water users' associations, a special type of mutual irrigation company, entered into contracts obligating them to collect from their stockholders charges by the United States government for construction, maintenance, and operation of irrigation facilities.[13] The associations were to assume operation of the irrigation works when the national government deemed the transfer advisable. The arrangement often proved unworkable, largely because of the necessity for bringing individual legal actions to collect charges that were delinquent and because of the proliferation of contracts. Furthermore, landowners within the projects who had not applied for water rights could not be compelled to contribute. Within a few years, therefore, the bureau substituted advocacy of irrigation districts for its earlier encouragement of water users' associations. It began urging the amendment of state laws and the passage of national legislation so that irrigation districts could enter into contracts with the national government.

Both state and national governments responded. In 1922, for example, Congress authorized the reclamation bureau to contract

---

[12] For a discussion of earlier national laws, such as the Desert Land Act and the Carey Act, and subsequent legislation encouraging irrigation, see Roy E. Huffman, *Irrigation Development and Public Water Policy* (New York: Ronald Press, 1953), especially pp. 18–32.

[13] Wells A. Hutchins, H. E. Selby, and Stanley W. Voelker, *Irrigation-Enterprise Organizations*, Circular No. 934 (Washington: U.S. Department of Agriculture, 1953), p. 26.

with irrigation districts on a joint liability plan. Under this repayment system all the land included became collectively liable for
the entire project cost, instead of each acre being liable for merely
its proportionate share. In addition, this law did not make the
obligation a first mortgage on individual farms, and thus facilitated
borrowing from governmental agricultural lending agencies which
required a first mortgage. Upon the establishment of the necessary
legal bases, the Bureau of Reclamation locally advocated the sub-
stitution of irrigation districts for existing or contemplated water
users' associations. The bureau came to favor agreements with
irrigation districts because the collection of charges could be enforced through the districts and because the number of contracts
could be reduced for a comparable over-all amount of service.
Currently almost all contracts pertaining to federal reclamation
projects are made originally or renegotiated between the national
government and irrigation districts. Furthermore, under the contract terms the national government actually determines the
amount and timing of the charges collected by the districts.
Through the various activities of the Bureau of Reclamation, the
national government has been directly influential in the creation
and growth of irrigation districts on reclamation projects.

The bureau has had additional impact on irrigation district development. As early as 1911, it became legally possible for the
bureau to contract with irrigation districts and other individuals
and groups not within reclamation projects. In this type of relationship some districts have contracted for part or all of their water
supply through the purchase of excess water not needed to meet
the requirements of land to be irrigated within the projects. Others
have contracted for the construction of irrigation or drainage systems by the bureau.

The national government has also had an appreciable financial
effect on numerous irrigation districts. Two illustrations indicate
its significance in this connection. The depression of the 1930's
caused many irrigation districts to default in bond payments, and
the defaults continued to increase until halted through federal
help. The aid took the form of refinancing loans through a recently
created national agency, the Reconstruction Finance Corporation.
Not all loan applications were granted, but the lending organiza-

tion approved the requests of many districts with good prospects and superior financial histories. Bonded indebtedness was retired at a fraction of the original dollar value and the interest rate was appreciably lowered. In addition, the refunding actions of the Reconstruction Finance Corporation enabled a number of districts to obtain loans at lower interest rates from private sources. The efforts of this agency therefore played a major role in the refinancing of irrigation districts; many districts were salvaged or had their financial condition greatly improved.

Irrigation has always been regarded as a phase of the national reclamation policy in the United States which should pay its own way through reimbursement of costs to the national government. Designed to help states in need of irrigation to help themselves, national participation in irrigation activities has been judged as an investment rather than a gift.[14] This judgment is in contrast to that concerning most of the construction costs of national flood control and navigation improvements, which are considered nationally beneficial and nonreimbursable. The one important concession to irrigation projects is that the cost is to be returned without interest charges. This principle of interest-free money is firmly entrenched in the national reclamation program, including its irrigation aspects, and has been of substantial benefit to numerous irrigation districts. It has enabled them to repay the national government without the heavy burden of interest charges and, during federal ownership of the project, to pay expenses for operation and maintenance. The interest-free plan extends also to delinquent repayment obligations.

The requirements regarding the length of the repayment period and the size of payments have varied. The repayment period has ranged from ten, twenty, and forty years to an indefinite period, with the forty-year plan being currently the most common. The amounts due at fixed periods were first based on an ascending scale with no reduction in the event of decreased income. When the depression of the 1930's necessitated a moratorium on repayments, the basis was converted to an adjustable scale geared to the fluctuating ability to repay as determined by the gross value of

[14] *National Irrigation Policy—Its Development and Significance,* U.S. 76th Cong., 1st sess., S. Doc. 36 (Washington: 1939), p. 10.

crops within the district. In 1939 Congress passed a law providing
two additional types of repayment contracts known as the Section
9(d) and Section 9(e) contracts. The first is a forty-year arrangement
with repayment of construction costs beginning after a ten-year development period. During the initial ten years only operation and
maintenance charges must be paid. Section 9(e) contracts pertain
to the furnishing of water by the national government for a short
period, or for a longer period not exceeding forty years. The rates
must cover operation and maintenance costs and the portion of
the fixed charges considered proper by the Secretary of the Interior.
These contracts are restricted to storage and carriage systems and
normally do not apply to distribution works. Under their provisions the cost of the works does not have to be repaid in forty
years nor does the contractor obtain water rights at the end of the
repayment period.[15] During the effective period of any type of
contract with the national government, an irrigation district cannot dissolve nor alter its boundaries without the written consent
of the Secretary of the Interior.

Sometimes Centers of Controversy

Irrigation districts sometimes become involved in turbulent controversies. Since their activities are basic to the welfare of the
areas they serve, the policies and actions of the directors or the
district voters are sometimes strongly and bitterly contested. In
several states the recall of directors is legally possible, and such
efforts have not been isolated occurrences. The number of directors against whom recall action is taken can be large, and the list
of charges can be comprehensive. For example, a recent attempt
concerned three of the five governing body members. They were
all charged with extravagance and incompetence in district management, as illustrated by the financial condition of the district,
and with improper utilization of a water supply already made
inadequate by the admission of outside dry land into the district.
Furthermore, the petitions stated that each director whose recall
was being sought "does not abide by the [state] water code as
proven by the superior court decision in the taxpayers' suit brought

[15] Alfred R. Golzé, *Reclamation in the United States* (New York: McGraw-Hill,
1952), p. 247.

to prevent payment of an illegal contract to which he was a party."[16]
For one of the directors, this was the second recall instituted
against him in less than four years.

In some instances dissension seethes for an extended period of
time. In one district two directors were recalled. This was followed
by an unsuccessful effort to recall a county supervisor who recommended a certain individual to fill out one of the unexpired terms
resulting from the recall! Then came a lawsuit to determine the
assessment policy of the district, which had been shifted from a
flat rate to an ad valorem basis. All these events occurred in slightly
more than one year. Another district in the same state has had a
stormier history during five recent consecutive years. The first
three years witnessed a county grand jury probe and indictment,
a recall election, an outbreak of fisticuffs at a board session, numerous mass meetings, hirings, firings, charges, and countercharges.
In the fourth year there were demands for reinstatement of a dismissed bookkeeper, and accusations by him regarding the preparation and holding of tea parties on district time, the overcharging
of a large number of water users, and negligence in the collection
of bills. Meanwhile the bookkeeper's successor was jailed on the
charge of grand theft. A private association of water users subsequently demanded the elimination of the general manager's authority to appoint and dismiss personnel without the approval of
the governing body. Soon thereafter a recall was started against a
director, with the candidate for his seat claiming that assessment
rates were excessively high. The candidate attributed this to an
inequitable and unrealistic contract to supply water to a privately
owned public utility for use in its hydroelectric operations. In the
fifth year the manager was dismissed, and a temporary replacement filled the post for many months.[17]

A policy first established in the national reclamation legislation
of 1902 and subsequently reaffirmed has also caused bitter disputes
in several areas. It is the limitation of the acreage to which water
will be supplied by a national reclamation project. Known as the
160-acre limitation and designed to foster the development of

---

[16] Sacramento *Bee*, Dec. 8, 1954.

[17] See *ibid.*, Feb. 3, 1953–Dec. 11, 1954 *passim*, for information about these two
districts.

family-sized farms, it restricts the amount of water which can be sold to that needed to irrigate a maximum of 160 acres in single ownership or 160 acres each for husband and wife. When the reclamation law was broadened in 1911 to allow the sale of water to private lands, the problem crystallized because the water restriction was applied to lands in private ownership whose total acreage was not controlled by national law, as were public lands.

The most vigorous opposition to the limitation on the amount of land eligible for irrigation water has emanated from three areas. They are the areas which can contract with the Central Valley project in California, the Valley Gravity project in Texas, and the San Luis Valley project in Colorado. Each area has sought to gain exemption from the restriction, but only the Colorado one has been successful. In a number of irrigation districts some of the owners of land in excess of the amount that can receive project water have fought negotiation of a contract with the United States Bureau of Reclamation by the district of which they are a part. Antagonism to negotiations with the bureau, as well as organized resistance to approval by the district electorate of a proposed contract for the purchase of water under the acreage limitation, has frequently been in evidence. Court litigation has occurred, with strong accusations of regimentation leveled at the bureau and anxiety expressed as to whether the bureau "is fostering a police style state in the guise of reclamation."[18] In California a joint legislative interim committee studied national-local irrigation relations, including contract provisions, in 1952 and 1953; in the latter year the committee chairman introduced an unsuccessful bill to prohibit irrigation districts from entering into reclamation bureau contracts containing the 160-acre limitation. Prolonged discussion and a detailed study of the feasibility of state ownership and operation of the Central Valley project have also occurred in California.

Differing opinions about the acreage limitation have been expressed by different observers. For example, one of them argues that the restriction guarantees extensive distribution of the benefits of national governmental reclamation efforts, while another contends that extending reclamation activities to privately owned

---

[18] Fresno *Bee*, Oct. 26, 1950.

lands has brought forth many new issues of social policy which need careful evaluation.[19] In individual local circumstances there have been proponents as well as opponents of contracts containing this restriction, and much controversy has ensued in some of the irrigation districts that can obtain project water through this arrangement.

SOIL CONSERVATION DISTRICTS

The soil conservation district, a new, widely used governmental unit, resulted from the belated formulation, in the depression of the 1930's, of a comprehensive attack on a growing, nationwide problem. In many sections of the country the productivity of the soil was fast dwindling through erosion and through unintelligent practices that reduced soil fertility. By this time, millions of acres of former cropland had been destroyed, millions more were in poor condition, and much of the remainder was vulnerable to erosion. This was evident in the large numbers of gullied crop fields, of streams and rivers carrying rich soil from upland farms, and of dust storms blowing across dry lands. Governmental recognition of the relevance of these problems to the national economy and to present and future public welfare crystallized in the depression years, and a federal survey in 1934 confirmed the extensive seriousness of the difficulties.

Although the national government had earlier shown concern by establishing erosion experiment stations, the Soil Erosion Service, and the Civilian Conservation Corps, its most important contribution to the rise of soil conservation districts occurred in 1935, when Congress passed an act directing the Secretary of Agriculture to establish the Soil Conservation Service. This agency

---

[19] Marion Clawson, *Uncle Sam's Acres* (New York: Dodd, Mead and Co., 1951), p. 194, and Mont H. Saunderson, *Western Land and Water Use* (Norman: University of Oklahoma Press, 1950), pp. 158–159. One author, in writing about the Central Valley project in California, has titled one of his chapters, "The Battle of the Contract." See Robert de Roos, *The Thirsty Land* (Stanford: Stanford University Press, 1948), chap. 8. Appraisals of the limitation feature in a specific state are found in Varden Fuller, "Acreage Limitation in Federal Irrigation Projects with Particular Reference to the Central Valley Project of California," *Journal of Farm Economics*, 31 (Nov., 1949), 976–984, and Paul S. Taylor, "Central Valley Project: Water and Land," *Western Political Quarterly*, 2 (June, 1949), 241–253.

was made responsible, in association with other organizations and in coöperation with local farmer groups, for launching a program of soil and water resource conservation based on intelligent land-use practices on private and public land susceptible to erosion. In turn, fulfilling these responsibilities called for the performance of various complementary activities, including contour farming, cover cropping, range and pasture seeding, woodland management, tree planting, farm drainage, and irrigation planning and utilization.

The Evolution of a New Government

The national government had decided that the soil conservation problem was of national concern, but in assigning the responsibility to the Soil Conservation Service it was recognizing that the program must also be cognizant of local needs and conditions. Various departments of the national government, including the Department of Agriculture, have provided for local decision-making and support without establishing new governmental units. In this instance, however, a different course was pursued. The utilization of local government was prompted by the obvious need for land-use regulatory authority in soil conservation activities, which could not be supplied by federal legislation. In addition, although admitting that there were already too many local governments, the Soil Conservation Service realized that the contemplated conservation activities would usually be concerned with territory in several counties and, less frequently, with an area smaller than a single county. It decided, therefore, that existing local governments were not well suited to carry out such functions.[20]

After making these judgments and undertaking soil conservation practices in experimental demonstration projects, the national government sought to implement its conclusion that a new local governmental unit was necessary. The Soil Conservation Service, its efforts bolstered by a program of national subsidy payments for soil conservation, first prepared A Standard Soil Conservation Districts Law in 1936. For the benefit of individual state legisla-

---

[20] Soils and Men, Yearbook of Agriculture 1938, U.S. Department of Agriculture (Washington: 1938), p. 300; A Standard Soil Conservation Districts Law, U.S. Department of Agriculture, Soil Conservation Service (Washington: 1936), p. 7.

tures, it spelled out in detail its suggested provisions for the creation, organization, and powers of the new government. The
national government then influenced the state legislatures to adopt
the proposal. This is clearly indicated in the foreword to the model
act, which stressed that under the recent national soil conservation
legislation the Secretary of Agriculture could require the enactment of suitable state laws as a condition of eligibility to federal
benefits. Finally, after the passage of state enabling legislation,
field workers of the Soil Conservation Service encouraged the
organization of soil conservation districts in local areas. In these
ways, some of them reminiscent of federal advocacy of housing
authorities and irrigation districts, the national government helped
to create a new type of local government. Significantly, too, its
interest in soil conservation districts has been a continuing one,
as evidenced by the substantial and sustained assistance that has
been rendered.

The urgings of the national government brought forth immediate responses, soon followed by widespread activity, at state and
local levels. In February, 1937, President Franklin Roosevelt sent
identical letters to all state governors recommending adoption of
the standard act. Various state legislatures promptly began to pass
enabling laws, and within six months the first soil conservation
district had been established. From the beginning, most of the
model provisions were incorporated into state legislation. By the
middle of 1938, twenty-two states had enacted laws and sixty-nine
districts, ranging in area from less than 30 to more than 4,000
square miles, were in operation. The number of adopting states
continued to grow and the number of soil conservation districts
increased steadily, even through World War II. In 1952, when the
Census Bureau counted the various kinds of governmental units,
it determined that there were 1,981 soil conservation districts
which were independent governments in thirty-eight states. At
the same time the Census Bureau revised its 1942 decision about
the governmental status of soil conservation districts in numerous
states. In the previous decade only those with authority to levy
property taxes had been recognized, and such units had been
found in only four states. Under the reclassification, all districts
possessing substantial fiscal and administrative autonomy, regard-

less of the right to tax property, were deemed independent.[21] The total has grown by more than 100 in subsequent years, and large majority percentages of all farms and ranches and of all agricultural land in the nation are now within the territorial boundaries of soil conservation districts. The principal areas not within such districts, though eligible under their state laws, are large sections of Indiana, Tennessee, Minnesota, North Dakota, Wyoming, Idaho, Oregon, and California.

Characteristics

The characteristics of soil conservation districts reveal that the national government has fostered an unusual governmental unit, unusual even among special districts which are often extraordinary. Not unexpectedly these districts have differences because of the large number of state laws, but in general they show great similarity owing to the influence of the model act. The initiation of a soil conservation unit is usually a simple matter. A small number of landowners or land occupiers, sometimes as few as ten to twenty-five, petition the state soil conservation committee, an agency expressly created to perform functions related to such districts. The committee, composed mainly or entirely of state officials concerned with various aspects of conservation, holds a public hearing and then determines the desirability and necessity of the proposed district and the appropriateness of the contemplated boundaries. Except in Massachusetts, the state committee submits the question to a local vote; customarily a simple majority of those voting is sufficient. The composition of the electorate eligible to vote on the question of forming a district and on subsequent issues differs in some states from the suggestion in the model act that resident landowners and occupiers form the basis. Instead, the voting privilege is frequently conferred only on landowners and is not extended to nonowner operators.

---

[21] The various figures illustrating trends should be considered approximations because of the varying definitions used by the same and different governmental agencies. For example, the Soil Conservation Service, disregarding these criteria, judges that there are independent districts in every state. Compare *Governments in the United States in 1952*, U.S. Bureau of the Census, Governments Division (Washington: 1953), p. 21, and recent annual issues of *Soil Conservation Districts*, U.S. Department of Agriculture, Soil Conservation Service. As throughout this study, the judgments of the Governments Division of the Census Bureau are used in this section for purposes of uniformity and comparability.

The usual governing body is a hybrid, consisting of three locally elected supervisors and two appointed by the state committee, all serving terms of three years. In recent years, however, some state laws have made the governing body entirely elective. The districts are generally endowed with two types of powers. The first, which is voluntary or coöperative, is concerned with setting up and carrying out projects designed to control and safeguard against erosion. Included are research, surveys, plans, demonstration projects, and engineering, all slanted toward prevention of erosion, and financial and material assistance to farmers and ranchers engaging in conservation work. The second type is compulsory and involves the adoption and enforcement of land-use regulations, sometimes called conservation ordinances, upon majority approval at a referendum election. Its purpose is to afford protection against the detrimental effects of land abuse by a minority. The mandatory land-use regulatory authority is not conferred by the laws of nine of the thirty-eight states that possess independent soil conservation units.

In line with the guides of the model act, the districts have extremely limited financing powers. They cannot issue bonds and, with the exception of those in California and Colorado, they lack the power to levy property taxes. Their funds are derived for the most part through appropriations from national and state governments. The main factor that preserves their status as independent governments and prevents their reclassification as adjuncts of other governments is their possession of the authority to require contributions from, or impose charges on, benefited landowners or land occupiers. However, the infrequency of their use of this power makes them borderline governmental units. This indefinite standing has been reinforced in states that have tended to increase the control of a state agency over the districts. In comparison with some districts, such as those concerned with water and power, soil conservation districts have limited finances and personnel.

Intergovernmental Relations

From the beginning soil conservation districts have been expected to function in the midst of extensive intergovernmental relations. The national Soil Conservation Service has had the most sustained contacts and greatest degree of influence. The extent of its importance to the districts was noted before a congressional committee in 1948 by the then president of the National Association of Soil Conservation Districts. He stated that "The Soil Conservation Service is the very life blood of the district. Everything depends upon it."[22] Over the years since the start of the soil conservation district movement, the financial assistance of the national government has been substantial. In a number of years since 1940, for example, the annual expenditures of the Soil Conservation Service for each district averaged in excess of $20,000. In addition, another national conservation program has given these districts indirect financial aid. Known earlier as the Agricultural Conservation Program of the Production and Marketing Administration, it is recently identified as the Agricultural Conservation Program Service.

Soil conservation districts obtaining aid from the Soil Conservation Service must request assistance and must meet certain requirements through written agreements.[23] In early years the amount of federal assistance depended on state classification rather than on local conditions. In 1937 the states were grouped into three classes to determine the amount of aid to be supplied by the national agency. Only those in the first two groups, whose laws completely or substantially embodied the model act provisions, were considered eligible for help. States whose laws differed too radically from the model act were placed in the third group, and their districts could not obtain aid. Several states were still in the third group when the categories of assistance were discontinued at the time of World War II. Since then they have not been reinstituted and districts in all states are eligible for full assistance.

Federal assistance to soil conservation districts is implemented through two documents, a first memorandum of understanding and a supplemental memorandum between a particular district and the Soil Conservation Service. As a condition to the first document, the district must establish the objectives of its program and the

[22] *Hearings before the Subcommittee on the Agriculture Department Appropriation Bill for 1948,* U.S. Senate Committee on Appropriations, 80th Cong., 2d sess., p. 1117.

[23] For greater detail on these agreements, see W. Robert Parks, *Soil Conservation Districts in Action* (Ames: Iowa State College Press, 1952), chap. 3, which has been used as the basis for much of the discussion of them. Professor Parks's book is one of the few comprehensive studies of a major functional type of special district.

service must judge them adequate to justify its coöperation. Although this requirement has come to mean primarily that some kind of local conservation program must exist, the content of the program is frequently influenced by suggestions from field representatives of the national service. After the district has fulfilled this stipulation, the national agency may enter into the first memorandum. The district agrees to establish a work plan and the effectuating procedures, to define in writing the obligations of farmers and ranchers receiving national conservation aid and their accountability in satisfying their commitments, and to supply information about its program and methods. The formulation of a suitable work plan is a condition to entrance by the Soil Conservation Service into the supplemental memorandum of understanding to make assistance available. There is, however, increasing acceptance of brief plans stated in generalized language.

The supplemental memorandum limits national aid to land whose owners have entered into agreements with the district, and to district-owned or -leased land for which a conservation plan has been adopted. The district further promises to keep up-to-date records regarding Soil Conservation Service materials, report annually on their distribution, and acknowledge the right of the service to impose added obligations when additional field equipment is made available. In return, the agency of the national government provides technical and material aid. Nearly all soil conservation districts have entered into supplemental memoranda of understanding. Before the national government furnishes assistance, the district must enter into an agreement with farmers and ranchers to determine individual obligations and responsibilities. Through the memorandum system, the national government seeks to guarantee the performance of certain specific acts by the districts. The government has shown great latitude, however, in establishing the initial district obligations and enforcing the completed arrangements. In setting the pattern of daily district operations, relations between district governing members and field technicians of the Soil Conservation Service have been much more influential than specific provisions of the formal documents.

In addition to the national government, other governments have significant contacts with the districts. Most important are the state governments and their soil conservation committees, whose roles were suggested in the standard enabling act prepared by the Soil Conservation Service. The state committees serve both as review agencies in formation proceedings and subsequently as facilitating organizations. They assist in various ways. They prepare hand-books on organization and administration, help establish financial systems, recommend equipment and property plans, and offer advice on records and reports. Furthermore, they hold joint meetings of district governing bodies; circulate pertinent information among districts, including data on legal protection; and assist in obtaining aid from other governmental agencies. A recent trend in some states has been to grant the soil conservation committee control over a varying range of district activities. This development, contrary to the original concept of state-district relations, further clouds the independent governmental status of some districts. On the other hand, another early recommendation of the national government has been followed. It is the appropriation of state money to aid the soil conservation district program. Such assistance is now common and has been growing, although the amount differs appreciably among the states. The annual total granted by all states, in part for the expenses of the state committees but predominantly for direct assistance to the districts, is several million dollars. County aid to districts is also increasing, but is still insignificant in comparison with national and state contributions.

Strengths and Weaknesses

How has the attempt to blend and balance national programming and local determination and support worked in soil conservation districts? Without question, the trend toward destruction of soil and water resources, which had reached serious proportions by the 1930's, has been reversed. Most farms and farm lands of the nation are within soil conservation districts, where scientific conservation practices have been made available to millions of farmers and ranchers owning and operating millions of acres of land. Much benefit has accrued from making acre-by-acre soil surveys, formulating and applying individual conservation farm plans, and maintaining the conservation system after the methods have been utilized. Although stating seven years later that the job was only about one-fifth completed, the chief of the Soil Conservation Service prophesied in 1945 that "In future years, when the districts have had more time to prove themselves, this enterprise undoubtedly will be regarded as one of the greatest accomplishments in the history of agriculture."[24]

Despite the progress in conservation, some major phases of the district system have not developed as anticipated and certainly cannot be viewed as unqualified successes. In the first place, one of the original reasons for fostering this new governmental unit has been almost completely unrealized, and a second remains substantially unfulfilled. The first was the need for compulsory land-use regulations to protect the well-being of the majority against a recalcitrant minority. A majority of the states passing soil conservation district legislation incorporated such authority in their laws, but an important number, including most of those acting since 1940, did not. Furthermore, a local approving referendum is always necessary to put land control into operation and only a handful of districts, most of them in Colorado, have taken the requisite affirmative action. The common stumbling blocks have been the requirement of a large majority and the restrictions on eligibility for voting. Advocacy by the Soil Conservation Service in written reports and through field technicians in favor of such regulations has had little apparent effect.[25] As a result, most districts exercise only voluntary or coöperative powers and make no use of mandatory authority even when it is available. A second major reason for creating soil conservation districts was the belief that their activities and needs did not conform to the boundaries of existing general units. District boundaries were to be determined by topographical factors, especially watersheds. This objective has not been ignored to the same extent as land-use authority, but nevertheless approximately one-half of the districts correspond exactly

---

[24] Hugh H. Bennett, "Soil Conservation among the 48 States," *State Government,* 18 (Oct., 1945), 174.

[25] *Land Use Regulation in Soil Conservation Districts,* U.S. Department of Agriculture, Soil Conservation Service (Washington: 1947). For information on the Colorado experience, see Stanley W. Voelker, *Land-Use Ordinances of Soil Conservation Districts in Colorado,* Agricultural Experiment Station Technical Bulletin 45 (Fort Collins: Colorado Agricultural and Mechanical College, 1952).

in area with single counties. Moreover, districts are increasingly being established on county lines.[26] Thus there have been serious shortcomings both in fulfilling a major functional purpose and in establishing the area of conservation activities.

Another departure from the aims of the movement has occurred in the composition of the district electorate. The standard act recommended establishing a broad basis of participation by granting the voting power in all district elections to both nonowner operators and resident landowners. Most of the states, bypassing this suggestion, have limited the voting privilege to landowners, at least in some district affairs. In a large majority of the states only landowners can cast ballots on the question of forming a district. In a substantial number only landowners can elect district officials. In addition, in most states permitting local adoption of land-use regulations, nonowner operators are disfranchised when the proposal appears as an election issue. Thus from the initiation of a district through the choice of elected officials and decisions about the extent of its activities, control is usually in the hands of a limited electoral group.

Key points in the evaluation of this effort to blend national programming and local determination are the role of the governing body members, the extent of participation by eligible persons, and the degree of local understanding of district government. The governing body members, usually called district supervisors, play only a small part in district affairs. Many of them have failed to assume their full policy and management responsibilities, either because they wanted to avoid the task or because field technicians dominated the scene. Supervisors often do little more than consult with conservation specialists and accept their recommendations. Participation in district elections is ordinarily at a low level. Many times, incumbent members are reëlected despite their lack of participation in district work, nominees are selected by professional conservation workers, and no opposing candidates appear on the election ballot. And finally, farmers and ranchers do not always

---

[26] Charles M. Hardin, *The Politics of Agriculture* (Glencoe: Free Press, 1952), p. 71. One of the points emphasized in the book is the competitiveness of the Extension Service and the Soil Conservation Service, both in the Department of Agriculture, in conservation activities. This study and the previously mentioned Parks volume discuss many of the deficiencies considered here.

understand district government. Many of them do not view districts as local governmental units endowed with authority to make local decisions, but rather as an activity of the national government through which people are told how to farm. This belief is strengthened by the greater acquaintance of local farmers and ranchers with the technicians of the Soil Conservation Service than with the members of the district governing body.

These weaknesses in lay governing board relations, popular participation, and public understanding are not unique to soil conservation districts, but this does not lessen their significance to a governmental unit designed to combine national policy with local initiative and support. The soil conservation district movement is yet young, but two of its closest observers differ as to its value. Professor Charles M. Hardin of the University of Chicago feels that neither the Soil Conservation Service nor soil conservation districts are adequate agencies if the various agricultural problems are to be handled as parts of a well-balanced program. However, Professor W. Robert Parks of Iowa State College concludes that the districts have provided a means for cross-fertilizing national and local experiences. Furthermore, they have shown great potentiality, he says, for developing a new working integration between national and local government and between the lay citizen and his government.[27]

DRAINAGE DISTRICTS

Drainage districts are extremely numerous and geographically widespread. Operating predominantly in rural areas, they outnumber both irrigation and soil conservation districts. There are approximately 2,200 of them, of varying importance and type, in thirty-two states. The services that drainage districts supply, therefore, vary from state to state and sometimes, as in Illinois and Nebraska, within the same state. Their most common purpose is to remove excess water from land already in farms and from swampland that can be made suitable for agricultural purposes. Such land improvement and reclamation are basic to adequate crop production, grazing, and soil fertility. Another purpose undertaken by drainage districts is to protect agricultural land from

---

[27] Hardin, op. cit., p. 103; Parks, op. cit., p. 224.

water overflow. The prevention of recurrent flooding differs substantially from draining away an overabundance of existing water.
A third purpose, handled mainly by drainage districts in western
states, is the removal of seepage and alkali from irrigated areas.
A separate district government may thus be created to remedy a
condition caused by another district, although some irrigation
units undertake both activities. Other drainage districts operate in
nonagricultural rural lands. As in certain sections of Missouri, they
eliminate water from mining locations. The diversity of functions
among drainage districts, which have in common only their concern over the problem of wet land, makes detailed analysis difficult.
The discussion therefore centers on broad characteristics and
trends.

Regional Concentrations and Growth

Drainage districts, embracing much of the land subject to, and
of the capital invested in, drainage operations, are of far greater
significance in some geographical regions than in others.[28] Their
importance also varies within the same region. In addition to these
districts, numerous other agencies undertake drainage, including
state, county, and township governments, and commercial, mutual,
and individual ownership projects. Furthermore, although the
problem of wet and potentially wet land is fairly common, the
greatest need and the largest response in the form of drainage
enterprises are found in the north central and lower Mississippi
Valley states. Drainage districts are important in Illinois, Kansas,
Missouri, Nebraska, and Wisconsin, but in the other seven north
central states county governments dominate drainage projects.
Among the lower Mississippi Valley states, drainage districts are
especially significant in Arkansas, Louisiana, and Mississippi. These
are the greatest regional concentrations, but districts are of scattered significance in twenty-four other states, most noticeably in

---

[28] The most general source of information about drainage districts is *U.S. Census
of Agriculture: 1950*, Vol. IV, *Drainage of Agricultural Lands*, U.S. Bureau of the
Census, Agriculture Division (Washington: 1952), which is the fourth in a series
undertaken at ten-year intervals since 1920. The data on districts must be used with
caution, since some organizations classified as drainage districts are not independent
governments. Also, there are divergencies between the numerical totals compiled
by the Agriculture Division of the Census Bureau and those tabulated by the Governments Division of the same bureau and used in this study.

North Carolina, Florida, and Texas, and in portions of the Rocky Mountain and Pacific Coast sections.

Drainage districts are among the oldest of special district governments. Originating in the early nineteenth century, they experienced their first major expansion in the closing two decades of the same century. Their growth continued until the outbreak of World War I, then tapered for a lengthy period including the depression of the 1930's, and revived in the 1940's. The various increases were not cumulative, however, for active districts that had fulfilled their immediate purpose could become inactive without formal dissolution, and others sprang up quickly in other areas. For example, from 1942 to 1952 many new drainage districts were formed and many existing ones become inoperative. The net effect was a slight increase in the number of districts in operation at the end of the period. In addition, in some states substantially less than one-half of the drainage districts organized over the years are currently functioning.

There are several reasons for the establishment of drainage districts. The problem became more and more of a governmental one as it became apparent that landowners who would benefit from a drainage project could not reach agreement, especially on the method of apportioning costs. A governmental mechanism was frequently necessary to provide enforcing and financing methods. The topographical factor, however, meant that the drainage area did not often coincide with the territorial limits of established governments. The difficulty became insurmountable when general units were legally or operationally unable to provide a function, either jointly or individually. The result was the development of a new type of government.

Many Variations

There is much variance in the size and operational nature of drainage districts. Some are intercounty and contain hundreds of square miles, but many are appreciably smaller than the natural drainage areas to be served. Some enabling laws impose a single-county limit, but territorial restrictions are usually self-imposed by the organizing petitioners. Numerous drainage districts are very small, including at times as little as a fraction of a square mile, and some

areas with a common topographical problem have so many districts
that the possibility of a comprehensive effort is greatly decreased.
The pattern in Arkansas, for example, indicates that many districts
were organized to include only consenting property owners instead
of to conform to topographical realities. As a result, water drained
from some of them was passed onto neighboring lands, where it
magnified the flood problem.[29] Drainage works range from open
ditches and tile drains to levees and dikes. Gravity flow is utilized
in some places and pumping in others. Many projects are simple
operations; others are complicated and expensive engineering
enterprises.

There is similar diversity in many other characteristics. This is
partly the result of assigning functions such as the removal of
excess water and the prevention of possible inundation to different
districts, all known as drainage units. The diversity, however, is
also the outcome of the enactment of separate optional laws to
provide exactly the same function in similar areas, a situation that
develops when interested groups appraise older district legislation
as unsuitable. Broad differences are readily apparent in the method
of initiating the formation of districts. Most commonly landowners
must give substantial support at the outset. Usually between one-
third and two-thirds of them, or of the total land, must be represented in the petition. Or the requirement may be a majority of the
landowners with a majority of the land. Nevertheless, in some instances as few as three to five landowners can start proceedings.
Irrespective of the proportion required, the possession of property
is rather consistently the requirement for participation in beginning the process.

There are, furthermore, marked differences regarding the agency
to receive the petition and the kind of action needed for establishment. The governing body of the county government and part of
the judiciary serve almost equally as recipients; their roles range
from checking the validity and adequacy of the signatures to
adjusting the proposed boundaries and other discretionary activities. In addition, the recipient usually decides whether the pro-

---

[29] Estal E. Sparlin, *Special Improvement District Finance in Arkansas*, Agricultural Experiment Station Bulletin No. 424 (Fayetteville: University of Arkansas
College of Agriculture, 1942), p. 32.

posal should be activated. Drainage districts in most states are therefore legally created through an ordinance, order, or decree issued by the county governing body or the court. Only occasionally is the question submitted to a referendum in the area. When it is, property owners are usually the exclusive voters, with the number of votes based on the size of their landholdings. Even less frequently a single official of a general government, such as a township clerk, makes the decision to form a district.

Wide variation is also noticeable in the selection and composition of district governing bodies. Election in the area is the most frequent method of selecting members, although again either the county government or the court may appoint them. Occasionally, as in gravity drainage districts in Louisiana, some of the board members are appointed by representatives of one level of government, and the rest by an official from another level. Boards almost uniformly have three members, though a few of them have five. The petitioners sometimes decide between the two alternatives. There is no comparable consistency in the length of terms, usually ranging from two to six years. Because there are commonly three members whose terms overlap, three-year terms are the most numerous, but they do not constitute a majority.

Drainage districts show substantial similarity in some financial aspects. Assessment in proportion to property benefits is the prevailing arrangement; only a few districts possess the authority to levy property taxes. Districts are also generally permitted to issue bonds and are restricted principally by maximum interest rates and maturity limits. Again, however, divergence is apparent in the bond-issuance procedure. Most often approval by the district electorate is necessary, but many times the decision rests solely with the governing body. When a popular vote is required, the necessary margin may be either a simple majority or an extraordinary one, with the former serving as the usual stipulation. After drainage districts are established, their most important intergovernmental contacts consist of advice and money grants. For example, numerous districts were financially assisted by the Reconstruction Finance Corporation during the depression of the 1930's, and some of those concerned with flood regulation have been aided by congressional legislation and by the United States Army Corps of Engineers. In general, however, drainage districts are subject to little or no supervision or control by other governments.

The diversity just considered in general terms is sometimes extensive in individual states. The situation prevailing in Illinois for many years provides a pertinent illustration. Two general drainage laws were passed in the late nineteenth century, the first in 1879 and the other in 1885. The original one, designed for use in bottom lands where periodic flood conditions were a major hazard, authorized drainage and levee districts. The second act, intended to eliminate excessive water in upland farm areas, contained provisions for the establishment of four types of drainage districts: one-township, union, special, and, under certain circumstances, independent subdistricts. The over-all result was that many of the details in the procedures for forming districts and in the methods of selecting governing bodies were different. Several years ago a firm of consulting engineers appraised the situation as one creating confusion and dissatisfaction, and stated with considerable moderation that previous efforts to modernize the laws had not been entirely successful.[30] Furthermore, the analysts were quick to point out that many persons and groups were hesitant to consolidate and simplify the legislation. Significantly, much of their reluctance and opposition stemmed from fear that revision of the laws might reopen matters already settled by court interpretation. The difficulty of unwinding illogical complexities is a lesson that cannot be learned too early in the legislative process, whatever the subject under consideration.

RURAL FIRE PROTECTION DISTRICTS: ILLINOIS

All except seven states permit local governments to undertake fire protection in rural areas, and the special district is the government most often designated. More than twice as many states grant the rural fire protection power to districts as to counties and townships combined. Furthermore, in fifteen states special districts are the only governments that can render this service. Most of the rural fire protection legislation, whether relating to districts, counties, or

---

[30] *Report on Flood Situation in Illinois*, Illinois Legislative Flood Investigating Commission (Springfield: 1947), pp. 5–6.

townships, has been enacted since 1920, and many of the district laws have been initially passed or revised since the 1930's.[31] The problem is a serious one in rural areas. Several thousand people are killed annually by fire in agricultural sections alone, and additional thousands are injured; farm property destruction totals almost $100 million. In some states, however, fire protection districts are more significant in urban fringes than in rural areas, although used in both.

Spectacular Recent Increase

Illinois provides one of the most significant examples of utilizing special districts for rural fire protection. The enabling law there grew out of the inadequacy of fire protection coöperatives, which existed mainly on donations. The need for adequate funds for equipment purchases and maintenance and for more equitable distribution of costs brought forth permissive legislation in 1927. By 1944 there were 100 fire protection districts in Illinois. The most rapid growth then took place. By 1950 the number had reached 300, and has continued to increase in subsequent years. About two-thirds of the Illinois fire protection districts are located in rural areas, often encompassing both rural communities and agricultural land.[32]

It is relatively simple to start the process of establishing a district. As few as 50 legal voters, or a majority if there are less than 100 eligible electors in the proposed district, sign a formation petition which is transmitted to the county judge. He may alter the tentative district limits after a public hearing, and then call an organization election. A majority vote is sufficient to create the district unless an incorporated place is to be within its territory, and then a majority must be obtained both inside and outside the village or city. Most of the fire protection districts in the rural areas of the state include a small incorporated community. Frequently the district idea is initiated by the incorporated rural com-

[31] John D. Rush, "State Legislation on Rural Fire Protection," in *Two Studies on Rural Fire Protection*, National Fire Protection Association (Boston: 1950), pp. 3–7; *Report*, President's Conference on Fire Prevention, Committee on Fire-Fighting Services (Washington: 1947), pp. 29–30.

[32] The most comprehensive written source of information is N. G. P. Krausz, *Organization and Legal Status of Fire Protection Districts in Illinois* (Urbana: University of Illinois College of Agriculture, 1950).

munity because it lacks a sufficiently broad tax base of its own and therefore favors the inclusion of farm lands within the proposed fire protection area. This is decidedly different from the experience in Nebraska, where fire districts are legally required to exclude incorporated localities from their jurisdiction. The Illinois districts have territorial flexibility since they do not have to follow county and township lines. They are found largely in the wealthier sections of the state, with very few functioning in the southern part where the tax base is low.

Selection and Powers of Trustees

As in numerous types of special districts in Illinois, the county judge is important to fire protection districts. He appoints the governing body, a board of three trustees, for staggered three-year terms, frequently accepting the recommendations of key people and groups within the district. Not more than one of the trustees may come from the incorporated rural community in the district unless it possesses more than half of the total population. Trustees must post bond, the amount and type of security being determined by the county judge. These governing board members are specifically prohibited from having a financial interest in contracts, property purchases, and other district business transactions. The direction and control of fire protection activities and personnel rest with them. They may annually levy taxes for purposes other than debt retirement in an amount slightly in excess of .1 per cent of the assessed property valuation. The average tax levy is somewhat more than one-half of the allowed maximum, and a substantial part of it is being used to pay for new equipment. The board may also incur indebtedness up to 5 per cent of the same valuation base.

Problems and Activities

The problems and activities of fire protection districts in Illinois rural areas that contain both small communities and agricultural lands reflect the distinctively rural nature of this governmental undertaking, and stand in marked contrast to those of a fire department of a medium-sized or large city. The typical district contains about 260 farms, each with an average of about five buildings, and about 240 village structures. More fires break out and fires cause more damage on farms than in rural villages within fire protection districts. The district usually operates from a single fire station situated in the village near the geographical center of the territory. Unless additional personnel and equipment are available at a sub-station, the area of the district, which may legally be any size within the state boundaries, is actually determined by certain re-quirements for obtaining fire insurance. No fire risk insured by pay-ments based on Class A or Class B ratings may be more than ten miles from fire headquarters, measured over roads capable of carrying fire equipment.

The area to be protected is nevertheless extensive. Most districts have between 50 and 100 square miles of territory to cover and between 100 and 200 miles of road to traverse, about one-fourth of them not paved, graveled, or oiled. Another frequent handicap is the absence of a prompt and effective means of reporting fires. Many farms lack telephones and even when telephones are present much time is lost because calls have to go through more than one exchange. In addition, very few districts have periodic inspections of farm buildings.

The personnel of the fire protection district is summoned for duty by a siren mounted at the firehouse or in another central loca-tion, or by direct telephone calls. Most of the ten to thirty fire fighters in a district are volunteers located in the village and sub-ject to call at any time from their place of business or residence. From seven to ten of them normally respond to a call, and for the time and risk involved they receive a nominal fee of $1 to $4 for each fire. The fire chief responsible for training the protective corps usually receives the same amount, sometimes augmented by a small annual payment.

Although some districts have three or four fire trucks, most of them have only one and have no separate water-supply truck. In many instances a single vehicle must be heavily loaded and must then proceed over roads of varying quality, the best of which may be in poor condition during several months of the year. Most dis-tricts depend on more than one water source, and some obtain an additional supply by installing cisterns, constructing ponds, or digging wells. Each district functions virtually independently of all other fire protection districts. Coöperative purchasing on costly equipment is almost unknown. Furthermore, residents want to keep a district as small as possible so that it will include only people and locations they know.

NOXIOUS WEED ERADICATION DISTRICTS: NEBRASKA

Unlike rural fire protection districts, which are found in many states, weed eradication districts are functioning in only a few, such as California, Utah, and Wyoming, and are extensively utilized only in Nebraska. They are therefore not numerically important among rural districts, but they do illustrate the use of the special district as an answer to an annoying land problem in a specific state. Furthermore, they have an automatic termination date, a feature that is unique among governmental units in the United States, and their activities reveal significant intergovernmental relations.

Landowner and State and County Government Action

In response to a serious problem, weed eradication districts have become extensive in Nebraska. In 1952 there were eighty-two of them, and others have since been formed. They are most numerous in the eastern half of the state but some also exist in the extreme western counties. As in many other kinds of rural districts, landownership rather than residence is a major qualification for participation in the creation and control of this type of district. In addition, the decisions of a state official, the director of the Department of Agriculture and Inspection, are vital to this governmental unit. The function of a district is to get rid of weeds that are noxious and therefore harmful or injurious to agricultural productivity. The enabling legislation was intended primarily to control or eradicate field bindweed, but several other kinds of noxious weeds are mentioned. Furthermore, the state director may designate other noxious weeds as coming within district jurisdiction. Thus, at the outset an official of the state government determines the scope of activity of weed eradication districts.

A small number of owners of adjacent land—twenty-five, or more than one-half of them if there are less than twenty-five—

initiates the formation process through petition.[33] The land proposed by the owners for inclusion in the district may be wholly outside or entirely within incorporated places, but it may not be partly outside and partly inside. The minimum area of a district containing unincorporated land is 1 square mile; that of a district composed of incorporated territory, 1 city block. Practically all Nebraska weed eradication districts are in rural areas where their limits may encompass parts of more than one county. After the petition is filed, the clerk of the county containing the entire proposed district or most of it notifies the state agricultural and inspection director. Again this official plays an important role. With such assistance as he desires from the agricultural college of the state university, he reports to the county board of supervisors or commissioners on the extent of infestation by noxious weeds within the proposed district, and recommends in a statement of reasons that the petition be granted or denied, in whole or in part. When the district is to contain unincorporated land, the county board holds a hearing, listens to evidence and objections, and considers the report of the state director. It may exclude grazing land from the district limits after determining that such land would not be benefited. Weed eradication districts are created by order of the county board and not by vote of the landowners or residents.

Major Types of Costs

Three to five supervisors—the actual number is decided at an organizational meeting—are elected as the governing board by the landowners and serve for staggered three-year terms. At a regular annual session, the landowners choose the supervisors and determine the assessments to be made to pay for the administrative costs anticipated by the elected governing body for the forthcoming year. However, in no instance may the amount be so limited as to obstruct the contemplated operations. In addition, the supervisors hold another meeting with landowners whose property is to be

---

[33] Since 1947, however, no local landowner initiation is necessary in unincorporated areas not a part of a weed eradication district and needing control of bindweed. Under such circumstances the state agricultural and inspection director may advise the county board about the necessity for a district, and the board may on its own initiative organize the governmental unit after a public hearing.

assessed for weed control and eradication. At the end of the meeting, the supervisors enact their control plans and assessment charges, sometimes after making modifications. All land in the district is subject to the administrative costs approved by the landowners at the regular meeting. On the other hand, only lands receiving eradication and control benefits, according to the individual farm plan developed and passed by the supervisors, pay service assessments. A landowner may eradicate and control noxious weeds according to the plan and with the approval of the supervisors. The assessment against his land is then credited with an amount equal to the cost of comparable work. If the landowner does not carry out the plan, the supervisors employ outside help for the purpose.

The state agricultural and inspection director has general supervision over all districts. He makes surveys and inspections and consults with the district supervisors. He recommends what he considers the best plan of control, and the members of the governing board may accept or reject his suggestions. Two methods of dissolving weed eradication districts are available. The first, similar to that used by various other types of special districts throughout the country, calls for petition by a majority of the landowners and affirmative action by the governing body of the county. The second is extraordinary among governments. It provides for the automatic dissolution of a weed eradication district twenty-five years after the beginning of the organizing action.

CHAPTER SIX

School
Districts

Independent school districts are dominant among governmental units directly providing public education below the collegiate level. They are the only governmental units performing this type of educational function in twenty-eight states, and the most prevalent in ten others. In six of the remaining states school district governments are in operation, but are less numerous than school systems administered by state, county, city, or New England town governments. They are nonexistent in four states where the schools are the responsibility of general local governments.

Substantial financial autonomy is a major factor differentiating school districts from other public school systems administered either by other governments or their agencies. For example, independent school districts need not submit their budgets to a general local government for possible modification, or have their locally determined financing supplied by another government. They are also distinguishable from the intermediate units, existing in most states, which supervise and furnish services to the independent school districts. Operating at a level between two or more school systems and state departments of education, intermediate units are not separate governmental units. Finally, independent school districts are distinguished from attendance units or districts, each of which is composed of the geographical area and the population served by a single school. Thus, the term is not used to identify a governmental unit, although at times the area of an attendance unit coincides with that of an independent school district. In larger school districts there may be as many as fifty attendance units. Therefore, the school districts that are the focus of this chapter

TABLE 4

POSITION OF SCHOOL DISTRICTS IN PUBLIC SCHOOL EDUCATION IN INDIVIDUAL STATES

School Districts Exclusively

Alabama	Illinois	Missouri	Oregon
Arkansas	Indiana	Montana	South Carolina
California	Iowa	Nebraska	South Dakota
Colorado	Kansas	Nevada	Utah
Florida	Kentucky	New Mexico	Washington
Georgia	Louisiana	North Dakota	West Virginia
Idaho	Michigan	Ohio	Wyoming

School Districts Predominantly

Arizona	New York
Minnesota	Oklahoma
Mississippi	Pennsylvania
New Hampshire	Texas
New Jersey	Wisconsin

School Districts in Minority

Connecticut	Massachusetts
Delaware	Tennessee
Maine	Vermont

School Districts Nonexistent

Maryland	Rhode Island
North Carolina	Virginia

SOURCE: The classification is largely derived from data in *Governments in the United States in 1952*, U.S. Bureau of the Census, Governments Division, State and Local Government Special Studies No. 31 (Washington: 1953), p. 18. The term "school district" as used here and throughout this book means an independent school district governmental unit, usually concerned with education below the collegiate level. The groupings are based on comparative numbers of school districts and other public school systems. The many state board school units in Delaware, treated as one school system by the Census Bureau because of their dependence on a single government (the state government), were counted separately by localities in the preparation of the table to make them more comparable with the material from other states. Activation of the first several regional school districts in Massachusetts since the Census Bureau determination necessitated reclassification of the state from the "school districts nonexistent" category to its present category. Similarly, 1955 legislation in Nevada shifted the state from the "school districts predominantly" category to the "school districts exclusively" category.

are not engaged primarily in supervising or providing service aid to other school operations nor are they merely centers of school attendance. They are independent governmental units possessing appreciable financial autonomy and functioning as direct suppliers of education.[1]

---

[1] See table 4 for the classification of specific states according to their comparative use of school districts, based on determinations made by the Census Bureau after a comprehensive enumeration of governmental units in the United States. Numerous school agencies, some bearing the word "district" in their official designation and many with independently elected boards, are judged by the Census Bureau not to be independent school districts but subordinate or dependent parts of another gov-

IMPORTANCE AND TITLES

Significant in Numerous Ways

School districts are highly important in many ways. Their functional significance is unquestionable; what they do is judged by many people and groups to be the most important of all governmental undertakings. These special district governments undoubtedly perform the most crucial local function that is usually beyond the jurisdiction of general local units. Collectively they serve a large area. Among governments territorially smaller than states, school districts together cover more land than any other kind of unit except counties and soil conservation districts. In area, therefore, they outrank cities, townships, towns, and all other types of special districts except those devoted to soil conservation. Furthermore, the extent of their activity is great, considered either alone or on a comparative basis. This is demonstrated by number of employees, annual expenditures, and total outstanding debt.[2] School districts had 1,455,000 employees, or almost 20 per cent of the public employees in the United States, in October, 1955. They ranked second in number of employees, with approximately three-fifths as many as the national government and more than any other class of state or local governments. They spent $8,192 million in the fiscal year ending in 1955, an amount equivalent to 7.5 cents of each public dollar expended. Standing fourth in this category, they followed national, state, and city governments in that order. Their outstanding debt at the end of the same fiscal year was $7,259 million, or approximately 2 cents of every dollar owed by all governments in the country. Again they were fourth, trailing national, city, and state governments in that order. The relative amount of school district debt is low, principally because the

---

ernment, because this government is empowered to alter their budgets or provide the locally determined finances. This classification should not be confused with one frequently utilized by educational specialists and known as basic administrative units. The latter is concerned with areas, rather than governmental units, of school administration. For example, under this grouping Florida and West Virginia are identified as county-unit states since the territory of the county is the school administrative area. However, governmental units exclusively providing public education below the collegiate level in both states are school districts, and these states are listed as school district states under the classification used in this study.

[2] For comparative information on the various governments, see table 1, p. 4.

national government alone owes almost nine-tenths of all governmental debt. Nevertheless, the total school district debt is surpris-
ingly low in view of recent school construction, part of which is
financed by locally derived funds.

A final reason for the importance of school districts should be
mentioned here. For many years they have been undergoing major
reorganization, involving numerous mergers of existing units. The
general results are a considerable decrease in number and a substantial increase in average size, changes which no type of general
government nor any principal type of nonschool special district is
experiencing. The trend is of such large-scale importance to school
districts—with possibly major implications for many other kinds
of governments—that it is given extended consideration later in
this chapter. Even if the development were not so significant, its
rarity would tempt the research investigator. During the history
of the United States, governments have tended to increase rather
than to decrease in number. The opportunity to analyze a type
that is decreasing is therefore unusual and impressive.

An Array of Official Titles

School districts function under an extremely wide variety of official names, some of which indicate the different levels of education provided. If numbered and lettered classifications are counted
as only one title in each state where they are used, eighty-four
legal designations exist throughout the United States. This is exclusive of specially created school districts, such as those in Chicago, Milwaukee, and Fargo, North Dakota. There is no need to
present a complete catalogue of official names, for examples from
several states will sufficiently indicate their diversity. The words
"school district" generally appear as the final part of each title, but
they are omitted here to avoid unnecessary repetition. Excluding
the Chicago School District, Illinois has ten types: common, community consolidated, community high, community unit, consolidated, consolidated high, high, nonhigh, township high, and
special charter. Minnesota has seven types: associated, common,
consolidated, county, independent, joint, and ten-or-more township. California has still more types: city elementary, regular elementary, union elementary, joint elementary, joint union elemen-

tary, city high, union high, joint union high, county high, unified, and junior college. The most frequent title, utilized in eleven states, is common school district. Others, used in six to ten states, are city, consolidated, county, joint, and county high. In seven states school districts are categorized in certain classes, identified by numbers or letters and based on such criteria as population of the city in which located, student enrollment, or assessed property valuation of the district.

Although school districts are not always readily understandable by their titles, they may indicate one or more of their major characteristics. The designation may identify the level of education provided, such as elementary, secondary, or collegiate (usually junior college), or a combination of two or three of them. It may show a merger of previously separate school districts. It may indicate that the district overlaps a general local government, such as a city or a county, or another type of school district. It may show that the district is within a single county or township, or that it embraces parts or all of more than one county or township. Several illustrations from California reflect specific use of labeling for these purposes. Many of the California school districts contain the words "elementary" or "high" in their names, and thus are classified as providing one of the two principal levels of education. The word "unified" also identifies the educational scope; it means that both elementary and secondary schools, and sometimes junior colleges, are provided. The five types of elementary districts in themselves clearly show the other three general characteristics. A city district embraces the territory of a charter city and a regular district is any one other than a city district. A union school government represents a merger of at least two regular districts. A joint unit is intercounty and a joint union operation is both intercounty and includes two or more previously independent regular districts.

AREA AND ORGANIZATIONAL FEATURES

Area Complexities

There is much divergence in the area characteristics of school districts. Many of them are approximately or exactly coterminous with a general local government, usually a city or a county and less frequently a township or a New England town. In Florida, Nevada, and West Virginia each school district covers an entire county; in many large cities the limits of school districts parallel those of the city government. In a number of states, including Alabama, Georgia, Kentucky, Louisiana, and Utah, some school districts coincide exactly or approximately with a general local unit. This happens when the territory of a school district embraces all of a county except some or all of the cities, which must or may have school districts territorially coextensive with their limits. A somewhat similar arrangement exists in Indiana, where each township and each city are separate school units. Under other conditions, a city school district may have almost the same area as a particular city. At times a school unit must consist of two or more general governments, such as cities or New England towns.

On the other hand, many school districts do not resemble any general local government in area. This is most noticeable among many rural school districts, each of which covers only a small amount of territory. Sometimes the area of a general local unit or of one type of school district is a factor in determining the area of another school district. Some districts must precisely overlap or be included within the boundaries of another kind of school unit. Others must include the entire areas of two or more different types. The requirement that the area of a school district exactly or nearly parallel that of a general local unit in itself broadens the territorial range of school districts because of the wide dissimilarities in the boundaries of counties, cities, townships, and New England towns. The frequent lack of such a stipulation enables many school districts to mark out extremely small areas; the option has been extensively used. The result is wide variance in the areas of school districts, which extend from a few to more than 5,000 square miles.[3] The national average is about 18 square miles, substantially more than the average for city governments but less than one-fiftieth of the average for county governments. The size and nature of the area are important factors in deciding how many individuals shall be served by a school district and what financial resources shall be

[3] *Your School District*, National Commission on School District Reorganization (Washington: National Education Association, 1948), p. 15.

available to pay for the services rendered. Thus enrollments and financing ability also cover a broad range.

Directors and Administrators

A school district is almost always governed by a group, most frequently known as the board of education or the board of school trustees and chosen by direct election of the local voters. Occasionally, however, nonelective methods are utilized. Appointing authorities include the grand jury, the other school boards in the area, the governor, the district judge, the governing body of the county, the mayor, the city council, the mayor and the city council, and the councils of the cities within the district. In some places the county superintendent serves as an ex officio board member. School boards usually have from three to seven members, elected for terms of three to seven years at separate school elections. In the township school district in Indiana a single trustee is elected. Nationally the membership range is from one to twenty-one with an average of five.

The school governing body, functioning within the legal framework of state constitutional and legislative provisions, has ultimate responsibility for and considerable discretion in the affairs of the district. Fundamentally it is responsible for the scope, intensity, and quality of the educational program. It employs and dismisses teachers, often subject in the latter duty to tenure safeguards. It hires and discharges nonteaching personnel. It prepares and adopts an annual budget and determines the local school tax rate. It issues bonds, usually after having submitted the proposal to the voters. It chooses building sites and authorizes construction plans, normally in conformity with state requirements. These functions are illustrative rather than all-inclusive, for, in the words of a New England school board member, "The legal powers given to school boards include authority to make all reasonable rules and regulations for the government and management of the schools, for the discipline of pupils and teachers, and for the admission and even exclusion of children for sufficient legal cause."[4] School board

[4] George T. Contalonis, "Some Powers and Duties of School Boards," *American School Board Journal*, 129 (Oct., 1954), 28.

management decisions are ordinarily final and, unless authority is abused, the courts do not review their actions.

A sample survey of the composition of school boards released in 1954 indicates that their membership comes predominantly from occupational groups classified as proprietors, managers, and professionals. Members usually are men, have children in public school, and possess income and formal educational training substantially above average. They spend the equivalent of about one full day a month on board duties.[5] To aid the boards in fulfilling their official obligations and responsibilities, a superintendent of schools is often selected to serve as chief executive officer; in larger districts he has a sizable staff. Starting in 1837 in Buffalo and Louisville, this administrative position has grown from minor importance to major significance. Accountable to the board for many phases of educational administration, the superintendent also serves as its chief policy advisor and frequently makes recommendations. Many of the early superintendents were selected by the school board from its own membership, but the position has been increasingly professionalized in the twentieth century. Larger districts now often make a new appointment only after a nation-wide canvass. A continuing problem is the high turnover of superintendents. In six recent years, for example, more than one-fifth of those in twelve Midwestern states were new in their jobs each school year. The tenure protection for teachers is not applicable to superintendents but many of them sign contracts of one to four years' duration. A school superintendent frequently receives the highest governmental salary in the locality.[6]

INTERGOVERNMENTAL RELATIONS AND FINANCING

Local and Nonlocal Finances

Like all governments, school districts operate in the midst of intergovernmental relations. The importance of these relationships is well illustrated by the methods of financing district services. Less

[5] Robert H. Brown, "The Composition of School Boards," *American School Board Journal*, 129 (Aug., 1954), 23–24. See also "Status and Practice of Boards of Education," *National Education Association Research Bulletin*, 24 (Apr., 1946), 48–72.

[6] Information on the tenure of superintendents in the twelve states is contained in Francis S. Chase and Robert E. Sweitzer, "Midwestern Superintendents Swiftly Come and Swiftly Go," *Nation's Schools*, 51 (Mar., 1953), 55–58.

than three-fifths of all revenue obtained by school districts is derived from their own sources which consist very largely of local property taxes. In obtaining more than two-fifths of their money from other governments, principally states, school districts outrank all other classes of governments in the proportion of funds derived from external sources and in the total amount of such revenue.[7] For a long time, local property tax collections, hampered by low assessment levels, tax rate limits, and growing tax exemptions, have not kept pace with state revenue resources available for school support. Since the 1930's, therefore, school financing has tended toward increased use of state-collected funds and a correspondingly decreased reliance on local revenues. The development is continuing. The amount of money paid for school costs by state governments more than doubled in the five-year period ending in 1952-1953. Concurrently, state governments have increasingly utilized general fund appropriations for schools instead of earmarked revenues, a practice regarded as partly responsible for the substantial increase in school revenues during the postwar years.[8]

The shift to greater state support has been largely a shift from reliance on property taxes to dependence on other taxes, such as those on income and sales. School aid has become a very large item in many state budgets, varying from one-fourth to as much as two-fifths of total appropriations from the general fund. The aid takes various forms. Most common are flat grants paid without regard to the relative financial ability of districts. More recently, grants on an equity basis, which vary inversely with a selected standard of local fiscal ability, supplement flat grants in most states. The equity principle is extended to include minimum foundation aid programs, based on a uniform effort by all school districts and varying inversely with their ability to finance a state-prescribed level of minimum expenditure.

In comparison with state governments, the national government has contributed little money to school districts, and most of its aid programs are of recent origin. The expansion of federal assist-

[7] *Summary of Governmental Finances in 1955*, U.S. Bureau of the Census, Governments Division (Washington: 1956), p. 20.
[8] "State Legislation Affecting School Revenues, 1949–1953," *National Education Association Research Bulletin*, 32 (Oct., 1954), 152–153.

ance to schools is a widely discussed issue. Recently Congress considered, but did not pass, legislation involving loans, grants, and a reserve fund to aid in overcoming financial obstacles to the building of schools. So far direct national aid has been limited largely to partial support of the school lunch program, encouragement of vocational education, and construction, maintenance, and operation of school facilities in certain localities. These communities are ones especially burdened by the loss of taxable resources due to national ownership of property, or by increased enrollments resulting from greater federal activity in such matters as military installations and industrial plant contracts.

Additional Contacts with Other Governments

Significant intergovernmental relations concerning school districts are not confined to financial matters or to the contacts that grow out of financial aid programs. Again the most important relationships are with state governments, which exercise supervision, guidance, and leadership in many areas of activity. State supervision is channeled mainly through a state board of education (existing in most school district states) and a state superintendent or commissioner of schools who directs a state department of education (existing in all school district states). Among other functions they certify or license persons to teach, formulate broad educational policies, recommend supervisory and instructional methods through visits and conferences, decide upon regulations governing the apportionment of state funds for school purposes, prescribe or advise certain courses of study, provide school library service, supervise school building plans, and accredit schools. In many states school districts must file financial reports and evaluations, frequently on prescribed forms, with a state education or fiscal officer. More broadly stated, the states plan for educational improvement, conduct research on many different topics, appraise conditions and needs, explain school needs to the legislature and the public, provide leadership for the profession, and take the responsibility for regulation and administration.[9]

[9] *State-Local Relations*, Council of State Governments (Chicago: 1946), pp. 15–16; Arthur B. Moehlman, *School Administration* (2d ed.; Boston: Houghton Mifflin, 1951), p. 331.

An intermediate agency usually functions in the public education field between the state government and the school districts.
Most often headed by the county superintendent of schools, an
official of the county government, it assists the educational agencies and personnel of the state government in carrying out their
responsibilities, and performs other functions stipulated in state
laws. Among other duties, this intermediate agency conducts
school elections; carries out the formation, alteration, or merger of
school districts, ordinarily after local voter approval; distributes
state funds; maintains different records and accounts; and performs specified functions in connection with the licensing and
selection of teachers. It also administers school transportation,
supervises instruction, enforces compulsory attendance requirements, counsels on curriculum development and other matters,
furnishes specialized services such as audio-visual aids, and collects
data and makes reports to the state department of education.[10] In
summary, this intermediate agency is active in record-keeping,
supervision, enforcement, and leadership.

The nonfinancial relations of the national government with
school districts are more limited than those on the state and intermediate levels, and are carried on principally by the Office of
Education in the Department of Health, Education, and Welfare.
(The educational activities of other national departments and
agencies are seldom directly concerned with school districts.)
Besides administering certain federal aid programs, the Office of
Education conducts research and interviews, including the issuance of a biennial survey of education; sponsors conferences of
interest to school district personnel; and allocates surplus property
to state agencies for distribution to educational and other operations. Most of its contacts with school districts, except for its own
requests for statistical and educational program information, are
initiated by the individual district, and take the form of corre-
spondence rather than field visitation.

The interrelationships of school districts and other governments
are widespread. Various funds are allotted, often on a conditional
basis, by different governments, and the numerous state laws re-

[10] The enumeration of intermediate level responsibilities is based largely on *Your
School District*, pp. 64–65.

lating to school districts are frequently compiled into lengthy education codes. Despite advice, supervision, and regulation at various levels, school districts are relatively free from domination and control by other governments. State educational laws establish a minimum state-wide program and within its framework delegate broad discretionary authority to school districts. The state, intermediate, and national levels play an essentially advisory role, and mainly furnish encouragement for local initiative.[11] Although the freedom and independence of school districts are commonly acknowledged, words of admonition can be heard. For example, the assistant to the governor of Washington recently warned that a unit receiving the bulk of its support from another government "will find that the substance of its authority is eroding, that its control over policies is gradually shifting to the parent unit. . . . It is naive to expect that more than a mere facade of local autonomy can be preserved by a local body which subsists largely on subsidies from a central government."[12]

INDEPENDENT GOVERNMENTAL STATUS

The Origins

The independent status of many educational operations below the collegiate level is a condition of long standing. Before the Revolutionary War, however, a different governmental arrangement existed in New England. There the towns averaged 20 to 40 square miles in size, but only a small portion of the area was inhabited because colonists were required to live within one-half mile of the meetinghouse; subcollegiate education was provided by the town government. By the end of the seventeenth century, as the dominance of the religious motive declined, new settlements had arisen within the towns. Since they were located at substantial distances from meetinghouses and schoolhouses, the residence laws were either ignored or repealed.

---

[11] Harlan L. Hagman, *The Administration of American Public Schools* (New York: McGraw-Hill, 1951); Van Miller and Willard B. Spalding, *The Public Administration of American Schools* (Yonkers: World Book, 1952), p. 122; Moehlman, *op. cit.*, p. 26.

[12] Roger W. Freeman, "State Aid and the Support of Our Public Schools," *State Government*, 26 (Oct., 1953), 240. Mr. Freeman also strongly challenges the contention that high state support means high standards and dependence on local support results in low standards.

By 1725 most of the population had dispersed throughout the towns and formed new settlements which were fairly isolated. Their residents began to insist upon and acquire local rights. As a result, towns were divided into religious parishes, and road, militia, and tax assessment and collection subareas. Demands regarding education were also made. The first concession was to establish the moving town school, held in each parish and at the center of town for a specified number of weeks during the year. Next came the return to each parish of money locally collected for school purposes, along with permission to maintain a local school or school district, as it came to be termed. The final authorization of local powers necessary to establish independent school districts—election of school board members, levying of taxes, and selection of a teacher—soon followed. These powers were granted in Connecticut in 1766 and in Massachusetts in 1789. Thus was established the independent school district system which eventually featured the one-room school for students of all ages and served as the model for school organization in many parts of the United States.[13]

The General Controversy

School districts are used principally in the United States, although England earlier used them, and Canada and several other countries still do. In many sections of the United States, however, school districts are more deeply rooted than anywhere else.[14] And yet there is substantial disagreement as to whether their functions should be separate from general local governments or a dependent part of their operations. Much of the controversy, however, is waged on the level of generalized intellectual argumentation, and not by local governmental and school officials about the possibility of converting particular school systems to a different status.

The proponents of school independence from general local governments support their position in several ways. Education is so

[13] There was a somewhat similar development in many public higher educational systems, which frequently possess at least semiautonomy. In later years the pioneer school districts of New England largely shifted back to the dependent category. The historical development of school districts is traced in Ellwood P. Cubberley, *Public Education in the United States: A Study and Interpretation of American Educational History* (rev. ed.; New York: Houghton Mifflin, 1934), pp. 68–73.

[14] William Anderson, *The Units of Government in the United States* (rev. ed.; Chicago: Public Administration Service, 1949), p. 34.

important, so basic to other governmental functions, and so deserving of substantial financial support that it should be kept free of
the uncertainties of local politics. It is a state and not a local government function. Since it must stay as close as possible to the
people, it should not be removed one step from their control by
being made dependent upon another government. The opponents
counter by arguing that although they agree on the importance of
education, a single and comprehensive government should judge
the relative merits of the financial needs of the various public
services in the community. They deny that governmentally independent schools are subject to less political pressure than dependent schools, and that education is any more a state function than
many other local services, particularly public health, law enforcement, and public welfare. They believe, furthermore, that significant economies result from the integration of services, such as
purchasing, which are common to all functions. And finally, they
contend that a separate school government with independently
elected board members lengthens the ballot and makes the task of
maintaining accountability more difficult for the citizenry. These
opposing arguments have long been in use, and are frequently
restated or slightly recast. Over the years each has had little noticeable effect in convincing the opposing nonbelievers, although there
is no shortage of supporters publicly arguing the two viewpoints.[15]

A Coöperative Research Study

In view of the contrasting positions regarding the proper governmental status of schools, the findings of two analyses which considered these different opinions are worth noting. The first is a
unique and important book, the composite work of a university

---

[15] For early examples, refer to the articles by Lester Dix and Joseph McGoldrick
on "Should the Public Schools Be Independent of City Hall?" in *American City*, 43
(July, 1930), 118–120, and those by W. A. Bailey and Charles H. Judd under the
title "Should School Boards Be Abolished?" in *Public Management*, 16 (Jan., 1934),
17–19. For recent illustrations, see August W. Eberle, "Fiscal Independence: An
Answer to Political Scientists," *American School Board Journal*, 127 (Dec., 1953),
23–24, and Joseph F. Clark, "School Business Is Municipal Business," *Phi Delta
Kappan*, 32 (Nov., 1950), 102–104. For a sharp exchange of views, see an article by
Ernest A. Engelbert, a political science professor, "Educational Administration and
Responsible Government," *School and Society*, 75 (Jan. 19, 1952), 33–36, the
countering replies by an education professor and a city superintendent of schools
(*ibid.*, Apr. 5, 1952), and the rebuttal by the original author (*ibid.*, Aug. 2, 1952).

professor of education and a university professor of political science, whose professional groups are generally on opposite sides of the question. The authors studied independent and dependent school systems, undertaking field work in thirty-three cities of 50,000 or more population. Of their findings, apparently agreed upon by both scholars, several are pertinent to the controversy.[16] Two of them are that schools are not subject to greater political pressure when dependent, and that under such an arrangement both school and municipal services have been improved much more often than either has been impaired. These facts, it is pointed out, are not generally recognized because of the widespread impression that political machines greatly influence municipal administration. In addition, state aid to schools is not unlike state aid to other community services, and does not necessitate a separate government to control school expenditures. Then, too, differing court opinions as to whether education is a state or a local function clearly demonstrate that a state legislature may select whatever organization it wishes for the control of local school systems and may even vary its choice in different localities. The concept of education as a state function therefore does not imply that local school systems must be independent of a general local government.

The authors then give several arguments in support of dependent schools. They note that governmental simplification, with less service duplication and cost, would result, and that general local government, including the professional interest and spirit of its employees, would probably improve. And finally, responsibility for proper school administration could be more easily placed upon a single authority. The integration of schools and general local government, the writers believe, will arouse less opposition as city governments improve their efficiency and responsibility. They feel that council-manager government is evidence that this improvement is occurring, for in cities operating under this form public respect for city government is as great as, or greater than, that for school district government.

[16] Nelson B. Henry and Jerome G. Kerwin, *Schools and City Government: A Study of Municipal Relationships in Cities of 50,000 or More Population* (Chicago: University of Chicago Press, 1938), chap. 8.

A Series of Evaluations

The second analysis is found in a comprehensive administrative survey of the city of New York and its taxation and finance problems. The members of the Mayor's Committee on Management Survey, the group responsible for the studies, were appointed in January, 1950, and the summary volumes containing their recommendations were submitted in March of 1953. The committee spent more than $2 million, using most of the money to finance a large number of management survey contracts. Public education, one of the matters intensively surveyed, was called "the City's biggest responsibility, measured in terms of the fundamental importance of the task, the size of the budget, and the number of employees."[17] All aspects of the educational organizations and activities of New York City, except curriculum content and instructional methods, were studied. George D. Strayer, professor emeritus of education at Teachers' College of Columbia University, and Louis E. Yavner, a New York attorney, did most of the consulting work in this field. In addition to such phases of public education as housing, grade organization, plant utilization, operational functions, personnel problems, headquarters activities, decentralization, and administration of the municipal colleges, their report analyzed the subjects of fiscal and administrative independence. A separate study on the advisability of fiscal independence for public education in New York City was prepared by Robert M. Haig, professor of political economy, and Carl S. Shoup, professor of economics, both of Columbia University.

The basic question considered by both survey teams, and ultimately by the committee members themselves, was whether the local system of free public elementary and secondary education should be continued under the fiscal control of the city government or should be reorganized under a new school district completely independent of the city government. The consulting groups took entirely opposite views. In making recommendations on the fiscal relationships of the school board, the Strayer-Yavner report was prefaced by the conditioning comment that "The fallacy of

[17] *Modern Management for the City of New York,* New York Mayor's Committee on Management Survey (New York: 1953), I, 244.

such control [by the city government] is seen when it is considered that budgetary requests of the Board of Education are based on opinions of professionals trained in the field of education, then vetoed and manipulated by a staff [of the city government] untrained in educational concepts."[18] The report then went on to suggest a number of comprehensive changes. The school board should continue to have nine members, but they should be elected on a city-wide basis at off-year special school elections for twelve-year terms instead of being appointed, as at present, by the mayor from the various boroughs for seven years. In addition, a permanent nominating committee, composed of sixteen members designated by civic organizations, should select one person for each vacancy on the board. "Individuals and groups within the City," Strayer and Yavner advised, "should be given the opportunity to propose to this nominating committee, but the entire responsibility for every name listed should rest upon the nominating committee as a whole."[19] There should therefore be a separate school district which, through the independently elected board of education, should have responsibility for and control of school fiscal affairs. To realize such responsibility and control, the school district should be vested with four powers. It should operate under a tax limit separate from that of the city government, assume the burden of its own delinquent taxes, adopt an annual budget not reviewable by city officials, and levy its own taxes and issue its own tax bills.

Professors Haig and Shoup surveyed the subject of fiscal independence largely by analyzing recommendations in the Strayer-Yavner report. At the outset they noted that city officials responsible for school finances are elected every four years, whereas a majority of the proposed elected board of education could not be removed for eight years. The wisdom of independent taxing power and independent borrowing authority can be seriously questioned on the grounds of the allocation of government resources among competing services, according to these analysts, who doubted that any particular service should be exempt from direct comparison with other services. The fact that education is a state function, which is true of most city functions, does not mean that the city

[18] *Ibid.*, II, 482.
[19] *Ibid.*, II, 484.

government has overstepped the limits of its authority in school affairs. They concluded with the over-all judgment that "Fiscal independence of education is not strictly essential to the achievement of many benefits that could be hoped for from its adoption . . . , and it does have an unfavorable effect on the fundamental task of allocating scarce governmental resources among the many services a local government must perform. It would worsen, not improve, the mechanism for arriving at decisions that accurately reflect community desires and soundly apportion limited resources."[20]

In making its recommendations about public education below the collegiate level, the mayor's committee was thus confronted with conflicting suggestions from two teams of experts regarding an elected board of education and fiscal independence. On these matters, the committee members supported the Haig-Shoup findings and advocated continuance of the appointed school board and of fiscal dependence. They rejected the contention that an elected school board would be more responsible, more representative, and more democratic. Favoring the short ballot and the placing of responsibility for the quality of appointees upon the mayor, the group decided that prominent citizens would not subject themselves to the effort, cost, and possible abuse involved in campaigning for election to the school board. The committee also turned down the Strayer-Yavner recommendation for a nominating committee because of opposition to legally endowing private organizations with the power to nominate for public office. Instead, the committee urged the establishment of an advisory group charged with drawing up a list of available, high-caliber candidates for the mayor.

The committee was equally forceful in its decision against fiscal independence. It concluded that such autonomy would result in financial competition between education and other city governmental functions, and would make the city's fiscal structure even more complex. One central fiscal authority is needed, it stated, to weigh the comparative needs of different services and to bring them into reasonable balance. Before reaching these two basic decisions against an independently elected school board and

---

[20] Ibid., II, 496.

against financial independence, the committee held an all-day conference attended by delegates from fifty-seven groups interested in public education. The conference discussion confirmed the stand taken by the committee.

Little Current Change

The findings in the Henry-Kerwin book and the final recommendations of the New York administrative survey committee should not be interpreted as reflecting a general trend toward converting school operations to dependence on general local units. Professors Henry and Kerwin emphasized that there was more pronounced popular opposition to absorption of the schools than there had been to the earlier integration of other functions with general local governments. Many prominent citizens interested in good government, they pointed out, derided and vigorously opposed such suggestions. The authors concluded that they could discover no concerted movement for abolishing school districts and transferring their activities to other governments.[21] Their observations, made in the late 1930's, have equal applicability today. For the most part, independent school operations are remaining independent and dependent ones are remaining dependent. Although there is currently little shifting in either direction, the *status quo* should not necessarily be regarded as inalterable for all future time.

REORGANIZATION TRENDS AND METHODS

A widespread change has occurred in many school district governments, especially in recent years, but it has not involved their conversion to dependence on general local units. The development has stressed the merging of independent school districts rather than abandonment of independence. School districts apparently grew steadily in number from their original establishment in Connecticut in 1766 down into the twentieth century. Districts containing one-teacher schools within walking distance of all attending students were prevalent in the early years of the present century, when the number of separate school districts exceeded 100,000.

Downward trends in some states and further increases in others

---

[21] Henry and Kerwin, *op. cit.*, p. 3.

became noticeable in the 1920's, and since the early 1930's the nationwide total has steadily lessened. The decrease has been particularly rapid since 1947, with the total declining by about one-fifth in each of the three-year periods 1947–1950 and 1950–1953. The decline since the 1930's, spectacular in itself, is especially impressive because there was concurrently little or no reduction in other governmental units, except townships. Figures and percentages will emphasize the extensiveness of the movement. In 1932, the total of approximately 127,000 school districts constituted 72 per cent of all governmental units. In the next ten years more than 18,000 districts were eliminated, a decrease of more than 14 per cent. The number in 1942 was 108,579, which represented 70 per cent of the governments in the United States. The decline accelerated, and by 1952 there were 67,346 school districts, less than 60 per cent of all governments in the United States. The number of school districts therefore declined by almost 40 per cent in the latter ten-year period, and by almost 50 per cent in twenty years. Further decreases have occurred subsequently; in 1954, for example, the total was 59,631.[22]

The large-scale reduction in the number of school districts, known as the school district reorganization, merger, or consolidation movement or as the redistricting development, is chiefly the result of widespread unification of separate school districts. The terms "consolidation" and "merger" are used synonomously by the courts in describing these efforts, although exclusive use of the latter has been urged. The terms are used interchangeably in this book, principally because the word "consolidation" is more commonly utilized to identify the unification of other special district and general governments. This trend should not be confused with another development, the consolidation of attendance areas

---

[22] The nonexistence of comprehensive data for pre-1930 years, and the somewhat different bases of definition used by the sources, make the numbers of school districts only reasonably rather than fully comparable. Totals for the different years are derived from William Anderson, *The Units of Government in the United States* (Chicago: Public Administration Service, 1934), p. 1; the U.S. Bureau of the Census counts of governments in 1942 and 1952; Howard A. Dawson, "A Blueprint for Progress," *Phi Delta Kappan*, 36 (Oct., 1954), 55; and *School Districts in the United States in 1954*, U.S. Bureau of the Census, Governments Division, State and Local Government Special Studies No. 40 (Washington: 1955), p. 1.

within a school district, nor with internal reorganization of school activities and operations.[23]

Geographically Widespread

The school district consolidation movement has been geographically extensive, but there have been broadly different results in different states. The dissimilarity of the results is largely traceable to differences in the degree of interest in reorganization and to the nature of the reorganization efforts. In the period since the 1930's, when area reorganization has been most pronounced, there have been many school district mergers in a number of states, especially in Arkansas, Illinois, Kansas, Missouri, New York, Oklahoma, and Texas. Each of these states decreased its number of school districts by more than 2,000 between 1942 and 1952. In Kansas and Missouri, however, large numbers of school districts still remain. These two states, plus Iowa, Minnesota, Michigan, Nebraska, South Dakota, and Wisconsin, together have more than one-half of the school districts in the United States; each of them possesses from approximately 3,000 to slightly more than 6,000 districts. Furthermore, these eight states have more than four-fifths of the nation's nonoperating school districts (which legally exist but send students to other schools), and more than one-half of the one-teacher schools in the United States. In addition, they have more than one-half of all school districts operating only elementary schools.[24] Some of these states, especially Iowa, Nebraska, and South Dakota, and others such as Indiana, North Dakota, and Pennsylvania, have had only negligible school district decreases during the most recent quarter of a century, when the country was experiencing the most thoroughgoing consolidation movement in its history.

Early Accomplishments

School district mergers have occurred intermittently over many years, although this chapter is concerned primarily with the most

---

[23] There has been a great deal of criticism and appraisal of curriculum content, teaching methods, and other school matters in recent years. See, for example, C. Winfield Scott and Clyde M. Hill, *Public Education Under Criticism* (New York: Prentice-Hall, 1954).

[24] Dawson, *op. cit.*, p. 56.

comprehensive phase starting in the 1930's, and particularly with
the greatly accelerated stage beginning in the 1940's. Massachusetts, which in the late eighteenth century had pioneered with
Connecticut in the establishment of the small school district, assumed the leadership in school district merger in the following
century. As early as 1837, Horace Mann, the prominent New
England educator, called the common school district the worst
development that had ever happened in public education in the
United States. In 1869 the state legislature of Massachusetts authorized the consolidation of school districts, and thirteen years
later the districts were replaced by the towns which they had
originally supplanted. The consolidation idea spread westward
in the closing decade of the nineteenth century, and in 1892 Ohio
enacted a permissive redistricting law.

By the early years of the new century twenty states had authorized mergers. By 1915 Kentucky and Utah had accomplished
substantial area reorganizations. The United States Bureau (later
Office) of Education strongly supported the development. In 1918
and 1922, for example, it emphasized in studies of South Dakota
and Oklahoma that the small school district system was an almost
insurmountable obstacle to the school organization required by a
modern rural population. There were major accomplishments in
North Carolina during the 1920's, in Arkansas during the 1920's
and the 1930's, and in New York from the 1920's down to the
present.[25] Although much of the legislation was designed for use in
rural areas, one of the foremost nationwide achievements was the
abandonment of the system whereby a city had as many school
districts as schools. By 1930 the merger of all adjacent city school
districts operating in the same general area into a single unit had
taken place in most populous cities. Despite many enabling laws
and much discussion and study, the pre-1930 results of school
district reorganization were meager and inadequate.[26] Significantly,

[25] The merger movement in Arkansas extended from 1928 through 1932 and
started up again in 1948. It has been fairly continuous in New York since 1925,
when financial incentives were added to the reorganization law of 1914.

[26] Fred Engelhardt, William H. Zeigel, Jr., William M. Proctor, and Scovel S.
Mayo, *District Organization and Secondary Education*, Bulletin 1932, No. 17 (Washington: U.S. Department of the Interior, 1933), p. 42.

too, the states with the greatest need for change—those with an overabundance of small school districts—usually tallied the fewest accomplishments. In the closing years of the 1920's the district system was still so disintegrated that in a number of states school board members outnumbered teachers.

Increased Recent Concern

Serious interest and activity in area reorganization began in the 1930's, intensified in the 1940's, and have continued with great vigor into the present. At the beginning of this period substantial economic and social changes, which had been under way for some time, strongly indicated that the prevailing system of many small school districts was outmoded and inadequate for educational needs. The impact of these forces, some of them rooted in such technological developments as the industrial and agricultural revolutions, was especially evident in rural areas where most of the small school units existed. The decrease in the number of school children in farming areas, and the drift of people from farms to rural nonfarm and city locations, were important factors underlining the urgent necessity of reshaping school district organization. There were other reminders of the need for consolidation, such as the shift of workers living in farm areas from agricultural to nonagricultural pursuits, the gradual breaking down of personal and group isolation, and the decline of some rural locales and the rise of others because of paved roads and automobiles.

The economic depression that developed in this environmental setting served as an immediate impetus for reform. The financial stringency of the 1930's focused attention on the quality of the area organization responsible for spending money for educational services. Since the 1930's the proportion of school support derived from state governments has spiraled upward appreciably. The greater financial contributions have given state governments and particularly state legislatures more concern about the adequacy of school districts receiving the assistance, and have helped to sustain and expand interest in the adjustment of school district areas. Increased concern about reorganization has also been fostered by various professional organizations. They advocate larger school districts in order to provide better education in terms of such matters as curricula, instruction, and equipment.

Two Procedural Patterns

The accomplishments of recent years have been based primarily on state legislation rather than on constitutional provisions. Since the start of the most extensive development, states containing school districts have passed varying numbers and kinds of relevant laws, and have attained broadly differing degrees of success. Especially noticeable has been the diversity of approaches to the problem, extending from grants of permission for local action to various types of comprehensive programs. Many states have used more than one type of program, some for particular situations and others applicable generally as optional possibilities, or have shifted from one type to another. Despite the variety of techniques employed, several clearly identifiable patterns have emerged.

An approach that was prevalent before 1930 is still the only one utilized in some states. Appropriate legislation provides the legal means for merging school districts through local initiation and approval, often by majority consent in each affected district. States that have not supplemented such legislation with at least one additional method of area reorganization, in the period since 1930, have merely a legal device, not a real consolidation program. The effects of minor adjustments in these laws have been insignificant. As in earlier years, progress under these circumstances, in New Jersey, for example, has been very slow.

States that follow the second general pattern grant broad discretionary consolidation authority to existing county boards of education or to specially constituted county school reorganization committees. Some of these boards and committees can order a consolidation without a local popular vote. Others must submit their decisions to the voters only when specified conditions exist. This procedure also antedates the period of the most recent merger movement. It has been in operation in Texas since 1927, when county boards were authorized under certain circumstances to reorganize school district areas.[27] Kansas has made spectacular use

---

[27] States mentioned in these discussions have been selected because of their importance as examples or to demonstrate the use of a procedure in different sections of the country.

of this approach. Under a 1945 law county school reorganization committees were established in each county and empowered to issue merger orders. No popular consent was necessary unless the consolidation pertained to a city district of more than 15,000 population, nor was there any state review of proposals. The courts were the sole recourse for grievances. Although the legislation was declared unconstitutional two years later, a law validating the actions of the committees up to a particular date and decreasing the number of school districts by more than 2,500, was judicially upheld. Subsequently, the 1950 session of the Mississippi Legislature granted similar latitude to county boards of education to consolidate school districts. Since 1951 even wider discretion has been vested in county boards of education by the South Carolina Legislature. Each board, consisting of the county superintendent of schools and six appointees of the governor, is empowered to merge, either in whole or in part, any school districts in the county. This can be done whenever the board decides that it will be beneficial. Extensive activity under this legislation has sharply reduced the number of school districts. In other states the discretionary power granted to a county agency was restricted by direct local control. Under a 1947 Ohio act, a county board of education was empowered to effect reorganizations unless a majority of the voters of the affected area filed a legal objection. Invoking local judgment on the decisions of the county group is easier in Wisconsin. In this state the legislation of 1947, which conferred upon county school committees the right to require consolidations, was amended two years later to provide for a popular vote upon referral by the committee or petition by 10 per cent of the electorate.

In general, the number of mergers achieved through this second approach has been substantial. In individual states, however, the results have varied because of such factors as the vitality of the county organization, the intensity of public opposition when a regular channel for its expression is present, and the existence and usefulness of optional reorganization methods.

Compulsory Legislative Approach

The third and most drastic approach is mandatory state action, generally in the form of state legislation. With antecedents going back to such pre-1930 activities as those in Utah and North Carolina, the method has several variations. The most thoroughgoing is complete county-wide consolidation, adopted by West Virginia in 1933, by Florida in 1947, and by Nevada in 1955. In the first two states the law stipulates that each county may have only one school district, an independent government coterminous with the county limits. Thus West Virginia has fifty-five counties and fifty-five school districts, and Florida has sixty-seven counties and sixty-seven school districts. The legislation in Nevada contains a comparable provision and further permits a school district to contain an area larger than a single county upon agreement of the school trustees of the counties involved.

The second variation, similar but less comprehensive, is modified consolidation on a county basis. It requires the merger of most school districts in a county but excludes those located in particular city areas. Georgia exemplifies this method in its new constitution of 1945, which calls for the consolidation of all school districts, except certain city districts, in each county.

The third type of mandatory method, which is very unlike the other two, affects districts that are not meeting certain conditions or standards. Usually it applies to school units which do not operate schools or do not contain a specified number of students. Texas has abolished districts that have not maintained schools for two consecutive years and has added their territory to that of adjacent units. In Arkansas a law effective in 1949 consolidated all school districts in each county serving less than 350 students. Since 1941 New Mexico has had legislation granting the state education board authority to dissolve elementary school districts with fewer than twelve students in average daily attendance, and high school districts with fewer than thirty students in average daily attendance. The board is further authorized to consolidate such units with adjacent districts. Some states at times apply both standards. In 1947 the Oklahoma Legislature eliminated all school districts which were not directly providing education or had an average daily attendance of less than thirteen, and conferred power upon the state education board to join their territory to other districts. Various states frequently merge a nonoperating district or one enrolling less than a stated minimum number of students with an active district. The elimination of such a district, however, does not legally have to be coupled with consolidation. In either event, the area reorganization contributes to the numerical reduction of school districts.

Each variation of this third approach to consolidation is highly effective by reason of its mandatory nature. By way of illustration, West Virginia, Kentucky, and Arkansas have each merged hundreds of school districts by using a different variation. Condemned as unfair by some people and groups because local consent and participation are absent, the process is defended by its advocates as a justifiable exercise of state governmental power over school districts.

Comprehensive, Permissive Method

The fourth and final approach is comprehensive-planned-permissive reorganization, consisting of participation at county and state levels followed by local decision. It is the most recent development in school district area adjustment. The method was first employed in 1941 in Washington, which adapted and augmented some features of the earlier experience of Arkansas, New York, and North Carolina. In a relatively short time, the plan has been widely adopted. Prominent examples are California, Illinois, and Iowa in 1945; Idaho, Minnesota, North Dakota, Pennsylvania, and Wyoming in 1947; Missouri in 1948; Colorado and Nebraska in 1949; and South Dakota in 1951.[28]

The process involves three important elements, a county organization, a state agency or official, and a local election. The county organization is generally responsible for making a thorough study of the status of school districts in the county and formulating proposals for beneficial area reorganization. Usually the performance of assigned duties is legally required of the agency, although in some states—Minnesota and Nebraska are examples—it is optional and determined within each county. The responsibilities at the county level are allotted to one of two bodies. Occasionally it

---

[28] The New York program, which has been in operation for many years, includes state leadership and a local vote but does not include county level activity. Wisconsin has an arrangement somewhat similiar to this fourth approach, but a local vote is taken only at the request of the county committee or upon local petition and not as a regular part of the procedure.

is the county board of education, but more commonly it is a specially created county survey committee, frequently consisting of nine persons. The committee members are selected either individually, one by each district governing board, or collectively at a joint meeting of all the school boards. Laymen serve on most county committees and sometimes constitute a majority of the membership. Usually the county superintendent of schools plays a prominent role in the affairs of the county board or committee. Whether or not he is an ex officio member of the organization, he generally offers counsel and suggestions. The county superintendent is also customarily responsible for calling the election after the obligations of the state agency or official have been discharged.

Efforts at the state level usually supply leadership, guidance, and review of activities carried on by the county agency. They are centered in a specially constituted commission or in the state education board or superintendent. One trend, noticeable in Washington and California, for instance, is for the special state committee to be abolished after two to four years and its duties reassigned to a regular state education board or official. The special group usually includes six to nine members selected by either the governor or the state education board or superintendent. Generally some of the members are laymen. A fundamental objective of state participation, regardless of the type of agency, is to supply a perspective that is more than local in outlook. Frequently the role of the state superintendent of education in the state group is comparable to that of the county superintendent in the county group. The state agency or official responsible for the reorganization process furnishes advice to the county board or committee, often with the assistance of professional staff members, especially in technical matters. Occasionally the state agency is limited to rendering advice, but more often it approves or rejects plans submitted by the county agency.

The ultimate test of proposals made by the county board or committee is an election in the affected area, the third important element of this reorganization approach. Public hearings may be legally required at various stages in the formulation of the proposition, and sometimes an intelligent, long-range program of disseminating information is undertaken. Advocates are likely to intensify the campaign for education and support as the day of the balloting draws near. Although advice and assistance frequently come from the state level, local leadership is a basic requisite for obtaining an affirmative voter response.

Equally if not more basic is the nature of the voting procedure. The voting is always restricted to the area involved in the proposal, and a majority is always required, but the method of counting the ballots differs among states. Three different voting methods are utilized. They are, in order of increasing difficulty, an over-all majority in the area of the proposed district, separate majorities in the rural territory and the urban territory of the contemplated district (with varying definitions of rural and urban applied), and separate majorities in each of the districts directly affected by the reorganization plan. California is the only state to provide, in amendments to its original legislation, a less difficult voting method. An over-all majority is sufficient in California unless a single district in the proposed area casts a majority of the votes. In that event, separate majorities must be obtained in this district and in the combined area of all remaining districts. Between 1945 and 1947 Iowa had the most difficult requirement of any state ever to operate under this reorganization procedure—60 per cent majorities in each district affected by the proposal. In 1947, though retaining the same method, the state reduced the proportion of affirmative votes needed to one-half. On the other hand, Colorado, North Dakota, and Washington all shifted to the strictest alternative of separate majorities in each unit. Each of the three voting methods continues to be preferred by some of the states adopting the reorganization method after the first group of acceptances from 1941 through 1945. Since 1947 at least one state has made each alternative part of its original legislation.

The defeat of a consolidation proposal is not considered a permanently irrevocable decision. The same proposition or a somewhat similar one may legally be resubmitted, sometimes within a stated minimum period of sixty days to two years, or within a specified period of years. Often, however, there is no time limit and the decision to resubmit rests with the county board or committee. Numerous proposals have succeeded on second attempts, and in some states the percentage of adoptions is higher on second than first efforts. Occasionally, as in the Idaho legislation of the late 1940's, there is a deadline for voter acceptance of reorganization; after the time limit has elapsed, consolidation can be effected without a popular vote. The comprehensive-planned-permissive pattern has been acclaimed by many individuals and groups and endorsed by the influential National Education Association.[29] However, the approach has been effective in only a limited number of states, and in some, like Iowa and Nebraska, it has had an extremely poor record of accomplishment. The many reasons for the broad variance in the success of this process are discussed in the following section.

REORGANIZATION OBSTACLES AND AIDS

Both comprehensive and piecemeal school district reorganization plans requiring local consent have many features that serve either as impediments or as aids. As will be seen, these elements are often interrelated, sometimes as cause and effect. Although the emphasis here is upon obstacles, it should be kept in mind that their rectification usually converts them into accelerating factors.

Procedure and Performance Hurdles

Some of the handicaps emanate from the procedural steps included in or omitted from the various reorganization laws. They are therefore legislatively imposed hurdles of commission or omission. A particularly damaging one is the requirement of separate voter approval in each district that is to be part of the proposed school unit. The stipulation has been an effective block in Iowa and Pennsylvania, and in every other state that has employed it. Its effect is especially noticeable in Colorado, Washington, and other states where its replacement of the over-all majority rule has directly contributed to the decline in school district reorganizations and, frequently, to the entrenchment of inefficient districts. A somewhat similar technique hinders the initiation of a proposal or even of a survey. The law either specifies an extraordinary number or proportion of the voters or, as in Michigan, limits the initiatory right to the school board members within the county.

---

[29] A Model School District Reorganization Bill, National Education Association, Research Division and Division of Rural Service (Washington: 1948).

Unlike voting and initiating encumbrances, some barriers to reorganization are not purposely included in the legal procedure, but result from ambiguities in wording. Under such circumstances recommendations are made from time to time for clarification of sections pertaining to the post-reorganization disposition of assets and liabilities, including bonded indebtedness, and to the bonding capacities of new districts. The defect does not always relate to the more technical matters. For example, during the early experience with Minnesota's comprehensive permissive law of 1947, a state advisory committee decried the lack of clarity in the provisions on voting. It recommended that the law be made clear on a number of fundamental points, including establishment of precincts, appointment of election judges, types of ballots, and canvassing of votes as well as eligibility for voting.[30] At times the legal procedure is detrimental to reorganization attempts as the result of deliberate or unconscious omissions rather than difficult or ambiguous requirements. Illustrations are the absence of a time limit for the submission of plans and the lack of permission to submit a second proposition if the voters defeat the first one.

Other difficulties arise through improper regard for the intent and meaning of the basic reorganization law. One example is markedly prominent. Most of the recent comprehensive legislation spells out important professional and lay roles for participation at both the state and local levels. It is implicit in these circumstances that considerable leadership shall be exerted. In a number of instances, however, the guidance at both levels has been inadequate. Substantial differences in accomplishments in two states with comparable laws are sometimes traceable to wide disparities in state and local leadership, just as variations within one state are attributable to the caliber and extent of local direction. Insufficient vision by a state educational commission or department, dilatoriness by county superintendents, and unnecessary appeasement and compromise by local survey committees have each served as a potent impairing force in particular situations. Another hindrance sometimes occurs when optional laws are in effect in a state. There can then be too many laws on the same subject. What has usually

---

[30] For additional details, see *Report*, Minnesota State Advisory Committee on School Reorganization (St. Paul: 1949).

happened is that comprehensive legislation was passed subsequent to a milder act. In some states where the earlier actions were not repealed, or at least temporarily suspended, when the new program was adopted, numerous localities continue to bypass the new policy and make use of the older but less adequate law. All of the obstructions in this major group originate in legal procedures for reorganization and their implementation.

Counterpolicies and Financial Difficulties

Another principal category of obstacles arises from the failure of state governments to relate school district reorganization to other pertinent phases of government, particularly state financial aid to districts. Together with the content and the implementation of legal provisions relating to merger, state fiscal policies are generally the most powerful factors influencing area reorganization. Three such policies are detrimental to the redistricting purpose. The first is assistance to inferior districts which should be merged. Studies in the late 1940's in Indiana, New Mexico, South Carolina, Texas, and other states all noted that state financial assistance was bolstering the continuance of inadequate school units. Some state financial plans place a premium on the maintenance of established school districts. At times, therefore, state financing is utilized to solidify existing districts and to provide those supplying insufficient education programs with enough help to stave off needed reorganization. State aid can be damaging not only before but also after mergers. In Georgia, for example, the granting of additional funds to a certain type of district in 1951 caused some areas to withdraw from larger units and establish separate districts.

A second anticonsolidation fiscal measure is the imposition of financial penalties of various kinds on districts that reorganize. In their early years under the comprehensive plan, California districts that reorganized suffered reduction or complete elimination of state funds designed to establish a minimum educational program and to furnish supervisory services by the county superintendent of schools. Furthermore, the state distributed aid for transportation costs to the disadvantage of rural districts that consolidated. The prospect of losing annual state support ranging from a few hundred dollars to $250,000 naturally served as a strong deterrent to a number of school units interested in the possibilities of merging.

The third state fiscal policy which detracts from consolidation is the failure to provide financial incentives to encourage such procedures. The reasoning behind the provision of such inducements is that the state government should help to pay certain costs resulting from district mergers. Obviously the state's failure to guarantee such aid makes school districts wary of consolidation because they will have to bear the large costs alone. Financial incentives devoted to a variety of purposes, including textbooks and other instructional materials, teachers' salaries, and equipment, have been recommended by a number of individuals and groups, but those most commonly in use pertain to pupil transportation costs and building construction expenditures. Since 1925 New York has, through aid for both of these needs, fostered school district reorganizations. More recently Washington enacted a school building aid act which has been a powerful stimulant to area change. Some state legislatures became so convinced of the effectiveness of such inducements that they increased them after original adoption. Thus, Missouri enlarged its school construction fund in the early 1950's.

Using state financial assistance to nourish the continuance of highly inferior districts and to penalize reorganized school units, and avoiding its use to stimulate consolidation, suggest that these important parts of state policy conflict and work at cross-purposes with state reorganization programs. Some policies therefore negate rather than enhance or complement area adjustment plans. The result can be an undermining of the merger movement.

There are further financial problems, other than those just considered under state aid, which make up a large class of obstacles. Two of the most basic difficulties are apparent in the reactions to proposed mergers of wealthy and poor districts. The objection of the former is that their taxes will increase without compensating gains in the educational program. The antagonism of the latter is founded in the belief that extending the educational standards of the wealthier district to the prospective consolidated unit will raise their taxes. It is difficult to refute these arguments so long as the principal portion of district financing is derived from local property levies. Supplementation of conscientious local financing efforts with state funds that guarantee a certain intensity and quality of educational performance is the approach most often advanced as a remedy to this kind of opposition.

The disposition of assets and liabilities of separate districts that will be merged through reorganization also serves as a financial stumbling block. By way of illustration, a district possessing a small amount of debt is frequently reluctant to join with one having a much larger obligation when the law calls for the assumption of the total debt by the newly established district. The proper distribution of debt is a delicate matter and merger laws do not agree on a solution. Some of the laws specify that each merging district retain its own obligations, others require that the new district assume all indebtedness, and still others propose a method of debt distribution as part of the redistricting plan submitted to the electorate. There are similar difficulties when the problem of district assets enters into a merger proposal.

Misconceptions and Localism

Another group of factors obstructing district reorganization involves misconceptions about or inadequate comprehension of merger efforts. Sometimes people simply do not understand the characteristics and objectives of consolidation propositions, or the effects of previous ones. They are fearful and suspicious of the outcome of consolidation. Misunderstandings about the difference between school districts and attendance areas frequently lead to the conclusion that a reorganized district will mean one big school. Actually this decision is usually left to the local board of education, and consolidated school districts often operate more than one school. Frequently erroneous beliefs focus on the transportation of students. Whether or not based on the false conviction about one big school, many of the fallacies concern the length of travel time on buses. Other difficulties grow out of the feeling that buses and roads are unsafe. These misconceptions are often symptomatic of the previously mentioned insufficiency of state and local professional and citizen leadership. Unfortunately, studies and proposals are not always accompanied by adequate dissemination of facts. In certain instances the thorough explanations needed to allay acute transportation worries have not been forthcoming.

Although reorganization advocates sometimes study and discuss the merger idea too long, at other times they try to move too quickly without giving proper attention to an informational program. Education of the public about the consolidation of school districts must be patient and painstaking.

Extreme localism is a serious stumbling block and is often interrelated with other impediments, including lack of understanding. The existence of strong sentimental attachments is not unexpected since many school districts, especially in rural areas, originated through the combined action of a small number of families. Furthermore, it is difficult to argue effectively about the educational advantages of merger in the face of certain local attitudes. Many people of provincial outlook come to favor school district reorganization in principle, but want it utilized in other areas instead of their own. In more than isolated instances localism so pervades the thinking of survey groups that they reach contradictory conclusions: the present system of small districts is inferior but no corrective steps should be taken locally. The small school district is often a hub of rivalry and pride. At times communities in separate districts that would be merged suspect the moral standards of each other. Such mutual suspicions, sometimes fanned by clergymen with strict denominational viewpoints, are difficult to eradicate. One of the most frequent expressions of deeply embedded localism is fear of the loss of control. This fear is sometimes overpowering. In one instance area change was rejected as early as the discussion stage because of the supposed danger of concentrating responsibility for a reorganized district of approximately 100 students in a single board of education. Abdicating local control is sometimes an issue only when school district consolidation is proposed. This is strange indeed, because a number of districts that operate no schools transport students to other districts, and their residents have no control to abdicate.

Self-Interest, Reaction, and Inactivity

An unusual degree of localism is often difficult to distinguish from another reorganization obstruction, the selfish interests of individuals and groups. Arguments seemingly derived from extreme localism can be used for concealment of real motives. This is not always so, but neither is it extraordinary. Selfishness emanates from many sources and can have a formidable impact if several types are concurrently operating in a particular situation. Some teachers and school administrators who are insecure or incompetent resist change for fear of losing their jobs. Some elected county school superintendents oppose mergers openly or surreptitiously on the assumption that a positive role will endanger their reëlection chances. Some members of district school boards, realizing that they may possibly not be elected to the governing group of the new district, object because they feel that reorganization can reduce their prestige and influence in the local area. Some people and firms argue negatively because they believe that consolidation will be detrimental to their trade with the school district or business growing out of the location of the school, and therefore diminish their profits. Some nonresident property owners, fearing that taxes will be increased and that merger will result in no direct gain to them, attempt to influence the opinions and actions of local inhabitants. Although the actual reasons behind the antagonistic attitudes are not revealed, all of these kinds of opposition are self-centered and unconcerned with young people and their educational opportunities.

Still another handicap which sometimes materializes is unfavorable reaction to earlier mergers, generally those occurring two decades or more ago. How often this is a real reason rather than simply a professed one is virtually impossible to decide, but it has been brought forward in several states. The handicap appeared in Montana in recent years because of the judgment that some mergers in the 1920's were inadequate, and in Kansas in the mid-1940's because of unfavorable reactions to large consolidations of a quarter-century before which involved considerable expenditures for new buildings and extensive transportation costs. If reorganization is considered a continuing problem, this argument against it is important, for the nature and success of the merger actions of today can accelerate or impede those of tomorrow. A final obstacle is feared by all reformers whether they are concerned with area changes in school districts or alterations in other types of governments. It is inertia. A formidable hurdle in any circumstance, it is particularly difficult to overcome when encased in blind adoration of the *status quo*.

POST-REORGANIZATION ASPECTS

Positive Effects and Results

Adequate school organization is fundamentally so important that the extensive merger movement under way for a number of years has guaranteed the materialization of profound effects and results. Generally identified as the most crucial element in public school administration, the proper area size of districts is directly related to many other major aspects, including curriculum, instruction, guidance, and financing. Changes in district areas therefore affect numerous phases of school programs. The principal general objectives of reorganization are to furnish a broader educational program, create a more efficient unit of education capable of supplying better service for the money expended, and widen the base of educational financial support. Many studies substantially agree on the characteristics of satisfactory districts. There is general concurrence that a district should be able to provide an educational program employing a minimum of forty teachers from kindergarten through the twelfth grade (and preferably through the fourteenth year) for a minimum of 1,200 students ranging from six to eighteen years of age. If the school district is smaller, per-student cost for a comparable educational offering, it has been concluded, is relatively greater. Furthermore, another finding declares that the more students a district possesses up to approximately 10,000, the broader the program it can present at reasonable cost.[31]

The full effects of the area reorganization trend are impossible to appraise because many of the changes have been recent. The total impact may not be known for many years. However, the area merger development has been moving in the direction of the accepted standard of providing more efficient per-unit expenditures and broader educational opportunities. Here are some of the major results of the substantial reduction in the number of school districts

[31] Dawson, *op. cit.*, p. 59.

and of the resultant appreciable increase in the average area size of districts in the period 1947–1953.[32] The number of one-teacher schools decreased by more than 26,000. Districts employing nine or fewer teachers dropped by more than 37,000. Those limiting their offering to the elementary level were reduced by almost 22,000. Districts operating only secondary schools declined by approximately 100. Furthermore, a study published in the closing year of this period, which related to more than 500 districts reorganized largely within the preceding six years, indicates a number of ways in which the post-reorganization educational program has been broadened.[33] Almost three-fourths of the districts offering secondary level work added one or more courses, most often in industrial arts, homemaking, or music. Two-thirds of the reorganized districts added one or more courses to their elementary school programs, most frequently music or art. A significant number inaugurated other curriculum or school program services, such as psychological and standardized achievement testing, and visual aids. Almost one-half launched at least one or usually more curriculum-development and in-service education projects after reorganization. And finally, almost nine-tenths of the districts created through mergers have teaching staffs with a higher level of college preparation, a change substantially affecting the quality of the educational offering.

Reorganization is not only progressing toward lower per-unit costs and broadened school programs but also toward a wider base of financial support for education. Gross local tax variations formerly present among small districts have been equalized in the enlarged area. Also, nonoperating districts have been abolished and their territory attached to functioning units, and their residents have thus been forced to contribute to school support. Many of the districts providing no educational service have been serving as refuges for people and groups wanting to evade or keep down financial contributions to schools. In the 1947–1953 period, approximately 2,800 such districts were eliminated. There are other major results of this widespread merger movement, occurring

---

[32] Howard A. Dawson and William J. Ellena, "School District Reorganization," *School Executive*, 73 (July, 1954), 39–42.

[33] C. O. Fitzwater, *Educational Change in Reorganized School Districts*, U.S. Department of Health, Education, and Welfare, Office of Education, Bulletin 1953, No. 4 (Washington: 1953), pp. 34–43, 47–48.

mainly in rural areas and bringing about larger school districts and frequently larger schools or attendance areas. One is the effort to create reorganized districts that coincide with the natural community area within which people obtain their basic services and satisfy their principal interests. Another is the expanding significance and the strengthening of the intermediate units or levels which assist and supplement local school districts. These numerous lines of development demonstrate that the movement is varied and far from superficial in its effects and results.

Continuing and Emerging Problems

Like many reforms, the school district reorganization movement has brought on new problems before completely solving the original ones. Basically, many of the area changes do not meet widely accepted standards, and an adequate level of attainment has not been reached in most states. Conditions existing in 1953 clearly reveal these shortcomings. There were in excess of 11,000 nonoperating, dormant school districts, constituting more than one-sixth of the total number of school units. Hundreds of them still legally existed in some states. The size of most school districts continued to be relatively small. Approximately one-third of those operating had nine or fewer teachers, and only about one-twentieth met the widely advocated goal of forty or more. Almost 49,000 one-teacher schools were still functioning, despite the elimination of many of them since the 1930's. The sharpest decline had occurred in the least rural states and in those with larger districts. The use of separate districts for elementary and secondary levels of instruction persisted. Only one in every four active districts provided education from kindergarten through the twelfth grade. These conditions indicate that the result of merging two or more inefficient districts has often been a new district which can more easily afford its inadequacy.[34] In addition, there has at times been unintelligent combining of the entire territory of a few districts, instead of comprehensive recasting of the area boundaries of more districts on a sounder basis.

Another original, persistent problem is that of reorganization itself. There is insufficient realization that school district organiza-

---

[34] Dawson and Ellena, *op. cit.*, pp. 39–42; Kenneth E. McIntyre, "The Progress and Problems of Redistricting," *American School Board Journal*, 128 (Mar., 1954), 38–40.

tion must receive continuing attention. Newly arising conditions and changing needs call for readjustment of district areas. As in numerous reform movements, the arousing of more than temporary public interest and concern is difficult. However, this fleeting attention is sometimes prompted by the weak or temporary nature of state legislation and the attitudes of state and local educational leaders. The adequacy of district areas constitutes a recurrent problem of today and a potential difficulty of tomorrow.

Some problems, such as the community school district and the intermediate level of educational service, are of increasing significance. The conformity of school district boundaries to the limits of natural sociological areas has been an objective of the merger movement in most states. But such attainments have been limited in number, partly because of the difficulties of formulating an adequate concept of a natural community and of distinguishing the elements involved in delimiting such areas. There has been confusion over terms such as community, neighborhood, and trading area, which sometimes have been loosely drawn rallying points for campaign support rather than carefully formulated determinations. In addition, the necessity for a strong, expanded intermediate level has become more evident in many states, as numerous reorganized districts have demonstrated the need for assistance and supplementation of their activities. Nevertheless, its importance is not fully recognized, and operating officials and academicians have not yet reached agreement about its organization and functions, although recent progress toward these goals is noticeable. There are other emerging problems which might most aptly be described as areas richly deserving research exploration. Several analysts, after engaging in a symposium several years ago, warned that adequate knowledge was nonexistent on many of the problems and issues growing out of reorganization. More recently, a sociologist stressed that the merger movement had created problems of physical plant, finance, and educational programs, as well as the very crucial issue of community adjustment to a major institutional change.[35]

[35] "A Symposium on Needed Research in District Reorganization," *Phi Delta Kappan*, 32 (Apr., 1951), 356–359; Roy C. Buck, "School District Reorganization: Some Considerations for Sociological Research," *Journal of Educational Sociology*, 28 (Sept., 1954), 25–29.

The effects of attacking the many major problems that are parts
of area reorganization may not be fully comprehended for some
time. There has been much improvement, but it should not be
overestimated. The initial difficulties were numerous, and most of
them have been only partly surmounted. The original problems
continue to exist although reduced in intensity, and meanwhile
new or more critical ones have appeared. Very few areas have
agitated for a return to the premerger arrangement. Furthermore,
a healthy and encouraging atmosphere prevails because original
objectives, emerging developments, and varying effects are receiving attention. The present balance sheet seems to appraise the
large-scale reform undertaking as largely beneficial.

NEBRASKA: SLOW REORGANIZATION PROGRESS

Nebraska has approximately 6,000 school districts, the largest number in any state; Minnesota, in second place, has about 1,100 less.
Nebraska's school districts, almost as numerous as they were in
1890, together have more governing board members than teachers.
With the number of districts doubling between 1880 and 1890, the
multiplication of small school districts was a natural development
in a predominantly rural state where families were large and transportation was poor. New social and economic conditions soon
appeared, and in the early years of the twentieth century the state
superintendent of public instruction several times urged redistricting. The suggestions had no noticeable effect. In 1919 a school district consolidation act, calling for county-wide reorganization, was
passed. Although the law was so worded as to be virtually mandatory, it produced negligible results. After eight years during which
there were only 164 mergers, the number of districts began to rise
again, exceeded 7,200 by the 1930–1931 school year, and remained
over the 7,000 mark for more than a decade.

The official Nebraska Legislative Council issued studies in 1942
and 1945 which clearly demonstrated the need for school district
area adjustment. The earlier report indicated that conditions had
changed greatly since the time when so many districts had been
established. The number of farm families and the number of children in each farm family had declined while appreciable improvements in transportation facilities had been made. In addition, by

1942 the assessed valuation of farm lands had decreased by more than two-fifths in the preceding twelve years, and by more than one-half since the peak in 1920, when there was a school district for every thirty-seven students. Concluding that unreconstructed rural schools could not be supported at the level of earlier years without substantially raising school taxes, the Legislative Council argued that without reorganization either taxes must increase or the quality of the educational program must decline. The council's analysis of 1945 showed that more than one-fifth of the rural districts were not operating schools, more than one-fifth of the functioning districts had five pupils or less, and the practice of transporting students to a neighboring district was noticeably increasing.[36] Furthermore, in twenty years elementary rural districts had lost about 60 per cent of their enrollment, and in 1945 there were approximately 4,500 one-teacher schools in existence.

Legislative Actions

A positive response to the obvious need for widespread redistricting came two years later, when a bill featuring a strong form of the comprehensive-planned-permissive method of reorganization was introduced in the state legislature. It provided for the preparation of a county-wide plan of district reorganization by county committees, and for acceptance or rejection of the plan by a state committee. Specific merger proposals agreed upon by the two groups were then to be submitted to a single, over-all vote of the electorate within the entire affected area, and another proposition was to be presented if the first was rejected. The proposed law further called for state aid, in the amount of $500 for each classroom unit, to districts reorganized under the act and to other districts approved by the state and county committees as adequate without reorganization. The bill was drastic both in its requirements and in the increase in state support to school districts, which were receiving the lowest amount of such assistance in the nation and were relying heavily upon local property taxes. After the section on state aid was deleted by the committee on education, the bill surmounted all legislative hurdles until its final reading in the

---

[36] *Public Education in Nebraska below the College Level*, Nebraska Legislative Council, Research Department, Report No. 20 (Lincoln: 1942), pp. 19–20; *Educational Problems in Nebraska, ibid.*, Report No. 28 (Lincoln: 1945), p. 21.

state's unicameral legislature, when it was defeated by a margin of two votes. The Legislative Council was ordered to prepare another study, and its findings emphasized the long-time trends of substantial decline in rural school enrollment and of growth in the number of districts which were dormant, transported students elsewhere, served only one to five students, or provided merely one or a few years of instruction. These conditions, it noted, conclusively showed that the existing system of school district organization fostered great inequalities in educational opportunities and tax burdens.[37]

Although the bill enacted in 1949 followed the comprehensive-planned-permissive pattern, it took account of the opposition to its predecessor and differed from it in four important details. The preparation of a reorganization study is discretionary with the county committees. The state committee is advisory only. All rural territory affected by the proposal votes as a separate unit, as does any high school district that is included in the plan. No state aid designed to encourage redistricting is available. At the time of the law's passage, a milder type of reorganization was and continues to be available. The county school superintendent may alter district boundaries upon petitions signed by 55 per cent of the voters of each affected district, and may attach to other districts those with less than three voters or with no students in attendance for 160 days, or those failing to send students elsewhere.

The Results

The reorganization law of 1949 has had little effect.[38] Although about 900 districts were eliminated in the five years immediately following the legislation, most of the consolidations materialized through the petition approach or through actions by county superintendents in merging depopulated districts with active ones. In addition, much of the reorganization achieved by these two means has been piecemeal and has not been based upon a plan formulated for a substantial part or all of the county, an objective antici-

[37] *Report No. 25*, Nebraska Legislative Council, Sub-Committee on Redistricting (Lincoln: 1948), pp. 5–7.

[38] *Report No. 50*, Nebraska Legislative Council, Committee on the Reorganization of School Districts (Lincoln: 1954), pp. 20–37; *A Report on the Reorganization of School Districts in Nebraska*, Nebraska State Committee for the Reorganization of School Districts (Lincoln: 1953), pp. 20–27.

pated in the comprehensive legislation. The state committee established under the 1949 law has been quite active. On the other hand, many of the ninety-three county committees—formed in all counties except the one having a county-wide school system—have been dormant and therefore indifferent or hostile. In 1953, for example, one-fifth of the county committees transmitted no report to the state committee, an action required by law. Furthermore, during the same year approximately one-third of the reporting committees spent no money and slightly more than two-thirds made no tours or visitations. In some counties committee members have been elected specifically because of their opposition to district reform. Antagonism to reorganization centers around several factors: fear of paying higher taxes and of losing local control, belief in the unnecessariness and impracticability of area reform, and reluctance to change.

A major reason for the slow tempo of school redistricting in Nebraska is that the comprehensive reorganization method stands virtually alone, without the support of other state programs which would accelerate its use. A moderate degree of equalization was attempted in 1949 through enactment of a levy of not more than 4 mills applied to all taxable tangible property in every county. Although this effort served to encourage reorganization, it was judged unconstitutional by the state supreme court three years later. The moderate reorganization approach is much impaired by the meagerness of state aid to school district financing, the resulting dominance of local property taxation, and the tremendous variations in local property tax levies. The results of the comprehensive-planned-permissive reorganization process have been unimpressive. Its principal accomplishment has been to spur on redistricting under an earlier merger method, often utilized in order to avoid more thorough, orderly, and well-conceived area adjustment. However, the failure of the 1949 law should be viewed within the larger framework of the other inadequacies of state governmental policy.

ILLINOIS: RAPID REORGANIZATION PROGRESS

A spectacular reduction of almost 500 per cent in the number of school districts has occurred in Illinois since the inauguration of the sustained, comprehensive merger program in 1945. This out-standing accomplishment has replaced the dubious distinction previously held by the state. At the time of the official count of governments by the Bureau of the Census in 1942, Illinois led the nation with 12,138 school districts, a total exceeding by more than 3,500 the number in Kansas, which was in second place. In 1945 the state still had approximately the same number of districts, about five-sixths of them at the elementary level and most of the remainder limited to high school grades. Most districts covered only a few square miles and possessed a single one-teacher school. Less than 1 per cent furnished education from the first through the twelfth grade. The dominant pattern, therefore, was the dual system of school district organization, consisting of many hun-dreds of high school districts territorially superimposed upon ele-mentary districts. Furthermore, there were nine major types of school units. But by 1954, nine years after the merger program was launched, Illinois school districts totaled only 2,557; a decrease of more than 25 per cent occurred between 1952 and 1954 alone. The reorganization in Illinois is definitely tending in the direction of units providing at least twelve grades of instruction.

Legislation and Leadership

The legal means for merger had existed for a number of years. However, although the first consolidation of elementary school districts occurred in 1905, the state-wide results in the intervening forty years were negligible. For example, for fifteen years before the program of the mid-1940's was started, the number of districts had remained at approximately 12,000, and meanwhile the pro-portion of districts not operating schools had risen from an in-significant percentage to one in five. A series of official and private studies on the need for school district reorganization spanned many years of the twentieth century, down into the 1940's.

The evidence presented aroused the Illinois Agricultural Asso-ciation to action in 1944, and, with the help of the Illinois Educa-tion Association, it succeeded in having comprehensive-planned-permissive legislation enacted in 1945. This act differed in two important particulars from a somewhat similar law passed four years earlier. It provided for the establishment of a state commission to assist local survey groups, and it did not terminate the local committees after the short period of two years. The new legislation ordered each county superintendent of schools to convene the governing board members of all school districts in his county to determine if they desired to establish a county-wide school survey committee. If their decision was favorable, they selected the nine committee members, none of whom could be a professional educator or a school employee. The law further specified assistance and guidance to the committee by the state advisory school reorganization commission, preparation of the county committee's final report by a designated time, and submission of merger proposals for majority approval of the voters. When incorporated places of at least 500 population were included, two separate majorities of voters—those residing in such localities and those living outside—were required.

The state commission soon realized that additional legislation was necessary to encourage and facilitate the establishment of districts providing education from the first through the twelfth grade. In 1947 the community unit school district law was passed, increasing interest in and strengthening the comprehensive machinery that had recently become available. Initiated by petitions signed by at least 100 voters, or by recommendation of the survey committee, the new type of district must contain a minimum of 2,000 people and an assessed valuation of $6 million. Empowered to include all or parts of districts to be supplanted, encompass territory in more than one county, and provide education below and above the twelve-grade range, a community unit district is created by obtaining a majority of the total vote in both urban and rural areas. There is no limitation on the frequency with which elections may be called. The community unit district law has served as a double catalyst to the earlier legislation. It eliminated the cumbersome, tedious process of dissolving the old districts in the area to be reorganized by providing for their automatic dissolution upon approval of the proposition. By 1949, for example, more than 200 districts of the new type had been established, superseding some 5,000 old districts and averaging in excess of 110 square miles in area. The law further broadened the thinking and perspective of the county survey committee members by supplying the legal means for extensive area change. The local groups began to plan increasingly in terms of the best possible organization rather than within the framework of what would likely be immediately acceptable. Upon adoption of the law, the study participants clearly saw the opportunity to furnish, according to a prominent state educational consultant, "signal leadership to the whole reorganization program."[30] With their assumption of the role of lay leaders in education, the reorganization program, which had remained largely inert during its first two years of existence, quickened with amazing rapidity. Although it was a voluntary matter, eventually all except one of the 102 counties in Illinois created local committees. Considerable assistance has been rendered at the state level, including research, informational, and appraisal activities by public universities and colleges.

A study made a few years after the passage of the community unit school district act graphically showed the many benefits accruing to areas which had converted to the new type of district. Here is a representative sampling. A broader, more integrated educational offering at considerably lower per-pupil cost was available. Music, art, physical education, and vocational training were added to the programs of numerous students who formerly lacked such opportunities. Special education of exceptional children and of those with physical handicaps was added. New impetus was given to visual education. The curriculum was affected to a greater degree by the impact of community problems and needs. A stimulus was given to the adult education and kindergarten programs. Transportation was more economical than under the previous system of separate elementary and high school operations. Uniform accounting procedures were installed, resulting in simplified bookkeeping and improved budgetary practices. Nevertheless, reorganizations sometimes caused problems. One of them was the school building deficiency, created in part by the consolidation of attendance centers and the enlargement of the school program. The second was a misunderstanding by some people about the services and activities of the new district of which they were a part. In summation, however, the analysts deemed the total education

[30] M. R. Sumption, "School Board Members Give Leadership in Reorganization in Illinois," American School Board Journal, 117 (Aug., 1948), 120.

program to be substantially improved in terms of effectiveness, adequacy, and economy. Two years later the executive secretary of the Illinois Education Association solidly supported this favorable appraisal. He concluded that the advantages of reorganization were now unquestionable in view of the achievement and service records of community unit school districts.[40]

Implementing Aids

The comprehensive-planned-permissive program and the community unit district act have been bolstered by other acts of the legislature. Several examples illustrate the forms such assistance has taken. In 1945 the legislature relieved districts providing both elementary and secondary work of three financial penalties: substantially less taxing power than the combined rates of elementary and high school districts serving similar areas; greater difficulty in qualifying for special state aid; and smaller bonding capacity than that available by combining the potentials of comparable separate elementary and secondary units. In the twenty years before the legislation, the number of first-to-twelfth-grade districts had decreased by almost one-half. In the year that these financial disadvantages were eliminated, the state law establishing the local tax rate necessary to qualify for state equalization aid was revised to give an advantage to districts furnishing both elementary and secondary education. Two years later, another legislative act raised the average daily attendance levels required in elementary and high school districts for eligibility for state aid. Other more drastic legislation followed in 1951. The law called for all school districts not maintaining schools for two consecutive years to dissolve and annex their territory to adjoining districts. Its immediate effect was the abolition of more than 600 districts.

The Illinois experience in school district reorganization is an excellent illustration of the implementation that must be given to the formal reorganization process. The legal process in itself was formulated with a number of moderate provisions. These included local determination of the need for a survey committee, the ad-

[40] H. M. Hamlin and M. R. Sumption, *New Community Unit School Districts: Practices and Problems,* Bulletin No. 45 (Urbana: University of Illinois College of Education, 1951); Irving F. Pearson, "It's Your Responsibility," *Illinois Education,* 41 (Mar., 1953), 258.

visory role of the state group, and the double majorities required in joint urban and rural area proposals. Probably the mild nature of the procedure would have deterred positive action in Illinois, as it has in Nebraska, if it had not been amply supplemented. But important support did come forth in the form of outstanding local leadership, imaginative state guidance and perspective, and intelligent legislative actions. These gave real impetus to the merger movement. The current status of school districts and the reorganization movement itself are not without criticism in the state.[41] Some reconstructed districts are still too small in size. State financial support is frequently deemed insufficient. The inadequacy of pupil transportation reimbursement has been a significant element in retarding change in certain areas. The 5 per cent bonding limit hampers some merger efforts. Concern over these shortcomings reflects a healthy sustained interest in the continuing problem of reorganization. Despite the defects, Illinois has made remarkable progress in school district reorganization in a relatively short time.

[41] See, for example, Irving F. Pearson, "Problems in Education Which Are of Legislative Concern," *Illinois Education*, 43 (Nov., 1954), 108–110; *Illinois School Problems*, Illinois School Problems Commission No. 3 (Springfield: 1955).

CHAPTER SEVEN

Dependent
Districts
and Authorities

Some entities that are not independent special districts resemble them in some particulars and are at times mistaken for them. Although these dependent districts and authorities are not the main concern of this book, they deserve separate consideration principally for purposes of clarification and also because they are increasing in number and importance. The fundamental distinction between such operations and special district governments is the former's lack of sufficient fiscal independence or adequate administrative autonomy or both. Their high degree of dependence upon a controlling governmental unit takes several forms. Many of them, with sometimes popularly elected governing bodies of their own, are subordinate rather than independent because of their fiscal relationship. Their financial requirements may be subject to official review and revision by a governmental unit, or the only source of their money may be funds from a government. Others have insufficient administrative independence; their plans and programs may be scrutinized and modified by a government.

A more extreme subordinate administrative arrangement is to have officials of a government, most often governing body members, serve as the entire membership or main part of the governing body of the dependent entity. Some subordinate agencies lack both financial and administrative autonomy. Furthermore, some have no governmental structure at all, but are simply areas delineated and administered by a governmental unit for the collection of special taxes or service charges. Entities in the latter group, variously known as special assessment and improvement districts and service areas, are created to finance additional or more intensified services in specific portions of the territory of general local governments. They should not be confused with the numerous subdivisions established by general units throughout their entire jurisdiction to facilitate such matters as the administration of justice and the conduct of elections.

Dependent districts and authorities are not always clearly distinguishable, and the titles have sometimes been employed interchangeably by state legislatures. Authorities, however, more frequently engage exclusively in revenue-producing enterprises financed solely by revenue bonds and service charges and rates, with or without support from governmental grants.[1] In certain states, notably New York and Pennsylvania, authorities cease to exist upon the expiration of their indebtedness, and their property reverts to the government that created them. Dependent districts and authorities are adjuncts of governments such as counties, cities, townships, towns, states, and special districts. In the last category, for example, conservancy districts in Colorado and school districts in several states have such arrangements. Counties constitute the unit to which dependent districts and authorities are most often subordinate. Towns are also prominent in this connection in New York State, and states and cities are especially important in relation to many authorities.

POINTS OF CONFUSION

It is easy to confuse some dependent agencies and operations with special districts that are independent governments. Many of them have the same functions and names as special districts. There are perplexing interstate differences. Although housing authorities, soil conservation districts, and school districts are generally independent governments, each category is subordinate in some states. To illustrate, local housing operations are separate activities in thirty-six states, but are dependent in Arizona, Kentucky, Michigan, New Mexico, and New York. Furthermore, bewildering differences may be present within the same state. This is because

---

[1] Some writers discuss authorities without considering their independence or dependence. Those possessing sufficient autonomy are special district governments and have been discussed in other chapters.

enabling laws at times permit optional methods of organization, and the independence or dependence of a district is determined by the alternative selected. Two automobile parking district laws passed in California in 1941 afford an example. Under the first act, districts are created and guided by the governing bodies of cities and are therefore subordinate. Under the second act, they have governing bodies selected by the voters and possess separate fiscal and administrative powers and are thus independent. Yet, both of them are identified as automobile parking districts! Justifiable cause for perplexity can also be found in a single locality. Six taxing districts are functioning within the territory of Norwalk, Connecticut. The first, second, third, and sixth have separately elected governing bodies which decide upon fiscal needs and are independent special district governments. The fourth and fifth taxing districts, however, are governed by the city council as adjuncts of the city government, and exist solely to provide a means for differential taxation. Even when the governing body of a general local government serves in an ex officio capacity as the governing group of a dependent entity, the dependent status of the operation is not always clear. Separate financial accounts may be maintained and most contacts with the public may come through administrative personnel rather than the board of directors. Thus, there may be little realization that the arrangement does not constitute an independent government. Administrative and financial autonomy, and not functions and titles, are the only accurate determinants of whether an organization or activity is independent or subordinate.

In different forms, and with different frequency and importance, dependent entities and activities exist in every state.[2] Collectively performing many of the identical services undertaken by special district governments, they further parallel special districts in operating in the same categories: metropolitan, urban fringe, coterminous, rural, and school. An additional similarity to special districts is that dependent agencies are not new, although their utilization has been increasing rapidly during the past twenty years. This fast growth has been most noticeable in municipal authorities in Pennsylvania. Functioning under many of the same names as special

---

[2] A partial list is contained in *Local Government Structure in the United States*, U.S. Bureau of the Census, Governments Division, State and Local Government Special Studies No. 34 (Washington: 1954), beginning at page 10.

districts, dependent entities and activities are also like them because their titles generally include either the word "district" or the word "authority." Most authorities, however, are adjuncts of other governments, although one of the important exceptions is housing authorities. On the other hand, districts are much more often independent governments. Therefore, for want of better terminology and in the interest of differentiation, organizations and operations somewhat resembling special districts but lacking adequate administrative or financial independence, or both, have been designated as dependent districts and authorities. To illustrate more specifically their nature and significance and to distinguish them further from special districts, case studies of two states are presented. First, the diversified kinds of dependent districts functioning in California are considered. This is followed by an analysis of municipal authorities in Pennsylvania, where they are most used.

DEPENDENT DISTRICTS IN CALIFORNIA

California, which stands next to Illinois in number of independent nonschool special districts, also ranks high in its utilization of dependent districts. Furthermore, it employs all the common forms of dependent districts; a representative sampling is presented here to indicate the nature of the development. A minority have their own governing bodies but lack either sufficient fiscal or administrative autonomy, or both. The dependence of a district possessing a separate governing body is most frequently caused by the requirement that a governmental unit review and possibly modify its fiscal requests. The customary reviewing agency is the county board of supervisors. The predominant arrangement is demonstrated by public service districts and county recreation districts, both of which have their financial requirements ultimately determined by the county supervisors. Less often, fiscal subordination is the result of a government's supplying the district with the major portion or all of its money. Such a situation is present in municipal building commissions (districts). In some instances lack of sufficient independence grows out of a government's authority to scrutinize the proposed program. Here horticultural improvement districts serve as an example, for their plans must be submitted to the governing body of the county. Occasionally both financial and administrative independence are not present to an adequate degree. Vehicle parking districts, for example, are subject to control by the creating county or city government at various stages, including the acquisition of property, the making of improvements, and the incurring of debt.

Frequency of Ex Officio Governing Personnel

Most dependent districts in California are governed by a group composed wholly or principally of officials chosen initially to serve an independent governmental unit. The most prevalent arrangement is to have the governing body of an independent unit serve ex officio as the directors of a dependent district. All the major classes of government in the state function in this way, although not to the same degree. State officials make up the board of the California Toll Bridge Authority. City councils constitute the governing bodies of municipal lighting maintenance districts, municipal sewer districts, and one kind of municipal water district. Union high school library districts are governed by the trustees of union high school districts, and a particular variety of junior college district is the governing concern of the board of directors of a high school district. The governing body of a municipal utility district simultaneously serves a certain kind of sewage disposal district. By far the most frequent ex officio group, however, is the county board of supervisors. At this point it should be noted that it is sometimes difficult to distinguish between dependent districts, governed by ex officio governing bodies, and dependent districts or areas, frequently known as service areas or special assessment or improvement districts, established solely by such governing bodies for the collection of additional taxes or charges. The major distinction is that dependent districts of the first type frequently have their own working personnel separate from that of the controlling government. Conversely, the controlling government usually has its regular employees perform the duties in dependent districts of the second type.

The numerous dependent districts governed by county boards of supervisors in California are functionally extensive and geographically widespread. Many hundreds of them are operating in

four-fifths of the counties in a broad range of land-use situations.[3]
Ten to twenty dependent districts of a single kind are active in a
number of counties, and in one county there are eighty-six engaged in the same function. They most frequently undertake fire
protection, flood control, sanitation, sewer maintenance, and water
supply. Less often they furnish air pollution control, drainage,
police protection, sewer construction, storm drain maintenance,
and recreation, parks, and parkways. Occasionally they perform
garbage disposal, harbor improvement, parkway maintenance, and
road maintenance.

The most noticeable feature of many dependent districts is their
functional similarity to independent special districts. With some
frequency, both dependent districts and independent special districts are engaged in the same function in the same county, sometimes in adjacent areas. The result of the limited service scope of
individual dependent districts is, not unexpectedly, that most of
them are small financial operations. A significant minority, however, annually obtain sizable revenue, amounting usually to hundreds of thousands of dollars, and in more limited instances to
millions. Regardless of the total money involved, the responsibility
for its legitimate and wise expenditure rests with the board of
supervisors. The board thus has similar obligations in the county
government and in dependent districts. The combination of duties
sometimes gives supervisors a burdensome work load.

Los Angeles County Illustrations

Some dependent districts governed by county boards of supervisors undertake consequential activities which are very basic to
the areas they serve. Included among those of a vital nature are
three functional examples in Los Angeles County.[4] The earliest
one grew out of a major disaster in the county's coastal plain,

---

[3] *Annual Report of Financial Transactions Concerning Special Districts of California*, California Controller (Sacramento: 1956), pp. 123–214.

[4] Winston W. Crouch, *Intergovernmental Relations* (1954), pp. 89–96, 103–105;
Edwin A. Cottrell and Helen L. Jones, *The Metropolis: Is Integration Possible?*
(1955), pp. 18–22, 42–47; James Trump, James R. Donoghue, and Morton Kroll,
Fire Protection (1952), pp. 28–45. These monographs are volumes 15, 16, and 6,
respectively, of the series, *Metropolitan Los Angeles: A Study in Integration*, published by the Haynes Foundation in Los Angeles.

which was subject to periodic flooding catastrophes. In 1914 a serious flood causing many deaths and injuries and millions of dollars of property loss pointed up the need for a comprehensive program. The response came in the following year with the passage of a special state legislative act creating the Los Angeles County Flood Control District. The county board of supervisors was designated as the governing body of the district and numerous other county officials, including the auditor, county counsel, purchasing agent, and treasurer, were required to perform for the district the same duties undertaken for the county government. Subsequently, under an amendment to the act, the district contracted with the county for a complete personnel service program. Employees of the flood control district, however, are not employees of the county government. District personnel is separate from that of the county government and is directed by a chief engineer.

The territory of this dependent district consists of slightly less than three-fifths of the county and excludes the northern desert portion and the offshore islands. Covering two complete watersheds and part of a third, it encompasses all the cities within the county and much unincorporated land. It is authorized to undertake both flood control and water conservation. The dependent district, after heated controversies over the financing and construction of large masonry dams, shifted to building check dams to avoid the effects of severe floods, and to formulating and carrying out a conservation program. Its activities changed somewhat after 1936, when Congress made the United States Corps of Engineers responsible for major flood control construction projects in various parts of the United States, including Los Angeles County. Since then the emphasis of the county flood control dependent agency has tended in several directions. The district maintains channel improvements, debris basins, and many completed projects, and keeps up spreading areas which allow waters to be retained in natural reservoirs. It works on the headwaters of watersheds, purchases rights of way, and pays road and bridge realignment costs to facilitate flood control construction. Since voter sanction of a multimillion dollar storm drain bond issue in 1952, the flood control district supervises and comprehensively reviews projects designed by city governments for construction within cities.

The activities of the Los Angeles County Flood Control District are financed through property taxes, bond issues, grants from governments, and miscellaneous rentals and sales. Although its taxes for construction and maintenance purposes are limited to 15 cents for each $100 of assessed valuation, extra money must be raised to satisfy interest and principal requirements on bonds voted by the district electorate. The district is a big operation, employing more than 1,100 full-time people, expending almost $4.5 million annually (exclusive of capital outlay for land and permanent improvements), and possessing an indebtedness at the close of the 1954–1955 fiscal year of approximately $67 million.

The second oldest illustration of dependent districts significant to many people in Los Angeles County consists of county fire protection districts. The impetus for their creation was the need for a positive program to handle structural fires in rapidly urbanizing, unincorporated areas. In 1923 the state legislature passed a law permitting the formation of fire protection districts through initiation by the county board of supervisors or by the property owners of the proposed area, followed by a public hearing and a board resolution. Since 1927, however, when the state law was changed, majority approval of the local electorate has been required. Quick, extensive use was made of the law in Los Angeles County, and in the first fiscal year after its passage thirty-one county fire protection districts were established. From the beginning, these dependent districts were geared into the county government. The county board of supervisors serves as the governing body and has responsibility for employing and dismissing personnel, purchasing equipment, determining the tax rate, and levying an annual tax. In addition, the county forester and firewarden, whose department includes the mountain fire battalions which are direct units of the county government supported by general county funds, is the administrator for the districts. The affairs of each district are kept separate from those of other districts, and the administration and personnel of the districts and the department generally are distinct. For example, district employees not above the rank of captain are employees of the district and not of the county, and must maintain residence within the district territory. There are two principal exceptions to this separateness. Supervisorial positions above the status of captain in fire districts are occupied by county employees, and the title to district property is vested in the county government. Money raised by the annual tax levied by the county board of supervisors, however, must be spent for fire purposes within the district area.

Since 1931, when a state legislative amendment enabled the territory of county fire protection units to include noncontiguous land, these dependent districts have expanded steadily in area, population served, and personnel employed. Although it is possible for cities operating under generally applicable state laws to be parts of such operations, a recently incorporated community, Lakewood, is the only one functioning under the arrangement. The total area of the districts, consisting almost entirely of unincorporated territory, has been growing, and in 1948 exceeded 200 square miles for the first time. In several recent years hundreds of annexations were completed through petition of the local property owners and action by the county board of supervisors. Although both the department and the board of supervisors came to favor a single district for the whole county in the mid-1940's, the absence of supervisorial power to charge differential tax rates in various sections of one large entity on the basis of varying needs served as an effective deterrent. Then, too, certain local areas were opposed to the idea. Under an alternative plan which was substituted and has been successfully used, the county board gradually consolidates the various districts as they approach the same tax rate. Numbering thirty-four at the inauguration of this policy, county fire protection districts had decreased to six by 1954. One of the districts, known appropriately in view of the merger objective as the Consolidated County Fire Protection District, has an annual income in excess of $4.5 million.

The most recently established important dependent district in Los Angeles County is concerned with air pollution. On numerous warm, dry days air pollutants are held in suspension at a low altitude level because of topographical and meteorological conditions, and the outcome is an irritating haze known as smog. The situation, aggravated by the heavy influx of people, industries, and automobiles, and threatening the health and comfort of inhabitants, had become a matter of widespread attention by 1944. After a study was made under the direction of the county board of supervisors, inspectional and regulatory ordinances were adopted, enforcement was assigned to the county health officer, and an office headed by an air pollution control director was established. These county efforts, however, applied only to the unincorporated areas. Although the supervisorial board urged the cities to enact comparable laws, slightly less than one-half of them complied. The attempt at coöperative enforcement, successful only in part, induced the California Legislature to act in 1947. It considered, among several possibilities for a stronger organization, an independent special district encompassing parts or all of four counties, and direct, comprehensive administration by the county government. The former was defeated partially because citrus growers feared that such a government would interfere with orchard heating. The latter was turned down because of opposition by the cities. The law that was enacted authorized the board of supervisors in any county in the state to create at its discretion an air pollution control district coterminous with the county boundaries. It further stipulated that the county supervisors were to be the district governing body. An air pollution control district is not a regular department of the county government but is dependent basically upon the governing body of the county and is financed through general county taxes.

Such a district was organized in Los Angeles County in late 1947 and began actual operations in April of the following year.[5] Possessing county-wide jurisdiction, this dependent district conducts research, licenses equipment and industries, and enforces antipollution regulations. The problem with which the district deals is of considerable magnitude and periodically raises community and individual antagonisms. There is fairly general acceptance that the district operations have lessened the difficulty, but there is frequent contention that its progress is not rapid enough. Uneasiness about the relationship between smog and lung and functional diseases has brought on demands for immediate, complete solutions. During extended smog periods mass protest meetings have been held, featuring speeches, discussions, urgings of major and minor changes, and sometimes accusations of incompetency. In

---

[5] Four other counties in California have subsequently established similar organizations. An air pollution district, different in structure, has also been established in the San Francisco Bay counties.

early 1955, after an internal reorganization, the number of court actions against violators rapidly increased. From time to time some city officials have strongly advocated that the district cease to be an adjunct of the county government and instead become a separate governmental organization in which the cities have direct representation. The district is expending more than $1 million yearly.

County Service Areas

The newest addition to the variety of dependent districts and operations in California is the county service area, a subsidiary of the county government possessing no governmental structure of its own. The creation of this financing mechanism arose out of disagreement over the method of providing certain services of a municipal type in unincorporated urban areas. In 1950, delegates to the annual convention of the League of California Cities, the official representative of most cities in the state, concluded that various county boards of supervisors were responding to demands by unincorporated urban residents for intensified urban services, and were financing them through general county funds. This meant, it was stated, that cities and strictly rural areas were being obliged to subsidize municipal-type services supplied by county governments in unincorporated urban areas. To rectify the inequitable situation, the league suggested that the state pass legislation prohibiting the use of general county monies for such services and compelling persons and property in benefited areas to pay the cost by establishing a local special district or by annexation or incorporation. A bill introduced in the 1951 legislative session required counties to impose a tax on unincorporated areas when they received county services at a higher standard than those provided in rural areas. In a setting of bitter charges by city and county officials and their representatives, the proposal was defeated in the upper legislative house and the subject was referred to a legislative interim study committee.[8]

Two years later the legislature passed the county service area

---

[8] The general report issued by the California Assembly Interim Committee on Municipal and County Government is *Final Report . . . Covering Fringe Area Problems in the State of California* (Sacramento: 1953). More detailed studies on five counties were also published.

law, following collaborative efforts by the League of California
Cities and the County Supervisors Association. Recognizing that
counties have a responsibility for providing extended services in
unincorporated urban areas but that such areas should pay, the
legislature established an additional, permissive method of acquisition and financing. A county service area, which is a taxing jurisdiction of the county government, is organized to pay a local,
special tax for receiving specific intensified services from the
county government. The services are extended police protection,
structural fire protection, local park, recreation, or parkway facilities and activities, and other services authorized to be performed
by counties and not supplied on a county-wide basis both within
and outside cities. A county service area is formally established
by resolution of the county governing body which determines the
boundaries and the services to be provided. However, its creation
can be initiated only upon request of at least two of the five members of the county board of supervisors, or through a petition signed
by a minimum of 10 per cent of the registered voters of the territory. Furthermore, such a proposal must be abandoned by the
board if written protests are lodged by either registered voters
totaling 50 per cent or more in the proposed area or owners of a
minimum of 50 per cent of the property value in the territory. In
addition, if the protests are made by at least 10 per cent but less
than 50 per cent of the registered voters of the area, the board
either halts further action or submits the question to the voters.
A majority of those voting must cast affirmative ballots in order
to enable the supervisors to pass the appropriate resolution. If
the written protests are sufficient in quantity or if the majority
opposes the resolution, county services in the area currently found
by the board of supervisors to be of an extended nature are
stopped.

In effect for a relatively short time, the law has been used to
create only four county service areas, one for street improvement
in one county and three in another county for structural fire protection.[7] Difficulties have already arisen in connection with the

[7] Robert O. Bailey, "Summary of the Use of the Community Services District
Law and the County Service Area Law" (speech at annual conference of the League
of California Cities, Los Angeles, Oct. 18, 1954) furnishes a general analysis of
these service areas.

utilization of this newest kind of dependent district, which is a taxing jurisdiction without separate governmental organization and personnel. The most difficult problem is that of accurate differentiation between basic and extended service. Also important in some situations is the requirement that projects needing large capital outlays must be financed solely by direct taxation and not by bonds or other means. The theory of the county service area law seems to hold promise as an alternative to independent special district governments, but its realization is not imminent.

MUNICIPAL AUTHORITIES IN PENNSYLVANIA

There has been a spectacular development of dependent entities known as municipal authorities in Pennsylvania since the adoption of the general enabling legislation in 1935. The most extensive utilization of municipal authorities has been occurring in Pennsylvania localities, although there are somewhat parallel developments in a number of other states, at the state as well as the local level.[8] Pennsylvania municipal authorities are organizations authorized to engage in a wide variety of commercial, revenue-producing enterprises which are financed by revenue bonds, service charges, and rates, sometimes supplemented by government grants. Taxation is not permitted and special assessments are available only to authorities undertaking sewer construction. Despite considerable operational freedom during their existence, authorities are adjuncts of existing governments rather than independent entities because their property automatically reverts to the creating local governments when their indebtedness is paid within a period not exceeding fifty years. Furthermore, the government sponsoring the establishment of a municipal authority can at its discretion acquire the authority holdings by passing an ordinance or resolution and assuming the financial obligations. The lack of use of this permissive power does not in any way diminish this aspect of legal subordination.[9]

---

[8] For illustrations from another state, see *Report of Activities for the Year 1953–1954 and First Interim Staff Report on Public Authorities Under New York State,* New York Temporary Commission on Coördination of State Activities (Albany: 1954). A general consideration, largely devoted to state authorities, is *Public Authorities in the States,* Council of State Governments (Chicago: 1953).

[9] Gayle K. Lawrence, who has written the most extended study of these entities, supports the position of the United States Bureau of the Census that they are not

Evolution of the Law

The municipal authority movement started in the depression years of the 1930's. It developed from federal aid and work programs for financing revenue-producing projects, coupled with the highly restrictive borrowing limitation on local governments and the unworkability of the local revenue bond law. The result of the dilemma was the establishment of an instrumentality whose obligations are payable exclusively from its revenues and are charges neither against its property nor against the taxing power or credit of the state or of the creating local government. The original legal basis, enacted in 1933, was applicable only to Allegheny County (Pittsburgh), but it was quickly broadened two years later when permission was extended to all classes of local governments in the state except school and other special district governments. The enabling law was amended at each subsequent biennial legislative session, with some of the changes giving authority operations a greater functional and governmental scope. The most significant amendments extended the right to two or more local governments to collaborate in organizing an authority, and added the power to acquire waterworks and water distribution systems. A rewritten, superseding law, the Municipality Authorities Act, was passed in 1945 and is the present legal foundation of municipal authorities. Most of the amendments have been minor ones, but there have been the important changes of adding school building projects to the list of permitted undertakings and of granting school districts the right to create authorities.

This discussion of the enabling law demonstrates that the term "municipal authorities" is a misnomer in that it suggests a too restricted scope. Since the legislation was first expanded in 1935, the power to create authorities has been available not only to all cities but also to all counties, townships, towns, and boroughs. In addition, the right was extended to school districts sixteen years later. Thus municipal authorities can be established by all kinds of local governments, acting alone or in combination, with the

independent units of government. "Use of the Government Corporation as an Administrative Device by American Local Government, with Special Reference to Pennsylvania" (unpublished Ph.D. dissertation, University of Pennsylvania, Philadelphia, 1951), pp. 85, 103.

exception of a limited number of nonschool district governments.[10]
The establishment of a municipal authority rests formally on the
judgment of the governing body of the sponsoring local government or governments. The process is simple, involving no expression by the local voters at the polls. An ordinance or resolution is
adopted, and is published at least once in a legal periodical and at
least once in a newspaper of general circulation in the county.
Articles of incorporation are then filed with the Secretary of the
Commonwealth who, upon finding them in conformance with the
legal requirements, issues a certificate of incorporation which com-
pletes the steps necessary to bring the authority into existence.
Local governments can later withdraw from joint authorities if no
authority indebtedness has been incurred, or can become part of
them if the authority consents.

The authority governing body is selected by the local government or governments that created the entity. If a single local government incorporates a municipal authority, its governing body
chooses the members, normally five in number serving staggered
five-year terms. When an authority is organized by two or more
local governments, its governing body has not less than five members and includes at least one representative selected by each sponsoring government. The main restriction on eligibility is that appointees must live within the territory of the local governments
selecting them. In the early years a substantial number of authority
governing body members were officials of the creating governments, but more recently there has been a decided trend away from
this practice, fostered in part by a state supreme court decision in
1942 prohibiting commissioners of third-class cities from such
officeholding. To an increasing degree the appointees are lay persons of high community prestige. The governing bodies of the
creating local governments determine the compensation, which is
usually nominal or nonexistent. Members are eligible for reappointment, and may be removed only for cause by the county court.

[10] The discussion here is concerned with municipal authorities organized under
the general acts of 1935 and 1945. There are other local authorities, devoted to
parking and urban redevelopment, which are based on separate acts. Low-cost
housing projects were eliminated in 1937 from the list of activities that could be
undertaken by municipal authorities, and new housing legislation was enacted. The
U.S. Bureau of the Census recognizes city and county housing authorities in Pennsylvania as special district governments.

Broad Powers

Legally, municipal authorities may undertake a broad range of activities. They may acquire, hold, construct, improve, maintain and operate, own, and lease, either as a lessor or lessee, many different kinds of projects. Included are public buildings devoted entirely or partially to public uses, such as public school buildings, and to revenue-producing purposes; transportation, marketing, and shopping centers; terminals, bridges, and tunnels; flood control projects; highways, parkways, traffic distribution centers, and parking spaces; and airports and their facilities. Also permitted are parks, recreation grounds and facilities, sewers, sewer systems, sewage treatment plants, steam heating plants and distribution systems, incinerator plants, waterworks, water supply works, low head dams, hospitals, subways, and motor buses when utilized within the territory of a local government. The sole restriction placed on authority projects is that they must not duplicate, wholly or partly, or compete with existing enterprises serving substantially the same purposes. School districts are limited to public school buildings and other projects for school purposes. The organizing government may specify the activities to be undertaken or it may remain silent and allow the authority complete freedom in the choice of functions. After the formation, however, the sponsoring local government may increase or decrease the authority's functional range. In total, the authorizations are broad and diversified, but there are significant omissions of functions like electric utilities, gas, power, and telephone, which offer good revenue-producing possibilities.

In many aspects of their internal operations the municipal authorities have more latitude than the local governments in the state. Their property and income from bond sales are tax exempt. Bonds may be sold at either private or public sale and are not subject to state approval. Authorities may issue either term or serial bonds and amortize them over a maximum period of forty years. They do not have to submit their budgets to an agency of the state government, and only those engaged in water projects must transmit financial statements to the state. However, the state's attorney general may examine the books, records, and accounts;

an annual audit must be made by a certified public accountant; and a yearly financial statement must be published. Acquisition of private utilities must be voluntary and sanctioned by the state public utility commission and two-thirds vote of the governing body of the creating local government. Authorities have the exclusive and very important power to set their own rates. Although the rates may be challenged in court on the grounds of unreasonableness or lack of uniformity, such cases have been rare.

The municipal authority law is widely used. Several hundred authorities are in operation and have issued bonds totaling several hundred million dollars, and numerous others are organized but have remained inactive as a result of inability to work out a suitable plan of financing. Once activated, very few have ceased operation. The largest numbers of authorities have been created by boroughs, which constitute one kind of municipality in the state, and townships, many of which are functionally similar to cities and boroughs. This is not unexpected since together they represent more than one-half of the local governments in Pennsylvania. Cities, which are far less numerous than boroughs and townships, are making substantial use of the enabling legislation. Authorities are located predominantly in urban areas and are found in most sections of the state. Most of them have been established by a single local government, but few confine their operations to the governmental boundaries of the sponsoring government. Furthermore, particularly in the post–World War II years, there has been increased reliance on intergovernmental aspects as more joint authorities have been organized. One such operation has ten participating local governments.

Many activities authorized in the state enabling law have remained unused. Most authorities are engaged in only one activity, a few in two or three. Then, too, most of them are concerned with only one of the three most common projects. Before World War II, the efforts were largely devoted to waterworks. More recent years, however, have witnessed the inauguration of a state-directed stream pollution abatement program and the addition of school buildings to the authorized projects in response to the swelling need for more school structures. Sewage disposal facilities and public school buildings have thus joined waterworks as the most prevalent activities. Interestingly, only the first of these three was permitted when the legislation was broadened in 1935. Nearly all sewage disposal plant construction and waterworks acquisition and building in recent years have been undertaken by authorities, which only occasionally handle such projects as airports, parking lots and garages, flood control operations, and nonschool buildings.

A Controversial Development

Unlike dependent districts about which there is little discussion, critical or otherwise, by observers and governmental officials, municipal authorities in Pennsylvania have become a controversial topic.[11] Supporters argue that municipal authorities give to public ownership the elasticity, continuity, and efficiency of private commercial management. Not hampered by the inflexible restrictions on local governmental borrowing, and reasonably free from partisan politics because of their staggered terms, the governing bodies of authorities usually attract high-caliber personnel who show great zeal and sustained drive for their responsibilities. The ability of authorities to secure highly competent technical advice makes for increased efficiency and earnings. The necessary dependence on project income rather than on taxing power also stimulates greater efficiency. In segregating proprietary or business services from traditional governmental activities, the authority mechanism, it is felt, has made possible the assessment of costs for such services to directly benefited users while at the same time preventing an unjustifiable diversion of earnings to support general governmental operations. Furthermore, advocates urge as a principal merit of the municipal authority system its ability to cross political boundaries and to make intergovernmental coöperation a more widespread reality. Authorities have extremely promising potentialities, the reasoning continues, in solving interstate problems.[12]

Opponents argue that municipal authorities further fragmentize government affairs, causing duplication and waste, uneconomical limited-purpose operations, uncoördinated efforts, greater com-

---

[11] Similarly, there is substantial argument elsewhere, of both a general and specific nature, over the merits of the current and potential utilization of state and local authorities.

[12] These, however, are interstate rather than municipal authorities and are frequently considered to be special district governments.

plexity, and increased difficulty of citizen comprehension. Emphasizing that authorities unduly disperse power and control, they note that the governing body members are distant from public accountability and are difficult to remove. Rather than being judged as helpful intergovernmental devices, municipal authorities are berated as stopgaps which deter thorough solutions and needed legal changes. In addition, authority financing is appraised as not affording sufficient safeguards to the public and as being excessively costly because interest rates are often higher than those for local governments. Strong criticism is also voiced against two practices employed by some authorities.[13] One is the practice of placing authority operations in the hands of a private management firm, which guarantees a minimum gross annual return in exchange for a fee amounting to as much as 10 per cent of the yearly gross receipts. The other is the practice of leasing authority holdings back to the creating government on a rental basis.

Pennsylvania municipal authorities have been evaluated, on the one hand, as high-grade, useful, and precise instruments of public service, and on the other as the seat of political patronage and bank-dictated finance. Several years ago Tina Weintraub and James Patterson of the Bureau of Municipal Research of Philadelphia undertook a thorough study of Pennsylvania municipal authorities. Authorities, they decided, are not cure-alls but do offer a practical means of transcending government boundaries to provide necessary regional services. If no need of this sort is present, there must be strong specific justification for the establishment of another new public organization with special financing. Otherwise, the function should be allocated to an existing government and financed through regular means.[14] Despite continual controversy, municipal authorities have in a relatively short time become an established agency of Pennsylvania local government.

---

[13] Lawrence, *op. cit.*, pp. 223–224.

[14] Tina V. Weintraub and James D. Patterson, *The "Authority" in Pennsylvania: Pro and Con* (Philadelphia: Bureau of Municipal Research of Philadelphia, 1949), p. ix. For examples of supporting arguments, see Charles F. LeeDecker, "Special Districts in Pennsylvania," *Municipal Finance*, 24 (Feb., 1952), 107–110, and Harold F. Alderfer, "Is 'Authority' Financing the Answer?" *American City*, 70 (Feb., 1955), 115–116. For critical comments, refer to Carl H. Chatters' statement following that of Dr. Alderfer in the same issue, and James C. Charlesworth, "Why Many Cities Are Too Small," *American City*, 69 (Nov., 1954), 86.

CHAPTER EIGHT

Status
and Prospects

Special districts in the United States unquestionably constitute a class of governments which is already important and is expanding in significance. This is apparent in their large number, many types, geographical dispersion, varied functions, extensive finances, and numerous personnel. Furthermore, these units affect human activities in numerous situations, and various phases of the governmental system. Although occasionally recognized in the earlier decades of the century by a few isolated observers and writers as an emerging separate category of governments, and designated in the current decade by the United States Bureau of the Census as one of the most striking recent governmental developments, special districts are still widely overlooked. The reason for this incongruity is that individually they are usually not large governments, but collectively their operations and influence are large-scale.

Special districts are consequential. They are also different. Deviating in many ways from most kinds of governments, they present a number of extraordinary patterns. Some of their features are completely unusual and others are different in the sense that they are present more commonly in special districts than in any other class of governments. The differences between special districts and other governments are demonstrable through a consideration of representative characteristics.

Conspicuous among the unusual aspects of special districts is the limited scope of the functions they may individually perform. Here are governmental units originally designed to be public agencies individually restricted to one or a very few activities. No other class of governments, including townships which have been experiencing a decline in functions, was similarly conceived. Furthermore, special districts render services to the virtual exclusion of enforcing regulations, much more so than other governments. Although each is of narrow functional scope, together they embrace an extremely broad range of matters of public concern.

Outstanding, too, is the frequency of their area flexibility. They can usually overlap one another, a permission not granted to other classes of governments, and they overlie other units to an extensive degree. They often initially contain and subsequently add territory without regard to other existing boundaries covering part or all of the same land. They usually have exceptional latitude as to locale and areal extent. Most of the pyramiding of governments at a specific location is caused by special districts. Unlike other state and local governments, some districts are interstate. Some are international. Many are coterminous with a general or special district unit, a practice otherwise in use in only a few cities and counties which are consolidated. Some have noncompact territory and a few lack an explicitly defined area. Some must include another government within their boundaries, which are at times determined by the population and legal limits of the included unit. An area practice of school districts is unparalleled. Through numerous mergers, the most comprehensive area reorganization ever to occur in the history of the United States has been under way for some time. The long tradition of increasing the number of governmental units is being broken by substantial subtractions.

District organization is often extraordinary. A skeletal structure exists in practice in many instances, and frequently the governing body is granted complete power to shape the operational framework according to its own desires. Whether the organization is large or small, it is more often fully integrated under the governing body than in other classes of government. The contrast is most distinct in comparison with counties, an overwhelming number of which feature numerous officials chosen independently of the governing board. Furthermore, there is seldom a division of responsibilities among two or more basic parts. For example, special districts have no elected executive resembling a governor or a mayor. Few district officials are elected. Most often only the members of the governing body have elective status, and much more frequently than in other governments the incumbents run without opposition. In many districts no official is chosen by the electorate.

The extensive utilization of appointment in selecting governing body members is a particularly prominent differentiation in organization. Sometimes the appointing authority, such as the governor or a judge, functions in a larger jurisdiction than the area of the district. In other districts the directors are selected by combinations of appointing authorities from different branches or levels of government, each generally choosing a certain number separately. Both of these selection procedures are expressions of a theory of accountability to the people most directly concerned, which can in operation be very remote from them and extremely difficult for them to use effectively. Also unknown elsewhere is the requirement in some districts that part of the governing body select the remainder of its membership.

Other structural and operational district arrangements are highly uncommon among governments. A governing body characteristic unique to certain districts is the absence of a specific term of office, and in several district types the electorate has the extremely rare opportunity of deciding at the organizational election whether the governing board shall be elected or appointed. One operational process unfamiliar to governments in general is the stipulation of unit or bloc voting by governing body members who represent specific areas within the district. Although unit voting is not unknown in legislative actions of other governments, it is mandatory only in these special districts. Another unusual technique is to apportion voting strength among the members on the basis of assessed property valuation represented, instead of following the traditional standard of equal individual voting power.

An especially odd feature of some district governments is their theory of representation, which bases participation in important matters on property ownership. This means that the voting power of adult residents is not the same. The criterion is used with some frequency, especially by rural districts. It may be a standard of eligibility to sign petitions and vote to create a district, to select governing body members, to serve on the governing board, and to participate in decisions authorizing particular district activities. Sometimes the property ownership requirement is extended to permit nonresidents who possess property within the district to vote, or to authorize plural voting, which makes the number of votes per person dependent upon the amount of district land he owns. In some districts, therefore, a few individuals may have a majority of the votes and control the operations.

Using property ownership as the basic test for eligibility ignores the generally accepted concept of citizenship and residence as the fundamental determinants. Property ownership long ago disappeared as a condition of participation in most general governments; its principal remaining nondistrict utilization is in some local bond issue elections. Although usually regarded as a vestige of a past era, it has been made a part of some new district legislation during the last quarter of a century. Under the property ownership rule, broadly based citizen action is expressly prohibited, and under multiple voting it is further diluted. Property ownership in general, and the plural voting or stockholder principle in particular, help to make some special districts the most private of governments.

Some district relations with other governments are extraordinary. The foremost illustration is the national government's direct advocacy of new kinds of government, most noticeably soil conservation districts and housing authorities. Also prominent is the legal stipulation that specified officials of a general government must carry out similar duties for a district without financial reimbursement to the general unit. Although this obligation occurs in some city-county legal relationships, it is much more prevalent in district relationships with other governments. Furthermore, although no government functions entirely apart from others, many nonschool districts operate very independently, free of supervision or review by other governments.

Special districts are out of the ordinary in other fundamental ways. Financing is an excellent case in point. Taxation is a common corollary of governmental operations, but nonschool districts place much greater reliance upon other financing means, such as service charges, and constitute the only group of governments not depending heavily upon direct taxation. School districts, too, are exceptional in obtaining an unusually large proportion of their money through transfers from other governments. There is also variation in such fundamentals as formation proceedings, activeness, and dissolution. Statute books carry more unused or outdated legislation for creating special districts than for all other governments combined. Special districts become inactive without formally dissolving, if the silence of the law prevents legal dissolution, more frequently than other governments. Most divergent from the usual governmental pattern is automatic dissolution after twenty-five years of existence, which applies to noxious weed eradication districts in Nebraska. This is unprecedented among governments, and unique among many extraordinary district characteristics.

Special districts are therefore important and unusual in many respects. Not all of their deviations from widely known governmental molds and practices are beneficial, and in total their characteristics are a mixed blessing. Although they have features of government which are not generally considered governmental, special districts are much more than governmental curiosities. Their greatest contribution is that, in responding to demands for action under the name and powers of government, they reveal much about the operation of the over-all governmental system of which they are an established part.

What are some of these matters that they reveal? Three of them are particularly indicative. First, many districts are the product of the unresponsiveness, whether voluntary or involuntary, of other local governments, and are symptomatic of weaknesses in them. Special districts therefore frequently result from the unsuitability of existing governments, especially in area and financing characteristics and in the lack of sufficient ingenuity and compatibility to work out intergovernmental agreements. Second, special districts may develop from the actions of other governments and private organizations which are making an increasingly specialized approach to public problems. This is most graphically revealed by functional specialists who, although not deliberately trying to undermine general local governments, want to see a service provided but are unconcerned about its best governmental location. Sometimes their advocacy of special districts is directly related to the inadequacy of general units. At other times it is rooted in a desire, also held by interested laymen, to keep or take a function "out of politics."

Keeping or taking a function "out of politics" is a phrase which is often employed very loosely. If by "politics" is meant extreme partisanship or personal patronage, its existence in some nondistrict governments as well as in some special districts is undeniable. If by "politics" is meant the formulation of policies, a special district does not take a function "out of politics," but it may change the policy-making or political emphasis since the group in control of a district may differ from the group in control of a general government where the function could be located. In both circumstances a special brand of politics (partisanship or policy-making) is utilized instead of a general variety. Significantly, too, policy-making activities are not carried on by special districts in isolation. Policies are not made without influencing the policies of other governments, particularly those functioning in the immediate area, because such policies require decisions on social and economic matters, and such decisions directly affect other governments and the people they serve and are in turn affected by comparable political actions of the other governments.

The creation of some special districts also reveals a third feature of the governmental system of the United States, the desire of some residents and property owners for local autonomy or home rule. At times related to functional specialization, this desire may be a genuine feeling for a small government whose people are intimately acquainted with one another and with the locale. On the other hand it may be only a camouflage for individuals and groups seeking to derive a special advantage. Whatever the motive, the feeling for autonomy is frequently an element in the governmental process. These three aspects of the general governmental pattern—unresponsiveness, activity of a specialized nature, and the home-rule objective—aid considerably in understanding the rapid development of special districts.

Many special districts can be validly criticized. One serious argument against them is the inability of the public to exert adequate control over them. Special districts have multiplied so rapidly that citizens no longer keep themselves well informed on this aspect of governmental affairs. At the same time, general multipurpose governments have been expanding their functions. Although conscientious citizens might conceivably have exercised effective control over a few governmental units, it was unreasonable to expect them to watch and regulate a multi-ring circus. The fragmentation of governmental activities while governments were growing in functional importance has greatly increased the difficulty of citizen control and, in fact, has made it almost impossible. Public control has been made even more remote and superficial by the theory of representation based on property ownership and the theory of accountability, under which the appointing agent operates in an area larger than the district, performs his selection duty as part of a complicated arrangement, or lacks the power to remove appointees without substantiating serious charges. Whatever the details, appointed governing body members are at best twice removed from the voters, and residents can seldom legally bring a direct recall action against any of them.

The basic problem would not be resolved, however, by making all district directors elective. Although such a change could make public control more direct, the lengthening of an already long ballot would immediately dissipate any advantage that might emanate from the alteration. Simply stated, there are too many separate governments, and special districts are largely responsible. If "grass roots government" means broadly based public control, it is frequently an illusion in special districts. A very important way to improve citizen control and to solve the problem is to have fewer special districts.

The lack of popular control in special districts leads to a further important charge against many of them. Citizens have too little interest and consequently too little participation in the affairs of most districts. The fragmentation of governmental functions, particularly when coupled with extraordinary area overlapping, creates confusion, misunderstanding, and indifference. For example, many people living in metropolitan areas believe that some types of special districts are actually parts of general local governments. The aim of substantial citizen interest in a democratic political process is vulnerable to extreme fractionization. Citizen disinterest is not wholly unknown in other classes of governments (where it is partly attributed to the scattering of public attention among different governments through the rise of districts), but it is especially marked in respect to special districts. There is usually a low level of public concern about rural districts, and an upsurge of interest is often temporary and very emotional. Very seldom is there much interest in coterminous, urban fringe, or metropolitan districts. Among special districts, school districts receive the most citizen attention, chiefly because of parent-teacher groups and because of the contact and research work of taxpayers' organizations, which realize the extent of school financial outlays. Such interest has recently been further stimulated, in various sections of the country, by controversies over curriculum content and teaching methods. Nevertheless, public participation in electing school board members is proportionately lower than in electing city officials and is at times scarcely perceptible, in part because of fewer contested elections.

The underlying reason for the low level of public interest and participation in many districts is not difficult to diagnose. Few citizens feel that they can afford to spend much time on governmental affairs, and responsibility is now so widely shared by many independent governments that thorough comprehension is not easy. In fact, it is hardly an exaggeration to say that a citizen, especially one living in a highly urbanized area, who took part in only the important activities of all the local governments affecting his welfare would not have enough time left to earn the money he has to pay those governments. Lack of sufficient knowledge, and the competing demands made on personal time by numerous independent governments, force citizens to concentrate rather than disperse their attention.

Except for the attention they occasionally give to school districts, most citizens focus on one or more of their multipurpose general governments, such as cities, counties, or towns. Within the broad range of functions of such governments, people can usually find activities and issues that concern them. Furthermore, they need not have a permanent concern about one function, but can shift from one governmental activity to another and still be trying to influence the same government and the same governing body members. In special districts, such a shift requires a transfer of attention from district to district, and experience gained in participating in one frequently does not carry over to others. What is the principal detrimental result of the lack of citizen interest?

It is that many districts function largely unnoticed and uncontrolled by the public.

In addition, strong disapproval of the superabundance of special districts is justifiable because their uncoördinated, splintered efforts disperse activities among many independent governmental entities. This piecemeal, unintelligent attack on the problems of government, and the lack of over-all administrative and policy planning which grows out of the proliferation of governmental units, hinder the orderly development and sound utilization of the resources of an area. The approaches of different governments to a common problem often conflict and work at cross purposes, thus dissipating needed energies. A special district that handles only one aspect of a many-sided problem may do so with harmful results. Far too often has a special district tried to alleviate one difficulty and has simply succeeded in creating another. Interference with natural drainage by flood control work performed independently is a prominent example. Also, the functions of some special districts, such as housing authorities, may impinge upon related programs of general governments, which are powerless to require a coördinated attack on basic problems.

Another outcome of the lack of coördination among governments is the irrational competition for public monies, for which many special districts can be condemned. The only legal restriction on this practice is the existence of tax limits. Heedless of the needs of other special districts and of general governments in the area, each district has its own fiscal policy and makes its own demands upon the total financial resources of the area. There is no over-all financial planning and no method of intelligently weighing the relative merits of competing demands. Emotional competitiveness frequently prevails instead of rational comparative consideration.

Furthermore, special districts are often indefensible because, as a result of being too small, they are uneconomic. They do not benefit from the financial advantages that accrue to larger governments through the widely accepted administrative devices of personnel pooling and central purchasing, maintenance, and repair. These omissions are glaring in many districts, particularly so in urban fringe districts. In small governments operations are often more costly and services more expensive and less efficient than in larger units. The direct relationship of smallness of area to wastefulness in expenditure of money has been demonstrated frequently. The rush of state legislatures to pass laws designed to hasten the consolidation of school districts is a dramatic illustration. Many former urban fringes that have been annexed by cities have also experienced the benefits of economy through obtaining better service for each unit of cost. In fact, the belief that services would be cheaper has prompted a number of urban fringes to think seriously about joining a city government.

The expanding use of special districts has also been detrimental to general local governments. It has reduced their effectiveness through bypassing them or stripping them of particular functions. The withholding or removing of important responsibilities from these general governments, locally regarded as the fountainhead of direct service and regulation, does not make them better public instruments. The accelerated growth in types of special districts in recent years, somewhat paralleled by a resurgence of semi-independent administrative boards within some general units, seriously threatens the largely beneficial twentieth-century development of the integration of functions in general units under a single central authority. Because special districts are too numerous, and because they are only palliatives offering no long-range solution, they weaken general local governments and lessen the possibility of attaining a governmental system that is both responsive and responsible.

These criticisms of special districts should not be interpreted to mean that general local governments are nearly perfect and that special districts are alone accountable for deficiencies at the local governmental level. They do indicate that districts constitute an important problem of local government and that they are excessive in number and type. Reform is very much in order, but it is irrational to proclaim simply that all special districts should be abolished immediately or that a moratorium should be declared on the creation of new ones. The mere advocacy of elimination or diminution does not remove the causes that created special districts.

A reform program should therefore be related to the possibility of improving general local governments, whose deficiencies have greatly contributed to the rapid expansion of special districts. Again the problem must be viewed realistically. The history of general local units is one of additions rather than mergers, and during the present century the number of such governments has increased rather than decreased. The number of townships has been somewhat reduced, but the total number of county consolidations and city mergers has been negligible indeed. Except for the continuing downward trend in townships and the possible realization of some proposals for metropolitan area governmental simplification, it seems highly unlikely that thoroughgoing area consolidations of general units will occur in the foreseeable future. If this is an accurate forecast (and unforeseen technological factors sometimes make predictions about government unreliable), proposals for changes in the realm of special districts should be made within this framework. To strive for more general changes is one thing, but to expect that in the near future such changes will be widespread and will lead to special district alterations seems fanciful.

The first recommendations that are made here relate to school districts, the largest group of special districts. Area reorganization has been under way in many school districts for some time, but it has largely been consolidations of two or more districts rather than mergers of school districts with general units. The long-standing disagreement among some educationalists and political scientists over the merits of independence and dependence for school operations still exists, and recently there has been little conversion from one type of operation to the other. More significantly, the basic importance of education to democracy is related by many people to the continued separateness of school activities. This judgment is influential, whether or not it is correct, and there is no indication that school districts will yield their independence in the near future. School districts that have long been independent governments in many states are likely to continue so for some time to come, and recommendations for reform of special districts should be made in the light of this reality. But some immediately applicable suggestions can be made without necessarily precluding the long-range objective of integrating school districts into general local governments.

The current trend of merging school districts into larger district areas should continue and accelerate. The area reorganization problem was so immense, when attacked on a broad geographical basis in recent years, that some people have been overwhelmed by the results. The record is impressive and much has been done. But much remains to be done. Furthermore, reforms sometimes need to be redone. Thus, area reorganization among school districts should be quickened and already reconstructed districts that fall short of widely accepted standards should be realigned. Judicious direction and encouragement by state governments, including financial help, and the development of imaginative and farsighted local leadership will do much to facilitate the attaining of these goals. Fulfillment of these two objectives will in itself constitute a major special district reform, providing a strong contrast to the chaos of more than 100,000 separate school districts existing as late as the early 1940's, and will contribute greatly to broader, more efficient educational services.

Other important suggestions relating to school districts should be made. There should be closer intergovernmental planning and coördination between school districts and other governments operating in the immediate vicinity. Indications are that such actions are materializing more frequently in recent times. These efforts should be broadened in fields such as recreation, health, building utilization, and construction sites. Whether or not governmental functions are assigned to different governments, their primary purpose is to serve well the same body politic.

It is also an appropriate time for state governments to authorize comprehensive interstate studies to be undertaken jointly by social scientists and professional educators on the relative merits of independent school districts and dependent school operations. These inquiries should be directed especially toward determining the comparative quality of the educational offering, the relative per unit cost, and the extent of coördination between related governmental functions. Midwestern states with independent districts and New England states with dependent operations present an interesting comparison. In view of the prevailing public attitude, any serious effort to amalgamate independent school operations with general local governments would certainly have to be preceded by conclusive findings that the educational offering would be better and the per-unit cost lower. And even if such conclusions are reached, they may not bring about a general transformation, so deeply ingrained is the concept of school independence in some areas. In any event, these kinds of studies undertaken coöperatively by people from various academic disciplines seem very much in order. At least they will take much of the current consideration of the matter out of the realm of conflicting theories.

What about nonschool districts, many types of which are growing so rapidly? In contrast to the major suggestion concerning school districts—the merger of governments with similar functions—the basic recommendation about nonschool districts is that many of them should be absorbed into other types of governments. Nonschool districts that are coterminous with or smaller in area than general local governments should be made parts of those governments and stripped of all governmental autonomy. This can almost always be accomplished through state legislative action. To be effective such changes must be preceded by certain alterations in general local governments which should be more widely attainable than extensive area mergers. These governments must be granted authorization to establish service and financing differentials, instead of being required to give reasonably uniform service uniformly financed throughout an entire jurisdiction. They can then provide more intensive services in some portions to meet increased needs, and collect additional taxes or assessments from the people receiving them. In some states general local governments must also be freed of rigid tax and debt limitations. It is advisable in some situations to furnish the legal means for internal administrative reorganization. Districts that are coterminous with general units can be transformed without utilizing the service and financing differentials, since they cover exactly the same area. Districts that are smaller than general units can become areas within them, serviced by the regular departments and financed by special taxes or assessments determined by the governing body of the general unit. All of them (as well as all comparable dependent districts currently possessing a degree of separateness) will be fully integrated into general governments. Thus the district idea of additional service will be maintained, but within the framework of general governments.

Except for cities, which will frequently assume the responsibility for coterminous districts, counties (and towns in New England) will be the principal inheritors of districts because of their greater territorial inclusiveness. There is ample precedent for them to undertake the assignment. Counties are most frequently utilized in dependent district situations, and this suggestion is simply a modification of that system. Some counties can more advantageously assume the additional responsibilities by modernizing their administrative structure, although this might require state constitutional amendments. The most necessary ingredient in the plan's effectiveness, however, will be the wise use of authority by general local units and their governing bodies so that the various areas within their jurisdiction will pay the proper amounts for special services. This reform will substantially reduce the number of special districts, but more vitally it will eliminate one of their principal causes and will strengthen local government.

On the assumption that extensive area mergers of counties and other general units will not soon materialize, it is obvious that the recommendation just made will not eliminate all nonschool districts. Even if consolidations of general units do unexpectedly develop on a broad basis, special districts will still be needed for areas which are extremely large or which involve difficult jurisdictional questions. Some rural types are illustrative of the former and some metropolitan ones, especially those embracing land in two states, are examples of the latter. Although the broader use of intergovernmental contracts should be encouraged in some of these situations, a supplementary reform proposal is also to the point.

The suggestion is that many of the remaining single-purpose districts be brought within multipurpose district operations. This would require the elimination by state legislatures of much of the remaining district enabling legislation and its replacement by legislation possessing a multipurpose base. Voters residing in the areas should be permitted to choose what functions and powers they find necessary, but it must be legally stipulated that the multipurpose district can be used only a limited number of times—once or twice, for example—in an area. Otherwise, there might be many separate uses of districts for single purposes, and thus the multipurpose concept could be destroyed. The legislation should authorize a broad scope of functions, including land-use and regulatory powers, and should call for determination and control by the resident voters living within the district. In some instances when the district is authorized to perform activities of state-wide importance it may be appropriate to have some members of its governing body appointed by the governor. The legislation should further permit the establishment of service and financing differentials.

This reform program would be particularly valuable in metropolitan and nonmetropolitan urban fringes, although it is also applicable in some rural areas. The multipurpose metropolitan district, since it is not limited to revenue-producing activities, would be an effective public instrument for handling area-wide, especially interstate, difficulties. Furthermore, endowed with permission to create service and financing differentials, it could also cope with the urban fringe problem. In urban fringes that straddle county lines outside metropolitan areas, the multipurpose district with the differential feature would also be worthwhile if intercounty contracts could not be worked out. This recommendation for multipurpose legislation would reduce the overlapping of districts and the diffusion of authority and responsibility. In effect, it would establish another class of general governments which would be limited in number.

A number of less important and less meaningful suggestions can be made. One is to increase state supervision and reporting. A second is to broaden county governmental control over budget preparation and execution when districts are smaller than counties. Another is to revise the state laws to effect a greater uniformity in the basic characteristics and procedures of special districts. Still another is to require that the state or county government investigate requests for creating new districts. All of these moderate recommendations would improve the situation, but none of them would really come to grips with the basic difficulty. It appears, therefore, that the two major reform proposals—to make many nonschool districts parts of general local units and to convert many others to a multipurpose form—are needed to alleviate the growing special district problem. Each can be applied alone, but in combination they will be much more effective.

The reforms advocated for nonschool districts will encounter obstacles in many states. Public disinterest and confusion about districts are prevalent, and citizen opposition to the continuance of districts, when it exists, is usually stated in generalized terms. Other impediments are also sometimes present. Examples are the fragmentary approach by state legislatures to local governmental affairs; state-wide organizations of special district officials, some of which employ lobbyists; and various special interests that benefit from existing arrangements. Furthermore, the longer districts exist, the more difficult it is to pry them out of their increasingly entrenched position. It is often true, however, that the path of the reformer is not easy, and yet the history of the United States is replete with reform successes.

The state legislatures are the key to district reform. They bear the responsibility for an adequate local governmental system, and many types of special districts are reducing the adequacy and dissipating the strength of the other units of local government. The state legislatures can employ a state-wide outlook and understand the seriousness and total effects of the problems resulting from special districts. Furthermore, with rare exceptions the state legislatures, unhampered by state constitutional or local charter restrictions, have full legal power to eliminate or alter special districts. The challenge and the opportunity are theirs!

Local governmental renovation should be broader than special district reform and allied minor changes in general units. Governments exist and function in an intergovernmental environment. There is a need, often long-standing, in practically every state for comprehensive state governmental study and appropriate action regarding the modern-day sufficiency of all classes of local governments. Only the area weaknesses of school districts have received such attention in recent years. There is also a need for both the state and national governments to appraise the effects of their various programs upon local governments. Such analyses are appropriate and urgent, as noted recently by the Commission on Intergovernmental Relations of the national government and by

William Anderson, distinguished writer on American government, in his book, *The Nation and the States: Rivals or Partners?* Moreover, the evaluations of the status of local government should be made regularly by professional personnel of the legislative or executive branches of the state government, for these are not matters that should be investigated only during economic depressions or when their costs mount prohibitively.

In modifications resulting from such studies, the goal should not be governmental symmetry, but a system of government that is understandable, responsive, and effective. Absolute uniformity in the governmental systems of all states is not desirable. A degree of experimentation and variation should exist, but not to the point of inefficiency and wasteful financial exactions in the name of government. Special districts do represent a frontier line of adjustment to change, but governmental authority is powerful in nature and should not be granted indiscriminately.

By starting with a consideration of special districts, a number of state legislatures may be prompted to launch into broader analyses of the entire local governmental system. Although at present regarded as detrimental, the growth of special districts may sooner or later serve as the impetus necessary to bring about needed and long overdue changes across the whole fabric of local government. In the future, therefore, special districts may be evaluated as having been a necessary and vital evolutionary step toward a general advance in the adequacy and quality of government in the United States.

A Commentary on
Bibliography

Written sources relating to special districts range widely in value and availability. Many of them are fugitive materials that have been issued in limited quantity and frequently have not been included in the standard bibliographical indexes. Often they are descriptive rather than analytical, and contain merely incidental references to districts embedded in discussions of other aspects of government. An exhaustive (and probably exhausting) enumeration of the many hundreds of items investigated in the preparation of this study could be given here, but in the judgment of the author it would be more confusing than helpful because of the wide variations in quality. Instead, a brief list of the more valuable materials is presented and discussed. Excluded are reports and bibliographies pertaining to specific local areas, compilations of laws, and annual reports.

The most extensive, general data are contained in reports of the Governments Division of the United States Bureau of the Census. Outstanding among them is *Local Government Structure in the United States* (Washington: 1954), which includes a concise legal description of the characteristics of all types of special districts and other local governments. A corollary, largely statistical publication is *Governments in the United States in 1952* (Washington: 1953), which is similar in some respects to *Governmental Units in the United States: 1942*, issued nine years earlier. Other significant Census Bureau releases of a general nature are the periodic presentations on governmental finances and public employment (the monthly reports of the latter transferred to the U.S. Bureau of Labor Statistics in early 1955), and the brief report, *Special District Governments in the United States* (1954). All publications since 1952 by this division of the Census Bureau utilize a refined definition of governmental units. This is an important factor to consider in making use of earlier studies by the Governments Division and publications by other public and private organizations of national, state, and local scope. All data from other sources have been interpreted in this book in relation to the reworked definition.

Also pertaining to special districts in general is the ground-breaking, highly significant work of William Anderson, *The Units of Government in the United States,* published initially by Public Administration Service in Chicago in 1934. Concerned both with determining the essential characteristics of governmental units and with judging the adequacy of the present local governmental system, the monograph is evaluative and provocative. Twice revised, it was most recently reprinted with a new appendix in 1949. The Anderson definition differs somewhat from the new one utilized by the Census Bureau's Governments Division.

Several writers recognized the special district development in the earlier years of the current century. Their research furnishes historical perspective and in some instances shows a growing concern about districts. Four articles largely devoted to recently enacted district legislation in the states appeared under the same title of "Special Municipal Corporations" in the *American Political Science Review.* The first two were by Charles Kettleborough in the November, 1914, and November, 1915, issues, and the latter two were by Frederic H. Guild in the November, 1918, and May, 1920, numbers. Guild subsequently appraised the movement in "Special Municipal Corporations," *National Municipal Review,* 18 (May, 1929), 319–323, as did Kirk H. Porter in "A Plague of Special Districts," *National Municipal Review,* 22 (Nov., 1933), 544–547, 574. In addition, John A. Fairlie and Charles M. Kneier devoted a major portion (pp. 476–494) of a chapter as well as scattered sections in *County Government and Administration* (New York: D. Appleton-Century, 1930) to the features of various special districts existing at the time. These pages reflect an extensive searching of numerous state laws and periodical references, many of which are cited by the authors as footnotes.

A much larger portion of the written record is concerned with types of special districts, rather than with all of them. Some of the more valuable materials of this kind are considered here in the order in which the related classifications appeared as chapters in this book. Among the most helpful sources on metropolitan districts are chapters 14 through 16 of Paul Studenski, *The Government of Metropolitan Areas in the United States* (New York: National Municipal League, 1930), and chapter 6 in Victor Jones' monograph, "Local Government Organization in Metropolitan Areas: Its Relation to Urban Redevelopment," in Coleman Woodbury, ed., *The Future of Cities and Urban Redevelopment* (Chicago: University of Chicago Press, 1953); and the concluding section of part two of *The States and the Metropolitan Problem,* Council of State Governments (Chicago: 1956), prepared under the directorship of John C. Bollens.

Important, too, are Betty Tableman, *Governmental Organization in Metropolitan Areas* (Ann Arbor: University of Michigan Press, 1951), particularly for its two appendices identifying by place location and characterizing a number of metropolitan districts, and two reports of the Governments Division of the United States Bureau of the Census, *Governmental Units Overlying City Areas* (1947) and *Local Government in Metropolitan Areas* (1954). Both of the latter list numerous districts which are metropolitan in scope. Daniel R. Grant, "The Government of Interstate Metropolitan Areas," *Western Political Quarterly*, 7 (Mar., 1955), 90–107, deals with a phase of the subject which deserves increasing attention. A further relevant item is *Structure of Governments in Metropolitan Areas*, Illinois Legislative Council (Springfield: 1952). The reader is also referred to "Metropolitan Area Developments, 1940–1950," in *Municipal Year Book: 1951* (Chicago: International City Managers' Association, 1951), pp. 32–37, and related articles by the present author in subsequent annual editions of the same publication.

General written information on urban fringe districts is very scarce. Some of their aspects are discussed in John C. Bollens, "Controls and Services in Unincorporated Urban Fringes," *Municipal Year Book: 1954* (Chicago: International City Managers' Association, 1954), pp. 53–61, and "Fringe Area Conditions and Relations," *Public Management*, 32 (Mar., 1950), 50–54. The previously mentioned Census Bureau report, *Local Government in Metropolitan Areas*, tabulates all special districts, many of which are in the urban fringe group, by individual metropolitan areas. By its nature, however, the count does not include urban fringe districts in nonmetropolitan situations.

Data and analyses for the most prevalent example of coterminous districts, the housing authority, are much more plentiful. The publications of the National Association of Housing and Redevelopment Officials, including its periodical, *The Journal of Housing*, and special reports such as *State Enabling Legislation for Public Housing* (Chicago: 1940) and *Handbook for Housing Commissioners* (1950), are useful. Also meritorious are the association's publications, *Housing Officials' Yearbook*, published from 1935 through 1937, and *Housing Yearbook*, issued from 1938 through 1944. Since 1945 a yearly section on housing and redevelopment activities has been written for the *Municipal Year Book* by either staff members of the association or administrators of individual local housing authorities. Various reports of the national housing agency, known presently as the Housing and Home Finance Agency, are similarly helpful. An example is *Public Housing: The Work of the Federal Public Housing Authority*, National Housing Agency, Federal Public Housing Authority (Washington: 1946). Additional insights can be gained from congressional reports, an illustration of which is *Federal Housing Programs*, U.S. Senate, Committee on Banking and Currency, 81st Cong., 2d sess. (Washington: 1950).

Basic data on two major types of rural districts, irrigation and drainage, are found in U.S. *Census of Agriculture,* usually prepared at decennial intervals by the Agriculture Division of the U.S. Bureau of the Census. Two valuable interpretive monographs relating to irrigation districts and written more than twenty years apart are Wells A. Hutchins, *Irrigation Districts: Their Organization, Operation and Financing* (Washington: U.S. Department of Agriculture, 1931), and Wells A. Hutchins, H. E. Selby, and Stanley W. Voelker, *Irrigation-Enterprise Organizations* (Washington: U.S. Department of Agriculture, 1953). Additional interesting commentaries are contained in books such as Alfred R. Golzé, *Reclamation in the United States* (New York: McGraw-Hill, 1952); Roy E. Huffman, *Irrigation Development and Public Water Policy* (New York: Ronald Press, 1953); and J. Howard Maughan's selection in Orson W. Israelson, *Irrigation Principles and Practices* (2d ed.; New York: John Wiley, 1950).

An important aid in connection with a third major rural type, the soil conservation district, is *Soil Conservation Districts, Status of Organizations, by States, Approximate Acreage, and Farms in Organized Districts,* issued regularly from Washington by the Soil Conservation Service of the United States Department of Agriculture. Other significant reports of the service include *A Standard Soil Conservation Districts Law* (1936), *Land Use Regulation in Soil Conservation Districts* (1947), and, in conjunction with the Extension Service of the same department, *Aspects of Administration of Soil Conservation Districts* (1945). The views of a leader in the soil conservation district movement are expressed in Hugh H. Bennett, "Soil Conservation among the 48 States," *State Government,* 18 (Oct., 1945), 173–176. Important, sometimes divergent, analyses are W. Robert Parks, *Soil Conservation Districts in Action* (Ames: Iowa State College Press, 1952); his article written in collaboration with Herman Walker, Jr., "Soil Conservation Districts: Local Democracy in a National Program," *Journal of Politics,* 8 (Nov., 1946), 538–549; and Charles M. Hardin, *The Politics of Agriculture: Soil Conservation and the Struggle for Power in Rural America* (Glencoe: Free Press, 1952).

Unlike many other special districts, school districts have called forth voluminous writings and interpretations, chiefly from professional educators and school district governing body members. Only a broad sampling will be given here. Two organizations which are especially productive in this field are a governmental agency, the United States Office of Education, now located in the United States Department of Health, Education, and Welfare, and a private group, the National Education Association. Illustrative of the pertinent research work of the former is *Biennial Survey of Education in the United States, 1948–1950* (Washington: 1954); *Principles and Procedures in the Organization of Satisfactory School Units* (1939), by Henry F. Alves and Edgar L. Morphet; *Educational Change in Reorganized School Districts* and *Selected Characteristics of Reorganized School Districts*, both written by C. O. Fitzwater and issued in 1953; and *The One-Teacher School: Its Mid-century Status* (1950), by Walter T. Gaumnitz and David T. Blose. Indicative of the activities of the National Education Association are its regularly issued *Research Bulletin* (e.g., "Status and Practice of Boards of Education," pp. 47–83 of vol. 24, published in Apr., 1946); its *Yearbook* (e.g., *School Boards in Action*, released in 1946, and *The American School Superintendency*, published in 1952); the *NEA Journal;* and *A Model School District Reorganization Bill* (Washington: 1948). Another significant study released under the auspices of the association and prepared by the National Commission on School District Reorganization is *Your School District* (1948). The National Society for the Study of Education also regularly presents data in this field. Two editions of its *Yearbook*, published by the University of Chicago Press, are *American Education in the Post-War Period* (1945) and *The Community School* (1953).

Numerous periodicals add consistently to the abundance of information about school districts. Included are the *American School Board Journal, Nation's Schools, Phi Delta Kappan, School Executive,* and *School and Society.* In the matter of school district reorganization, Kenneth E. McIntyre has regularly reviewed recent developments in the *American School Board Journal,* at two-year intervals beginning in 1950. Other examples of worthwhile general summaries of school district area reform are *School District Reorganization,* Kansas Legislative Council, Research Department (Topeka: 1944); *School District Mergers,* Kentucky Legislative Research Commission, Research Staff (Frankfort: 1954); and Dorothy C. Tompkins, *Reorganization of School Districts* (Berkeley: University of California Bureau of Public Administration, 1951). The continuing reorganization trend is observable in *School Districts in the United States in 1954,* U.S. Bureau of the Census, Governments Division (1955). Relevant to some of the broader relationships of school districts are publications such as *The Forty-Eight State School Systems,* Council of State Governments (Chicago: 1949); Nelson B. Henry and Jerome G. Kerwin, *Schools and City Government: A Study of School and Municipal Relationships in Cities of 50,000 or More Population* (Chicago: University of Chicago Press, 1938); and C. Winfield Scott and Clyde M. Hill, *Public Education Under Criticism* (New York: Prentice-Hall, 1954).

In order to avoid extremely detailed listings, sources on special districts in individual states must be confined to those which relate to numerous or all types within a specific state. Very few state studies are devoted exclusively to special districts. Most of them discuss districts, sometimes only in a limited way, along with other governments, or explain the governmental pattern in which special districts operate. The following are suggestive of such research monographs and books:

Joseph W. Reid, Jr., *The Units of Government in Alabama* (University: University of Alabama Bureau of Public Administration, 1946)

Henry M. Alexander, *Organization and Function of State and Local Government in Arkansas* (Fayetteville: University of Arkansas Bureau of Research, 1947)

John C. Bollens and Stanley Scott, *Local Government in California* (Berkeley: University of California Press, 1951)

Winston W. Crouch, Dean E. McHenry, John C. Bollens, and Stanley Scott, *California Government and Politics* (Englewood Cliffs: Prentice-Hall, 1956)

Max R. White, *The Units of Government in Connecticut* (Storrs: University of Connecticut Institute of Public Service, 1953)

Clyde F. Snider, Gilbert Y. Steiner, and Lois Langdon, *Local Taxing Units: The Illinois Experience* (Urbana and Springfield: University of Illinois Institute of Government and Public Affairs and Illinois State Department of Revenue, Property Tax Division, 1954)

Kansas Legislative Council, Research Department, *Political Sub-Divisions of Kansas* (Topeka: 1949)

Emmett Asseff, *Special Districts in Louisiana* (Baton Rouge: Louisiana State University Bureau of Government Research, 1951)

Frank M. Landers, *Units of Government in Michigan* (Ann Arbor: University of Michigan Bureau of Government, 1941)

William Anderson, *Local Government and Finance in Minnesota* (Minneapolis: University of Minnesota Press, 1935) (Also see the more recent series of monographs titled *Intergovernmental Relations in the United States as Observed in Minnesota*, edited by William Anderson and Edward W. Weidner.)

Roger V. Shumate, *Local Government in Nebraska* (Lincoln: Nebraska Legislative Council, 1939)

Local Government in New Jersey, Princeton Local Government Survey (Princeton: 1937)

The Units of Government in Oregon: 1951, University of Oregon Bureau of Municipal Research and Service (Eugene: 1954) (An earlier edition was published in 1943.)

Stuart A. MacCorkle, *Units of Government in Texas* (Austin: University of Texas Bureau of Municipal Research, 1941)

State and Local Government in Utah, Utah Foundation (Salt Lake City: 1954)

Special Taxing Districts in the State of Washington: An Appraisal of Their Status and Operations, Washington State Legislative Council, Subcommittee on State and Local Government (Olympia: 1950)

Attention should also be directed to a series of books, now in preparation, on government and administration in individual states. Titled the "American Commonwealths Series" and published by Thomas Y. Crowell Company in New York under the general editorship of W.

Brooke Graves, these books give promise of contributing to an understanding of the special district development in specific states. The first five issued in the series are Wilson K. Doyle and Angus M. Laird, *The Government and Administration of Florida* (1954); Robert B. Highsaw and Charles N. Fortensberry, *The Government and Administration of Mississippi* (1954); Lynton K. Caldwell, *The Government and Administration of New York* (1954); Robert S. Rankin, *The Government and Administration of North Carolina* (1955); and Herman H. Trachsel and Ralph M. Wade, *The Government and Administration of Wyoming* (1953).

Additional books not in this series which are useful in comprehending the governmental setting of special districts include Pressly S. Sikes, *Indiana State and Local Government* (rev. ed.; Bloomington: Principia Press, 1946); Thomas C. Donnelly, *The Government of New Mexico* (Albuquerque: University of New Mexico Press, 1947); and Jacob Tanger, Harold F. Alderfer, and M. Nelson Geary, *Pennsylvania's Government, State and Local* (3d ed.; State College: Penns Valley Publishers, 1950). Others are Stuart A. MacCorkle and Dick Smith, *Texas Government* (2d ed.; New York: McGraw-Hill, 1952); C. Perry Patterson, Sam B. McAlister, and George C. Hester, *State and Local Government in Texas* (3d ed.; New York: Macmillan, 1948); Frank M. Stewart and Joseph L. Clark, *The Constitution and Government of Texas* (4th ed.; Boston: D. C. Heath, 1949); and Oscar L. Lambert, *West Virginia and Its Government* (Boston: D. C. Heath, 1951).

Finally, there are several general publications which do not concentrate on special districts but which aid in placing them in the broader perspective and governmental context in which they operate. Among the most thought-provoking are William Anderson, *The Nation and the States: Rivals or Partners?* (Minneapolis: University of Minnesota Press, 1955); *Report,* Commission on Intergovernmental Relations (Washington: 1955); *State-Local Relations,* Council of State Governments, Committee on State-Local Relations (Chicago: 1946); James W. Fesler, *Area and Administration* (University: University of Alabama Press, 1949); and John M. Gaus, *Reflections on Public Administration* (University: University of Alabama Press, 1947). Two publications containing numerous stimulating remarks about rural government and urban government, respectively, are Lane W. Lancaster, *Government in Rural America* (2d ed.; New York: D. Van Nostrand, 1952); and Coleman Woodbury's concluding essay in Coleman Woodbury, ed., *The Future of Cities and Urban Redevelopment* (Chicago: University of Chicago Press, 1953).

Index

Acreage limitation on irrigated land, 155–156

Administrative organization, 39, 248; in urban fringe districts, 105

Administrative planning, 255

Administrative units of education, 181

Agricultural districts. *See* Drainage districts; Irrigation districts; Rural districts; Rural fire protection districts; Soil conservation districts; Weed eradication districts

Agriculture, Secretary of, 157

Aid from other governments, 103

Air pollution, 51

Air pollution control, 236–238

Airport, 32, 51, 68

Alabama, 98; predominant method of selecting district governing body members in, 31; school districts in, 184

Albany Port District: method of selecting governing body of, 33

All-American Canal, 150

Allegheny County (Pennsylvania), 241

Anderson, William, 263

Annexation: by metropolitan districts, 69; by metropolitan districts in interstate areas, 88–89; by Metropolitan Sanitary District of Greater Chicago, 74–75; by Metropolitan Water District of Southern California, 85; by special districts, 29–30

Annexation by cities, 53–57, 101, 103; as inadequate metropolitan solution, 56–57; opposition to, 66; significance of, in metropolitan areas, 55–57; stringency of laws governing, 55

Area, 25–30, 248; of cities, 29; of city housing authorities, 127; of counties, 29; of county housing authorities, 127;

of drainage districts, 169–170; of irrigation districts, 145; of school districts, 183–185; of soil conservation districts, 165–166; of towns, 29; of townships, 29

Arizona, 116, 229; predominant method of selecting district governing body members in, 31

Arkansas, 142, 143, 168; drainage districts in, 170; rural road and bridge districts in, 140n; school district reorganization in, 200, 204; suburban improvement districts in, 28

Army Corps of Engineers, 172

Assessment areas, 102

Assessment districts, 229

Assessments, 149–150, 149n

Atlanta: annexation by, 54

Attendance units of education, 179

Authorities, 229

Baltimore: city-county separation in, 58; number of local governments in, 49

Baton Rouge: city-county consolidation in, 57, 58

Birmingham metropolitan area: rejection of city-county consolidation in, 58

Bi-State Development District (Illinois-Missouri), 64, 65, 68, 71n

Bloc voting, 249

Bonds, 43–44, 149–150

Boroughs, 58

Boston: city-county consolidation in, 57; mass transit in, 22

Boston metropolitan area: federation proposal in, 58

Boulder Canyon, 82

Boulder Canyon project, 82, 83

Boulevards, 138

Bridges, 27, 28, 68, 79–81

DATE DUE

JOSTEN'S 30 508